LIFE TRAVEL AND THE PEOPLE IN BETWEEN

Charleston, SC
www.PalmettoPublishing.com

Life Travel and the People in Between
Copyright © 2022 by Mike Nixon
Editors: Christian Coleman, Aissa Martell
Cover Design: Mike Nixon

First Edition

Hardcover ISBN: 979-8-9859452-2-5
Paperback ISBN: 979-8-9859452-0-1
eBook ISBN: 979-8-9859452-1-8

LIFE TRAVEL AND THE PEOPLE IN BETWEEN

A Memoir

Mike Nixon

THIS BOOK IS A MEMOIR. It reflects the author's present recollections of experiences over time. Some names, titles, and characteristics have been changed to protect privacy and identity, some events have been compressed, and some dialogues have been recreated.

Any views or opinions expressed in this book are personal and belong solely to the author. They do not represent those of the people, institutions, or organizations that the author may or may not be associated with in a professional or personal capacity. Any views or opinions are not intended to malign any religion, ethnic group, club, organization, company, or individual.

AND ONE FINAL DISCLAIMER:
The views expressed in this publication are those of the author and do not necessarily reflect the official policy or position of the Department of Defense or the U.S. government. The public release clearance of this publication by the Department of Defense does not imply Department of Defense endorsement or factual accuracy of the material.

FOR MY PARENTS, CARLA AND BOOKER. My siblings, Brionna, Deshaye, and Darion. And my loving wife, Kaori.

For my family who raised me. And for every family who adopted me by opening their homes and hearts to me.

For Rachel, this book wouldn't be possible without you.

For every wonderful person, I met along life's journey. For every mentor, traveler, volunteer, servicemember, friend, and stranger.

For everyone whose been there. This is for you.

INTRODUCTION

It isn't where you came from. It's where you're going that counts. —**Ella Fitzgerald**

I was born in St. Louis, Missouri, also known as the "Show-Me" state. There are several legends about how Missouri inherited the nickname, but no one knows for sure. Just like no one knows how to pronounce it. I pronounce it "Miz-urh-ee." Others say, "Miz-urh-uh." The early French explorers didn't know what to call it either. A Native American group referred to as *Oumessourit* lived along the Mississippi River when the Europeans arrived. And some French guy wrote the group's name as he heard the natives speak it. Over time, the pronunciation changed as different settlers came to the region. You can pronounce it how you want. Just don't call it "Misery," which it can be for those living in the inner cities.

I'm from a section of Saint Louis called Wellston, one of the poorest parts of Missouri. Deteriorated structures and run-down homes occupied my city like a graveyard of bones, a stark reminder that the town once had a lively soul. It may seem unimaginable to those who have never encountered them, but these cities are very real.

Once, I was a boy living across from one of those boarded-up houses. I had dirt floors inside of my home. In the wintertime, my family taped thick plastic sheets around the windows to keep the house insulated during heavy Midwest blizzards. Any time the cast iron radiators stopped working, my grandma used the kitchen oven to heat the house. My cousins and I, in the next room, watched *Home Alone* and our residence felt just as cozy as Kevin McCallister's.

I had a big and loving family that made my childhood feel golden. We were a young family. My mother was barely past her teenage years. I lived with all my relatives at one time or another. This included my grandma, aunts, and uncles. There was never a shortage of cousins or neighborhood kids to play with.

Life was innocent, but not without its challenges. My mother was studying to get a General Educational Development (GED) while working diligently to support me (her first and only child at the time). Then there was my father; he didn't exactly play midfielder for the inner-city lacrosse team. Another extracurricular activity led him to an unfortunate run-in with the law, and he learned a hard lesson. The good thing was he learned and avoided the perpetual cycle that ruins a lot of misguided youth.

At nineteen years old, my dad joined the United States Navy, which led him to the east coast. Several years later, the rest of the family joined my dad in Staten Island, New York. I was five years old. By the time I completed second grade, we were living in Virginia, and I had three siblings. It was challenging for my mother to work and take care of four children while my father was at sea. When fifth grade arrived, I was back in Saint Louis. Being closer to family provided some relief for my mom.

At eleven years old, I was more observant of my surroundings. The close-knit community that I knew as a child now felt like a nightmare. No one knows how bad something is until they have something to compare it to. For me, that was transferring from the city to the county school system. The schools in Wellston were falling apart, and eventually, they did. Today most of those schools resemble abandoned buildings or empty lots, including those I attended.

For the first time in my life, I went to a county school with predominantly White students. It was different for me because the city schools were primarily Black. In New York and Virginia, the communities and schools were diverse. At first, the novelty of attending a county school brought excitement. I had Spanish classes and participated in the seventh-grade band. I met new friends, and most of my peers treated me fairly. Some of my classmates invited me to their suburban homes on a few occasions.

In time, constantly seeing my reality shift between the city and suburbs hit me, and I shattered. I don't remember exactly how or when. Something about the bus ride from the suburbs to the city eroded my morale. Shortly after departing school grounds, the bus passed by elegant homes in safe communities. Thirty minutes later, I was walking past a liquor store with bars in the window and boarded-up buildings and praying I wouldn't have to fight any of the neighborhood bullies on the way home. When I got home, the adults were at work. I would do my homework if I understood it.

Sometimes, I stayed up late waiting for an adult to bring food or cook a meal, so I didn't go to bed hungry. Eventually, my grandma taught me how to cook. And cooking became one of my earliest passions. I was great at it. I wished I could've said the same thing about school.

By the eighth grade, my grades were the lowest they had ever been. I couldn't focus in school. My social life began to fade at school and in my neighborhood. There was something about going to the "White school" that made me lose credibility with the kids in Wellston. Likewise, something about being from the city distinguished me from the kids at school. I barely made it out of middle school.

Employment-wise, things were not going well for my mother. She decided it would be best to return to Virginia, where my father was stationed. In the summer of 2000, we moved to Virginia Beach, Virginia.

For me, moving back to the east coast was heart-wrenching. Again, I would be away from my extended family who played a huge role in looking after my siblings and me. As I got older, I realized it was the best decision. There was not much of a future for me in Saint Louis.

I had a childhood friend named Darrell, whom I met on the first day of fifth grade. He was also friends with my cousins. We'd have sleepovers and play Nintendo 64 all night. I cried when I learned that Darrell was shot and killed by as many bullets as his age; he died at seventeen. Undeniably, Virginia was the better place to grow up.

My family moved a lot, and our lives had little stability. By the time I reached high school, I had attended five schools. Before finishing high school, two more schools would be added to the list. I rarely had the chance to develop any long-term relationships with peers. It was always a different school, another neighborhood, and new faces. Deep down, I knew that my parents were doing their best to provide their children a better life than they had. For that, I'm truly thankful.

High school went much better than the previous academic years. I wanted to be an actor and took a theater class. I used to write and perform original monologues about Darrell that made the class laugh. My classmates and fellow thespians knew my comedic monologue series by the title *Where's Lil Darrell.* The reality was much more tragic. I enjoyed acting but memorizing scripts and practicing in front of mirrors were time-consuming.

Apart from courses, I was on the track and field team and flipped burgers at Hardee's part-time. Track and field kept me busy. It also allowed me to eat all the double chili cheeseburgers and curly fries, I wanted, and not gain an inch.

I loved eating. This was probably why I enjoyed my culinary arts classes and decided I wanted to be a chef instead of an actor. Eventually, I was accepted into a prestigious culinary arts university to study hospitality and culinary arts. But I couldn't afford it even with a partial scholarship, and I didn't know much about loans.

The problem with being the first is that you must figure out everything. In my case, I would be the first in my family to attend college. After missing out on culinary arts school, I was back to square one.

By the time I completed high school, I had graduated from flipping burgers to frying chicken and serving three-piece combos. "You want fries with that?" I seriously needed to find another job. My dream was to work in the hospitality industry.

CHAPTER 1
THE FRONT DESK OF THE WORLD

Life is either a daring adventure or nothing at all.
—Helen Keller

Today is the day I'm going to get fired. That's how I felt every day for two months, making mistake after mistake. I had been out of high school for nearly a year before landing the position as a Front Desk Representative at the Comfort Inn. The hotel wasn't anything fancy. There was nothing unique or impressive about its design or accommodations—no candle-lit therapeutic spa service or swanky hotel bar. In fact, it was a motel—a two-story building where guests accessed their rooms from the outside. I don't exactly know how the bigwigs at the corporate offices advertised the property; however, guests often complained upon arrival because they imagined they had booked a room at some five-star resort.

There was one great thing about the property; it couldn't have been in a more strategic location. Norfolk Naval Base, the largest naval base in the world, was only a short drive away. Heading in the opposite direction of the base led to Downtown Norfolk, Virginia, a center of commerce, government, entertainment, restaurants, and home to numerous shipping ports. The area had colleges and universities, too. Norfolk International Airport was a twenty-minute drive away.

All this meant that people from not only across the United States but also from across the world stayed at our hotel. Japanese college sports teams, who challenged the local university, stayed at the property. Contractors, both those working with the military and those doing business with local companies, were guests. Navy Sailors, college students, businessmen and women, truck drivers, runaway spouses ... I checked all of them into rooms.

Because of my encounters with thousands of guests, I have so many stories from my time at the Comfort Inn—wonderful and disheartening. I saw tears of joy from parents whose children were entering college, and I witnessed the tears of pain from those who lost friends to the War in Iraq. These touching experiences would help shape my decisions throughout my life.

On August 28, 2005, a guest came to the front desk. Although scheduled to check out, she had to extend her stay due to an unexpected flight cancellation to New Orleans. The woman was clearly upset as she expressed how much she was ready to return home. I could see in her face and hear in her voice how badly she wanted to go back to the land of Mardi Gras and jambalaya. Perhaps she missed her family or was just tired of feeling like a prisoner inside the hotel room. I imagine she felt like a prisoner of circumstance, as she felt bittersweet for her safety and watched as the events to come would change her life. The next day, Hurricane Katrina made landfall—the levees broke, and the muddy waters drowned the city. This guest probably never got to go "home" again.

I can't know precisely what Hurricane Katrina memory that guest carries, but I have one of my own.

Mr. Kincaid came from North Carolina. He worked for Norfolk Southern Railway. Occasionally he and his team stayed at the hotel while they were in Norfolk for work. Their visits ranged from a few days to weeks at a time. Mr. Kincaid was an older gentleman, energetic and friendly, and I considered him a mentor. He sent me cards and books whenever he wasn't at the hotel. Once, Mr. Kincaid sent me a book on personal finances and investing. Inside the cover, he left a note that read, "Learn and apply the information in this book. I guarantee you'll become a wealthy man."

That's the kind of relationship I cultivated with a few guests. They were like friends who came to stay at my place for a few days.

Months after Hurricane Katrina, work brought Mr. Kincaid back to the area. This time, he brought me several collared shirts and slacks. He explained that the clothes had come from department stores throughout New Orleans. After the storm, the stores considered them damaged merchandise and sold them to lower-tier stores throughout the country.

He told me, "These clothes are brand-new and unblemished. I know they'll look great on you!"

Technically, we weren't supposed to accept gifts from guests. Nonetheless, we made the guests feel like family, and they were adamant in expressing their gratitude by giving us food, among other things.

Once, I decided to show my gratitude by allowing a guest to borrow my car. He was a frantic and impatient older man waiting for his daughter to pick him up and take him out for dinner.

"She said she'd be here thirty minutes ago. Do you have a car I can borrow? I'll fill up the gas tank," he said.

Perhaps, it was the "fill up the tank" part that made me give my keys to this guest I'd never seen before. This was during President George W. Bush's days when $2.59 per gallon was considered expensive, so you probably understand why I'd toss my keys to a stranger. Even then, instant regret hit me as I watched my car leave the parking lot. Had I just seen my car for the last time? The police report I'd have to file was going to look very foolish.

A few minutes later, his daughter showed up. She said, "I'm looking for my father," and I knew exactly who she was. I told her that I had let him borrow my car to pick up food.

She looked at me in disbelief and said, "That was a stupid thing to do."

I felt miserable. Not knowing if I had the permission to ask why, I kept silent as a variety of wild scenarios ran through my head. Like, maybe he had dementia and wouldn't remember how to get back to the hotel or he was a schemer and planned to sell my car parts on the black market.

Twenty minutes later, the father returned with food. My car had a full tank of gas, and a few crumbs on the seats. Handing over my vehicle might have been risky, but I refuse to believe it's stupid to put my faith in the general goodness of people.

Before ever traveling outside of my country, or comfort zone for that matter, the world first came to me and subtly introduced itself through the people I met at the hotel. For example, I knew essentially nothing about the Japanese sports teams that I mentioned earlier. For all I knew, they had come from China. Places like China and Japan were as different as New Jersey and New York to me: distinct from one another but I didn't know in what ways. I was ignorant and had a limited worldview.

However, I was curious and fascinated with everyone who passed through the lobby because they all had a story. At nineteen years old, I felt like everyone's experiences and purpose overshadowed what I was doing. Japanese athletes were traveling the world, sailors were serving their country, business personnel were getting richer, and all the other guests were engaging in carnal pleasures. Even some of my coworkers were sneaking away from the front desk and getting it on with guests. What was I doing wrong? Although I enjoyed my work, their lives seemed much more fun and important than mine. The part of my job I enjoyed the most was getting them to share their stories. If I couldn't do what they were doing, I could at least ask them about their experiences and imagine a similar life. I learned that simple questions and listening went a long way. These skills would serve me well as I bounced around the world.

One day, a middle-aged woman and her daughter, who was around the same age as me, approached the front desk to book a room. The daughter was unquestionably attractive. I made conversation with all the guests, but I definitely wanted to talk with the ones whom I considered a prospective girlfriend. I noticed that the daughter wore a common type of tourist shirt, the kind with a country's name printed across the front of it. I'd seen a lot of similar shirts, but I'd never seen one from this country.

To make conversation, I asked the daughter, "Are you from the Banana Republic or did you just visit?"

"Excuse me," the daughter replied.

I repeated, "Were you born in the Banana Republic?"

After realizing I was serious, the mother and daughter burst into laughter. Using her sweet, motherly voice, the woman said, "The Banana Republic is a department store, silly!"

For neither the first nor the last time, I felt really stupid.

While the hospitality industry allowed me to meet and interact with thousands of people, outside of work, I really didn't do much else. I was now a freshman in college and had a few university friends, but we rarely hung out outside of class. Work was my social life. I worked as a professional extrovert, but I was an introvert in my personal life.

One of the biggest lessons I learned from working at the hotel was that the world was a larger and more fascinating place than I could ever imagine. Like the interesting stories of the guests, I wanted to be able to share captivating experiences with others about my interactions with the world. I just didn't know how to do it or where to start. That was until I met Sean.

The hotel guests gave me a sample of the world beyond my own little corner of it; however, Sean handed me the key to a vehicle that would change the course that my life was on. And Sean was the reason I quit my dream job.

Also, I should point out that the Banana Republic began as a store for world travelers to buy clothes suited for their travel. It was for explorers headed to banana republics[1]. So, I wasn't completely wrong.

---

1   The term was coined in 1901 by American author O. Henry. The phrase describes nations, typically South American countries, exploited by American companies seeking one export. For example, the United Fruit Company extracted millions of bananas from Honduras, hence the term.

CHAPTER 2
GO FOR LAUNCH

Each friend represents a world in us, a world possibly not born until they arrive, and it is only by this meeting that a new world is born.

—Anaïs Nin

Sean and I both attended Norfolk State University and were both business majors. That's basically all we had in common. I was a freshman, and academically, Sean was a year ahead of me. We were pursuing different degree programs within the same general major. Sean and I didn't even have any classes together. We became members of a campus business organization called Students in Free Enterprise (SIFE) by mere happenstance. I recognized him from the meetings, and we conversed occasionally. That was as far as our relationship went. Sean was a soft-spoken guy who made it easy to overlook him. One day, he disappeared, and I didn't even notice. I shouldn't say "one day" because I don't even know which day it was. He was at SIFE meetings, and then, he wasn't.

Unlike work and classes, SIFE brought excitement and purpose to my mediocre life, at a time when I felt like I was on the outside looking in. SIFE made me feel like I belonged and made a difference. SIFE was an international non-profit organization that worked with university students who desired to have a positive impact on their communities. Also, SIFE provided us with the opportunity to learn practical knowledge to become socially responsible business leaders.

The SIFE chapter at my university was heavily involved in the community. Some of our projects involved volunteering with elementary and middle-school students; we taught basic business concepts by utilizing Junior Achievement curriculum. We also organized field trips for high school students and performed consulting work with local businesses. At the end of the semester, our chapter representatives traveled to different states to present our projects at large-scale competitions sponsored by Fortune 500 Companies. SIFE chapters from universities all over the country competed at these events. The competitions measured which chapters made the greatest impacts in their communities and worldwide.

My team placed at the state competitions, allowing us to advance. We didn't make it too far beyond regionals, though. Some universities had done projects such as helping villages in remote places worldwide get access to clean water. They were really changing the world. I would have liked to think we were changing our corner of Virginia, but that didn't compare in my mind to the places these teams had been. Some had probably even built a few houses in *The Banana Republic*.

After returning from the competitions, our chapter would discuss future projects, especially projects that would have a significant impact on our community and be more competitive. At one of the meetings, we discussed ways that our chapter could collaborate with organizations in other countries to extend our impact overseas. If it gave other teams the advantage, it could do the same for us. Somewhere in the discussion, one of the members mentioned Sean's name. The only thing I remembered from that meeting was hearing, "Sean is in South Africa." He hadn't disappeared, but he might as well have been on the moon. The dark side of the moon felt as far from Norfolk, Virginia, as the south side of Africa.

**

ONE DAY, SEAN WALKED THROUGH THE STUDENT UNION BUILDING ON CAMPUS WHEN HE'D SEEN THE FLYER POSTED ON A BULLETIN. It was a simple printout covered in rectangles; each rectangle consisted of colorful patterns and represented a different country. At the top of the flyer, the message read, "Do you want to study abroad?" Sean's answer had been "Yes."

It was more than just a question, but rather a calling that captured Sean's imagination and ambitions—which led him to the Department of Global Affairs.

Sean spent weeks gathering everything he needed to apply to a study-abroad program. This assignment included completing the application, updating his resume, and preparing essays that answered questions, including:

Why do you want to study abroad?

Where do you want to study and why?

How does studying abroad fit into your personal and professional goals?

Once his documents were ready, he applied for a two-year study-abroad program in China through the U.S. State Department. Unfortunately, after all of Sean's efforts, he only received a rejection letter. Undeterred, he filled out another application, tweaked his previously written essays, and applied to a different program. This time, it was for an experiential learning program in South Africa, and Sean was accepted.

While Sean was performing awesome activities, such as wandering the streets of Soweto[2] and witnessing incredible sunsets from Table Mountain, I was engaged in my own set of actions. Besides working at the Comfort Inn, I picked up a side hustle of pressure-washing houses. Also, I was a sophomore in college and the Vice President of SIFE. My life had finally picked up.

Sean returned from South Africa in 2006 at the beginning of my second sophomore semester. YouTube had only been around for a year and a half so this was before people could upload 4K cinematic videos of their travel experiences. Nonetheless, Sean presented a PowerPoint slideshow highlighting his study-abroad experience at a SIFE meeting. The presentation included background music and photos of everything he had experienced while abroad.

Sean was a different person than I remembered before. He had always been an older man stuck inside a young guy's body, the kind of youth with wisdom beyond his age, but now he was more cultured and worldly for having lived in another part of the world. Sean had lived with several host families throughout his time in South Africa. This experience provided him with a unique understanding of the culture, including the food, beliefs, music, and people's daily interactions. For me, Nelson Mandela was a name in a history book. Sean had visited the anti-apartheid activist's home and the site where Nelson Mandela served his prison sentence. I enjoyed learning about the history and different aspects of South African culture from Sean.

---

2   Soweto is an abbreviation for "South-Western Townships." Created in the 1930s, Soweto was a segregated township for Black South Africans.

There was something that Sean knew, but I couldn't figure it out. He had something I needed, but I didn't know what it was. It was driving me crazy. I had my own set of essay questions repeating in my head.

Do I need to know more about South Africa?

Do I need to see more of his photos or hear more stories from his time in South Africa?

Do I need to develop a stronger friendship with this person I have grown to admire so much?

Something about Sean felt different from the guests at the hotel. They came from many faraway places and shared their inspiring stories with me. Sean was a mundane being. We were from the same world. I felt like Ordinary Mike, and Sean was Everyday Sean. We attended the same university and showed up to the same SIFE meetings. We cheered for the same teams, drove on the same roads, and ate the same food. Except he'd been to South Africa, and I just pressure-washed grime from the sides of houses. That's when I realized we had access to the same resources. I figured out what I needed from him: *"Hey Sean, how were you able to study abroad?"*

✳✳✳

AFTER SEAN TOLD ME ABOUT THE OFFICE OF GLOBAL AFFAIRS, I VISITED THE PROGRAM DIRECTOR THE NEXT DAY. The Director, Dr. Harris, questioned my academic standing, extracurricular involvement, personal interests, and reasons for wanting to study abroad.

Finally, he said, "Next year, we're sending students to Russia. How would you like to be one of those students?"

I couldn't locate Russia on a map, but I felt tremendous excitement just hearing the name of a different country. The next few weeks consisted of completing the application, writing essays, applying for a passport, and learning basic Russian phrases. I would need some new clothes, too; I probably would need some gear lined with sabertoothed tiger fur. Virginia gets cold, but it doesn't get Siberian cold.

Weeks later, I went to the Office of Global Affairs to update Dr. Harris on my progress. He told me to sit down. No good conversation has ever started with "sit down." No director has ever said, "Sit down ... we're going to have to give you a raise."

He explained that a different study-abroad program had become available. I could leave the next semester, a couple of months away; however, Russia would not be my destination but the Dominican Republic. I may not have remembered much as far as the Cold War, but I had at least heard of Russia. I didn't know anything about the Dominican Republic. Do they have bananas in the Dominican Republic? As far as I was concerned, the destination didn't matter. I was willing to go anywhere.

Since the program was only a few months away, I acted quickly to ensure that I was prepared to go. The application process was much easier the second time around. Once the application was approved, I resigned from my position as the Vice President of SIFE. I ended my pressure-washing enterprise and sold the equipment. A few weeks from leaving for the Dominican Republic, I submitted my two-week notice letter to my manager at the Comfort Inn. For the first time, I was going to leave the motel and live the kind of life the guests had told me about.

CHAPTER 3
THE TRAVEL BUG

Not all classrooms have four walls.
—Anonymous

H ispaniola is the second-largest island in the Caribbean. Two countries share the island, Haiti to the west and the Dominican Republic to the east. Historically, Hispaniola is the place where America, Europe, and Africa met (or collided). The first collision occurred when Christopher Columbus, his crew, and Africans arrived on the island inhabited by the native Tainos at the turn of the fifteenth century.

Five hundred and thirteen years later, on January 5, 2007, I was in a state of disbelief as the plane descended through the clouds. From the window, I saw endless coastlines highlighted with turquoise waters. As we approached closer to land, small and unfamiliar structures began to spring up from the green and brown patches of land. Moments later, the plane's wheels thumped against the ground, and the brakes brought the aircraft to a halt. There was loud applause as everyone clapped their hands for the safe landing. Not only was this my first time seeing people clap after a landing, but it was also my first time flying over an ocean. In addition, it was my first time in another country.

***

ULTIMATELY, THIS WAS THE FIRST EXPERIENCE OF A NEW LIFE, AND IT FELT AMAZING. I was no longer thinking about college, student organizations, disgruntled hotel guests, pressure washing, or anything from the past. I was standing on a line separating who I was and who I could be. For so long, I wanted to cross the line. Being in a new place where no one knew me provided the perfect opportunity to reinvent myself.

With many distractions behind me, I had an opportunity to reflect and address some insecurities that haunted me. As much as I attended classes and worked at the Comfort Inn, I spent a lot of time alone—not doing much of anything. There were so many moments in my youth where I thought that it would have been nice to hear someone say, "Hey, you want to join us?" or "Let's hang out." That hardly ever happened.

Music served as a great escape before I would ever travel to any foreign country; additionally, it was relatable. Sometimes, I would go to the theater to catch a movie. I'd listen to my music and go for a run, most times. Alternatively, I'd put on my headphones, lie down on my bed, and close my eyes. Gangster rap, '90s R&B or any of the oldies could always take me where I needed to be. Tupac, Luther Vandross, and Lauryn Hill were always riding with me.

***

ON MY SECOND DAY IN SANTO DOMINGO, THE DOMINICAN REPUBLIC'S CAPITAL, I STOOD OUTSIDE THE HOTEL WHERE I HAD STAYED THE PREVIOUS NIGHT. I stood alongside eleven other students participating in the same study-abroad program. An equal number of Dominican families waited to see which one of us belonged to them for the next few months.

I was handed over like a shelter puppy to an older, stout Dominican woman. She wore glasses and looked every bit like a librarian. She led me to a vehicle, where a driver waited for us. I placed my suitcase in the trunk. It was a quiet drive because my Spanish-speaking abilities were quite limited. Whenever the woman said anything, I communicated through smiles and head nods, again like a puppy wagging his tail, anxious for what's ahead. It was a short drive from the hotel to her home, a small apartment located above the community's pharmacy.

Once we arrived, a guy in his early twenties met us outside. The woman said, "*Maicol. El es mi hijo Israel.*" (Michael, this is my son, Israel.) For a week I called him by the wrong name because I thought she said, "My son is Raul." Although my Spanish sucked, Dominican Spanish didn't sound like Spanish.

"Hey bro, I can take your bags," Israel said in his Dominican accent as thick as mashed plantains.

The medium-sized fellow grabbed my luggage, and I followed him upstairs into the apartment. He led me to my new room and left me to unpack. It was such a weird feeling being a stranger in someone's home, not speaking their language, or understanding their customs. I thought, "Who in their right mind would let a stranger into their home for four months?" Shortly after I finished unpacking, Israel knocked lightly on the door and cracked it open before I could get to it.

He said, "I want to show you around the *barrio*." At the time, I didn't know what *barrio* meant. Israel didn't know the English word for *barrio*. Eventually, I learned that it meant neighborhood.

There was nothing too impressive about my new community. Still, I felt the excitement that comes from experiencing something new for the first time. One side of the street ended at the well-known and heavily trafficked avenue *La Independencia*, and the other side ended at George Washington Avenue. Across from George Washington Avenue was the Malecón or coast, and beyond that exhibited the contradictory ocean. Constantly, the water churned both violently and beautifully. I could walk there from my new home in five minutes.

I learned more about Israel than I did about the neighborhood during my tour. My new brother was an only child, just a day before I arrived. He lived with his mother, and now me. Two years my elder, he was a Senior at Autonomous University of Santo Domingo[3], one of the oldest universities in the Americas, where he studied construction. Israel dreamed of becoming a land surveyor, which he later accomplished. His hobbies included bumming around the beach, playing baseball, and jamming to reggaeton[4].

"Reggaeton? Is that Jamaican music in Spanish?" I inquired.

In the evening, Israel invited me to hang out with him and some of his friends. Hanging out with strangers on my first day in a new country seemed intimidating. "Nah, I'm good." I was not accustomed to going out and socializing. I declined Israel's invitation to avoid the awkwardness that possibly waited for me. The next time he invited me to go out, I rejected the invitation again. In Virginia, I'd wish people would ask me to go out with them more often. Now that I had the opportunity, I wasn't just letting it slip away; I actively slapped it away. Israel had remarkable persistence, and the only reason I eventually went out with him was that I figured it would make him stop asking.

---

3   Universidad Autónoma de Santo Domingo (UASD) was founded in 1866. However, it descended from a Dominican seminary founded in 1538. By many estimates, it is the third oldest university in the New World.

4   Reggaeton emerged in Puerto Rico in the early 1990s. The style blends Jamaican dancehall music with hip-hop, jazz, and several Latin American genres.

On a Friday night, we went to his church of all places to hang out with Israel's fellowship buddies. Nothing sounded less fun than going to church on a Friday night. Israel introduced his new little *hermano* from the United States to all his friends. They all seemed so genuinely happy to meet me, which seemed strange. *Who was I, and what did I do to be the recipient of so many bright smiles, handshakes and hugs?* Pretty girls approached me and gave me kisses—the standard Latin American "kiss on the cheek" greeting. No girl had ever done that before. These *Dominicanas* made conversation with me using broken English; their accents stole my heart. I was in love. Hallelujah, Jesus!

While watching guitar and piano performances, new friends served me snacks. Dominican bible study wasn't bad at all.

After church, we went to the after-party—more like an outdoor bar with too many tables to count. Dozens of well-dressed Dominicans socialized and drank. Some moved their bodies to the rhythm of the bachata and merengue music, setting the mood for the environment. Our table consisted of approximately twelve guests. From a crowded table in Santo Domingo, I couldn't even see where I'd left my comfort zone. When asked what I wanted to drink, I told the waiter, "I'll take a Virgin Piña Colada, *por favor.*"

I'd had a Virgin Strawberry Daiquiri a few years earlier, but that was the extent of my experience with "mocktails." I had no experience with actual cocktails. This night constituted my first exposure to any real nightlife or social scene, and I drank it in.

I was hardly a social person back home outside of work and college. Honestly, I had never been much of an articulate speaker. Since I didn't want to appear dumb or incoherent to others, I became withdrawn. I sent low energy out into the world around me, and I got low energy in return. Not having many friends to converse with didn't help my situation.

The Dominican Republic forced me into unfamiliar territory, both geographically and socially. Locals wanted to know where I was from and what I was doing in their country. I didn't have a choice but to engage in conversation. I was on the other side of the Comfort Inn desk for the first time. I was the world traveler, and they were the ones just hanging out at home. It was also an excellent opportunity to practice speaking Spanish.

There I was in the Dominican Republic, going to church, and enjoying happy hour with my big brother every Friday night. I had found my inner college party boy, far away from campus. Eventually, the Virgin Strawberry Daiquiris became Long Island Iced Teas, and the open-air bars became beaches. Before I knew it, my social circle, now including classmates from my study-abroad program, grew in numbers.

Being a foreigner in another country makes it easy to connect with other foreigners. Even if each person is of a different ethnicity or speaks a different language, they still have something in common—they're both strangers in a strange land. All my peers were from the United States, making it a lot easier to relate to one another's experiences.

I became good friends with most of my classmates. We spent many weekends relaxing on either Boca Chica or Juan Dolio beach, drinking Brugal rum. We discovered mom-and-pop eateries around the city. Our favorite food cart made empanadas[5] from scratch and served fresh fruit juices. The *jugo de mamón con leche*, or papaya milkshake, was something mean; I used to howl after drinking it. We visited museums, parks, and shopping areas.

---

5   Empanadas consist of a filling wrapped in pastry; they can be baked or fried. Robert de Nola wrote the earliest known reference to the dish in a cookbook from Galicia, Spain, in 1520.

We went on movie dates with stunning Dominican girls during the day—and the clubs at night.

No matter how much time I spent with classmates, nothing compared to the quality time with my host family. By living with a host family and hanging out with Israel, I was able to experience the amazement of being immersed in Dominican culture. On those blistering Dominican evenings, Israel would be shirtless, with no shame in exhibiting his hairy potbelly as he lay stretched out across the sofa. I would hear him slap his legs to kill the irritating bloodthirsty mosquitos. As he worked on his class assignments, I, like a proper little brother, would constantly interrupt him to ask for help with my Spanish homework.

"What does this mean?"

"How do you say this?"

"How do you say that?"

And sometimes Israel would stare at my Spanish assignments and go, "Yo, what the fuck is this? Huh, I don't know man. Nobody writes or speaks like this." It became apparent how difficult it is for any native speaker to properly teach their language to a non-native speaker.

My host mom would be in the kitchen making dinner. I could smell the divine aroma of *habichuelas* (stewed beans) and *pollo guisado* (braised chicken). Her voice wafted on the savory-infused air singing along to the classic bachata music that played in the background; no artist did it better than Juan Luis Guerra. With my host family, I had done more than "join in" or "hang out." I had built trusting connections and emotional ties. I had shared my dreams and myself. Now, I was a part of the family.

***

STUDYING IN THE DOMINICAN REPUBLIC WAS UNIQUE AND UNLIKE ANYTHING I'D EXPERIENCED PREVIOUSLY. The program allowed me to complete nineteen credit hours for general elective college courses. The courses included two Spanish classes and Caribbean Culture and African Heritage classes. Since each classroom size ranged from five to eleven students, we didn't have a choice but to interact as our professors encouraged discussion. We went on many educational adventures to escape those four-wall classrooms.

The study program integrated numerous excursions into the curriculum. For example, my classmates and I went on trips that allowed us to examine the socioeconomic statuses of Dominican people. We visited some of the wealthiest neighborhoods in Santo Domingo. Surrounded by high gates, the local currency could not purchase the large mansions. However, the U.S. dollar is an acceptable currency in many parts of the Dominican Republic. It seemed that no matter how far I traveled, there were still bits of America sprinkled everywhere, and the dollar was god.

We also walked around poorer communities made up of rusty shanty homes resting on the sides of hills. Fruit peelings, animal manure, and other types of debris lay scattered around the ground as we meandered through the town. I purchased fresh coconut water from a local vendor, selling natural fruit juices to make a living. He used a machete to slice open the top, right in front of me, before handing me the coconut and a straw.

The excursions allowed my classmates and me to experience every aspect of Dominican culture fully. For example, a Dominican tale tells the story of the devil's deportation from heaven to earth. As the fallen angel landed, he broke his leg. In the streets of La Vega, we watched the *Diablos Conjuelos* or limping devils dance around in their colorful, glittery, and extravagant costumes during the Carnival festival.

In parts of the Dominican Republic, people practice a religion that combines African beliefs with Catholicism. My classmates and I attended voodoo ceremonies. The idea of naked, uncivilized aborigines dancing around pits of fires never materialized. There were no dolls with pins or chalices filled with goat blood. Instead, I sat outside and watched through the window as the event took place. At the front, stood a table filled with candles and small statues of Catholic Saints. Unlike Catholic Masses, where gatherers are more conservative, the worshippers at the voodoo ceremony sang and danced. The event resembled that of every Baptist church event I had attended growing up except for the statues of Saints.

When I returned to my home in Santo Domingo, I shared the voodoo experience with Israel. He seemed very concerned about me.

"Huh? Don't play around with that stuff," he warned me.

"Have you ever been to a voodoo ceremony?" I asked him.

He replied, "No, but it's bad."

Israel's unease did not make me feel frightened of the experience. There's an ignorance that we all share—an ignorance that comes from inexperience, underexposure, and being afraid of what we don't understand or won't acknowledge exists. Nonetheless, it also was a true testament to Israel's protective nature that gave me a feeling of security and blanketed me throughout my stay.

Another memorable experience involved a nighttime trip to *El Bajo Mundo*, or The Underworld, in a town called Manoguayabo to attend a cockfight. In a million years, I would've never guessed that I'd be watching two roosters violently peck one another's brains out. My classmates and I read Michelle Wucker's book *Why the Cocks Fight*—a required reading for our Caribbean Culture class.

The purpose of attending the event was to explore the author's metaphor. The author compares the historical fight over Hispaniola (and how politics, economics, and society have been structured on the Caribbean Island) to a cockfighting arena. Bred by colonial powers including France, Spain, and the United States, the cocks were Haiti and the Dominican Republic.

The program introduced me to the concept of "the world being a classroom." For example, when we learned about Christopher Columbus'[6] arrival in the New World, we did so in Parque Colón (Columbus Park), located in the historic area of Santo Domingo. When discussing slavery and the African Diaspora, we walked around the slave plantations that once traded African souls for sugarcane profits.

Also, we experienced the Dominican Republic like tourists on a Carnival Cruise. Perhaps the most memorable was the trip to Puerta Plata. For the first time in my life, I stayed at a resort, let alone an all-inclusive one—all-you-can-eat and drink, all day long. Dominican Cha-Cha Slide lessons and beach yoga classes, all day long. The night my classmates and I arrived at the resort, the sky poured rain. While running from the van to the resort's lobby, my eyeglasses slipped from my face and crashed to the ground. I picked them up and returned them to my face. At first, I thought I was going blind in one eye but soon realized a lens was missing. However, nothing would ruin the experience.

After checking in, my peers and I changed into swimwear. We splashed around the large pools in the heavy downfall of rain, unafraid of lightning striking or thunder dominating the skies. The following days awarded us much better weather, and we had the time of our lives as we relaxed on the beaches, danced to the

---

6   Columbus landed in modern-day Santo Domingo on June 29, 1502. It was his fourth voyage to the New World.

sounds of bachata and merengue at nightclubs, and interacted with the locals.

I couldn't believe this was "studying" abroad.

***

THE EXPERIENCE WASN'T ALL BACHATA IN POUND-ING RAIN, THOUGH. One day, Israel invited my classmate Sam and me to visit family in the *campo* (countryside) near Punta Cana. Unfortunately, we didn't go to some destination filled with beach resorts that everyone thinks of when they hear Punta Cana. Instead, we took buses and crammed passenger vans to get to this town in the middle of nowhere. These were eight-passenger vans with double the capacity plus a couple of squawking hens.

Israel, Sam, and I arrived at a bus terminal, where we had to transfer. We went to the counter to purchase the tickets. The clerk sold everyone a ticket except me. Israel was absolutely Dominican, and Sam was acceptably White. But I didn't possess either luxury. The clerk inquired about my citizenship. After I said the United States, he asked to see some identification. I handed him a photocopy of my passport along with my Virginia driver's license. He turned down the documents and refused to sell me a ticket. Israel became enraged and yelled at the clerk. "*Hombre*, he showed you identification. Sell him a damn ticket. Holy fucking shit!" I'd never seen him with that kind of fire before. Soon after, the clerk sold me a ticket.

Initially, the clerk wouldn't sell me the ticket because my dark skin led him to believe I was Haitian. Although I had previously known the horrible and discriminatory practices against Haitians in the Dominican Republic, I was experiencing first-hand what it was like for the Haitians making a living in their neighboring country. As much as I wanted to resent Dominicans for what people who looked like me had to experience, I had to remember that not all Dominicans were like that. Furthermore, my brother Israel had just shown me that he would stand up for me if anyone treated me unjustly.

***

THE FINAL PIECE OF THE STUDY-ABROAD PROGRAM WAS THE INTERNSHIP. The program administrators had mistaken me for an education major; I was a business student. They assigned me to an internship working at an after-school program at Colegio Don Bosco. A few weeks later, the administrators realized their mistake and offered me the opportunity to intern with a local business; however, I declined and continued working at the school.

The Don Bosco program catered to kids living in impoverished communities. I worked with elementary-aged school kids. Many of them didn't attend school for various reasons. Some of the kids had to work and help support their families. Others faced violence, substance abuse, and neglect in their homes. With limited opportunities, they turned to the streets and became *niños de la calle* (street kids). The Don Bosco program provided an unconventional approach to schooling, allowing the kids to come in the afternoon. Daily, I'd see kids and teenagers selling food or washing the windshields of cars when the drivers caught the red light. I heard that the less fortunate children sniffed permanent markers or glue to get high. Ignorance allowed me to believe that poverty was a drunken old man pushing a shopping cart, filled with everything he owned, around the streets of Saint Louis. Here, it was women with babies sleeping on the streets. For this reason, I turned down the business internship because I knew that I would make a more meaningful impact working with the kids. My classroom partner was a free-spirited Canadian volunteer living in Santo Domingo. Together, we offered reading, science, and math lessons; more entertaining activities included arts and crafts, as well as sports. In addition, we'd go outside to play basketball, baseball, or soccer. However, it wasn't always fun.

Although of elementary school age, these were troubled kids. Sometimes they argued and fought. Once, I noticed one of the bigger boys pushing a smaller one. I told the bigger kid, "If you want to fight somebody, fight me." This four-foot "midget" grabbed my leg and tried to take me down. When the other kids saw this, they ran over and assisted the bigger kid. Hearing the commotion, one of the school's teachers ran into the classroom only to see a mountain of kids piled on top of me. "It's nothing," I played it off.

Afterwhile, the kids and I got to know one another very well. When I first started working at the after-school program, I noticed this timid little girl. Whenever I greeted or approached her, she'd turn away. It wasn't a good feeling for me, knowing that this child wanted nothing to do with me. I could only imagine what caused her to be so withdrawn. I don't think she ever felt entirely comfortable around me throughout my time there. On my last day working at the school, the little girl finally came over and gave me a big hug, and I placed my hand on her tiny back as she warmed my heart.

***

THE NIGHT BEFORE MY DEPARTURE WAS A FRIDAY. Instead of going to church, Israel and his friends took me to the Malecón to celebrate my final day in their country. Friday nights brought insanity to the Malecón. Thousands of people hung out, listened to music, purchased food from the vendors, drank, danced, and enjoyed life. There I was with a heavy heart, trying to enjoy myself while knowing that it would all disappear the next day.

Before going to the airport on my final day in the Dominican Republic, I went back to the Malecón to watch the endless ocean pressing against the mesmerizing Caribbean coast. The significance of going to the rocky coast was that it had been the first place I visited with Israel after meeting my host family. Therefore, I wanted it to be the last place I visited before leaving.

On the night of May 5, 2007, I returned to Virginia. When I woke up on May 6, I was in my old bed, and everything seemed familiar. It was as if the past four months of my life had been nothing more than a mere dream. I wanted to sleep more.

***

FINALLY, I HAD GONE THROUGH AN EXPERIENCE THAT, UNLIKE ANY OTHER, CHALLENGED MY NARROW WORLDVIEW AND GIFTED ME A NEW WAY OF SEEING THE WORLD. The study-abroad program was the best educational investment I had ever made. It did not teach me how to be a good student and pass tests; instead, it allowed me to open up, express myself (in and outside of class), and be more social. It taught me how to think (and do so critically) for myself and draw my own conclusions instead of, as my professor put it, "being an empty vessel waiting to be filled." More importantly, it allowed me to see that life is more fulfilling when we have the right people to help us enjoy it. The Dominican Republic had gifted me dozens of memories that I could only dream about experiencing again.

Four months away from the United States had impacted my life tremendously. As I found the words to tell people about my life-changing trip, no one had the attention span or relative experiences to hear and understand what I had gone through—not family, friends, or classmates. Sean understood. But to everyone else, I did not know how to explain to them that my life was now on a different trajectory. The experience left me with an indelible passion to travel, volunteer, and experience the world as never before.

***

LIVING IN THE DOMINICAN REPUBLIC GIFTED ME WITH A POETIC EXPERIENCE THAT I'LL FOR-EVER CHERISH.

My host mom worked long hours every day but often came home to a dark house with no running water due to city-wide power outages. The mosquitoes loved those sweaty, hot nights with dead fans.

Bathroom business was a confounding stanza. When the average person made $3 an hour, toilet paper was a luxury, and flushing it was a miracle. Don't worry because beside every toilet was a trashcan for used toilet paper; believe me, it wasn't as bad as it seemed. I never got used to the cold-water bucket showers no matter how sweaty and hot the nights were. But the cold water did make the mosquito bites feel better.

No matter how tipsy I felt after a night out in town, the raw image of poverty was a sobering pill. I didn't need Intermediate Spanish to understand an open hand, desperate facial expression, and the words, "*tengo hambre*." To say I'd be rich if I received $1 for every person asking for money is ironic because I'd probably be broke if I'd given 50 cents to every person that asked for it.

Infrastructure was as maintained as a McDonald's milkshake machine. The city was full of unfinished high-rise buildings, and the sidewalks were missing manhole covers. Cars drove through traffic lights but honked their horns in traffic jams. Still, I put my thumb up to catch a crammed *concho* (taxi) to meet a *chica* at the McDonald's downtown.

In the Dominican Republic, I learned what it meant to truly be American when asked, "Where are you from?"

"America," I had answered—only to be informed that America is two continents and many islands.

"I'm from the United States of America," I then corrected.

"Oh, so you're a gringo," he had replied.

"Do you know how to do the nigga dance?" one girl had politely asked.

"Uh, *weird question* ... I don't dance much, but I would love to learn bachata or merengue. Perhaps with you if you would like to go out. The coast is relaxing and romantic. I'll be leaving soon, but I love this country. And one day, I hope to return."

***

THE TRAVEL BUG HAD BITTEN ME, AND ITS POISON INFILTRATED MY DEEPEST ASPIRATIONS IN LIFE, LEAVING ME WITH A BURNING DESIRE TO TRAVEL. But maybe it was a sweet kiss instead of a bite, as the bug magically transformed into a beautiful woman. She must have been the Travel Goddess. Her face, ocean blue with greenish-brown continents spread across it, captivated my imagination. I stared into her eyes, and she stared into mine, filled with lovelight.

Whoever directed this scene in my life did so perfectly. I could vaguely hear the music playing softly in the background. It sounded like "I Could Fall in Love" by Selena.

Our eyes locked. I imagined all the places that I could go to and everything that I would do to have this mystical being. Indeed, I could fall in love.

CHAPTER 4
BIRTH OF AN ADVENTURE SPIRIT

A good friend is like a four-leaf clover;
hard to find and lucky to have.
—Irish Proverb

A week after returning from the Dominican Republic, I called my former manager from the Comfort Inn. In the months that I'd been abroad, he had transferred to a different hotel property located in Virginia Beach. However, since we had a great relationship and my old boss admired my work ethic, he hired me to work at the Fairfield by Marriott.

Studying abroad was a wonderful experience; however, it placed me $5,000 more in debt. In the grand scheme of things, my $8.50 hourly wage as a Front Desk Clerk was barely enough to get by. Shortly after being hired at the Fairfield by Marriott, to lessen the bondage of debt, I also applied for a job with a Fortune 100 retail-pharmaceutical company. Weeks later, I received a letter that read, "Thank you for your interest in our company, but we hope you applied for other jobs because you didn't get this one," or something like that. I felt devastated. Although I was working hard to reach my goals, I was not advancing. I had a decent grade point average. And yes, I had gone to the Dominican Republic and gained new experiences and skills. Now, the dream was over. The old way of life and the troubles I left behind had finally caught up to me, and I had to readjust to life back at home.

As life would have it, I had a few teammates from SIFE who landed internships with Walgreens, another retail pharmacy company. One of them had stayed with the company and became a well-regarded manager. I spoke with her about my interest in working for the company. My teammate talked to the Human Resources Manager at the regional office. Like magic, the HR Manager invited me to interview for their Management Trainee Internship Program. After doing well at the interviews, the company offered me a paid internship during the summer. After the three-month internship, Walgreens hired me as a full-time Assistant Manager. That experience taught me that relationships are just as valuable as education. Most times, the people in a person's network will hold more weight than words written on a resume.

Through the summer of 2007, I worked for the hotel and the pharmacy company. Once school began, I left the hotel industry for good. I had finally reached a financial milestone. I was able to pay down some of my loans and save money.

***

SCHOOL AND WORK CONSUMED A LOT OF MY TIME; HOWEVER, ONE OF MY FAVORITE PASTIMES WAS WATCHING BOXING ON LATE-NIGHT TELE-VISION. My favorite sports channel showed classic fights. This meant I could watch Muhammad Ali outclass his opponents, Mike Tyson instill fear in fighters, and Sugar Ray deliver masterful performances. Unfortunately, the channel that had once aired the classic boxing matches started airing World Extreme Cage Fighting (WEC). I missed out on classic boxing, but I fell in love with Mixed Martial Arts (MMA) after watching fighters like Uriah Faber, Dominick Cruz, Jose Aldo, and Ben Henderson.

One day, my manager, Henry, invited some coworkers to Hooters to celebrate his birthday. Usually, I kept my work life separate from my nonexistent social life. Still, I couldn't resist the urge to watch trained warriors duke it out. It was my first time going to Hooters, and soon I learned it wasn't the strip club that I imagined it to be. That night, the sports bar showed live Pay-Per-View fights. It was my first time watching the Ultimate Fighting Championship (UFC). A fighter named Anderson "The Spider" Silva headlined the event. Although Henry and I didn't watch any more fights together, he was responsible for converting me into a UFC fan.

Likewise, Dan and I met while working at Walgreens. Dan looked like a skinnier version of Eric Snowden, but that's about all both men had in common. Dan was the only person who was a bigger MMA fan than me. Dan knew everything about MMA. He taught me about all the fighters and their combat skillsets. Eventually, Hooters became our go-to spot. Dan and I cheered from tables filled with buffalo wings, celery sticks, and ranch dressing whenever there was a UFC event.

Being friends with Dan made me realize why I never really had many friends or hung out with others. In the past, whenever I invited others to hang out, they always found an excuse to cancel on me. I hated calling people to let them know that I was heading to where we planned to meet, only for my calls and texts to go ignored. I would rather do things alone than feel like I wasn't good enough for someone. I was somewhat of a one-man show before meeting Dan. That all changed when we started hanging out. Dan never flaked out on plans. A man of his word, he always showed up.

MMA wasn't the only thing we had in common; we both enjoyed adventures. For me, an adventure involved traveling to a different country, and the Dominican Republic had been my biggest and only accomplishment thus far. Although Dan had never traveled outside of the country, he was the MacGyver of adventure. He could turn a kayak, a toothpick, and duct tape into a road trip across America.

Road trips were a new concept for me. When I was younger, my family would drive from Virginia to visit our relatives in Missouri. Then there was the time I ran track in high school. My team took a "road trip" to the University of Pennsylvania to compete in Penn Relays, the largest track and field competition in the United States. I was the guy who ran track to stay in shape and never really posed a real challenge to anyone. Trailing behind other sprinters in front of hundreds of thousands of people wasn't the trip I wanted to remember.

Soon I learned that it was different going on a trip with Dan. Those previous trips had a destination, a time frame, and a route. With Dan, the adventure could be simply getting to the destination or enjoying the novelty of an environment I'd never experienced.

"I'm headed to the Outer Banks of North Carolina this weekend. You wanna go?" Dan asked right before the weekend.

In the Dominican Republic, I learned to be a "yes man." My motto became, "Don't be afraid to say 'No,' but say 'Yes' more." So, even though I didn't want to go, I joined my buddy. We walked through fishing towns with sandy streets; we explored seaside communities with colorful vacation homes, shops, and restaurants; and we climbed mountainous sand dunes and rode cardboard sleds back down.

Before long, I was enjoying and looking forward to the trips.

"I'm going on a kayaking trip to Back Bay National Wildlife Refuge. You in?" With his ever-present sense of adventure, Dan motivated me to explore horizons far beyond my ordinary boundaries. A brother couldn't even swim, let alone kayak. Despite that, I ended up paddling for miles through marshes and fighting the currents of the bay as we headed toward a small island where we camped out on the beach.

Dan taught me to appreciate the local scene. Eventually, I started taking my own day trips. Whenever I wasn't drowning in homework or working at Walgreens, I'd drive to nearby places such as Historic Jamestowne[7] and Colonial Williamsburg. Although I was never a beach enthusiast, I started going to Virginia Beach, even just to walk along the boardwalk and sightsee.

***

AS MUCH AS I ENJOYED DAN'S ADVENTURES AND MY NEWFOUND SOLO ESCAPADES, STILL I YEARNED TO TRAVEL ABROAD. At the time, the Dominican Republic was the only country I knew. Since studying there, I would visit a few more times. Even when I returned to the Dominican Republic, I spent most of my time hanging out at my host family's place and sometimes revisiting remnants of the past: restaurants, beaches, barbershops, and the university where I studied. The novelty and fun had passed.

Each time, I expected to pick up the excitement where it left off in 2007. Unfortunately, it was an impossible task. My classmates from 2007 weren't there. Israel graduated and worked full time, so we didn't spend much time together. I had expected to travel

---

7   Established on May 13, 1607, Jamestown was the first permanent English settlement in North America. For decades, it served as the capital of the Virginia Colony. After Jamestown burned twice in the 1600s, the capital was moved to Williamsburg.

back in time to all that I had previously known, precisely as I had known it to be, but again, the moment had passed. It was just a routine trip.

The simple reason for returning to the Dominican Republic so often is that it was the only country I knew how to travel to. Everywhere seemed so far away and out of budget. The Dominican Republic felt safe because I had friends there and knew how to get around. I hadn't yet developed the confidence to travel into unfamiliar territory. At least, I didn't have the courage to venture out into the world by myself.

In time, I started looking into volunteer travel opportunities through non-profit organizations. I figured these trips could provide a more unique travel experience than just being a typical tourist. Also, I'd get the chance to make a difference, which I'd wanted to do since being in SIFE. However, the volunteer programs appeared to cost more than the tourist activities, which seemed absurd. "Non-profit, my ass!"

After online research, I came across the Peace Corps. It appealed to me most because I would not only travel but also live and work in another country. As life would have it, a Peace Corps representative showed up at my university's career fair, like an angel ready to answer my prayer, during my junior year. Unfortunately, the angel was recruiting students who could travel within six months. Since I had several semesters remaining, this disqualified me.

Finally, in December 2008, I completed my undergraduate degree program with a Bachelor of Science in Business Entrepreneurship. The same month I graduated, I applied to the Peace Corps. After interviews, several essays, and rigorous medical examinations, I received an acceptance letter to serve as a Community Economic Development Volunteer in a country called Paraguay. Still, I had to wait a year and a half before leaving for Europe. *That's where Paraguay was, right?*

***

IN THE MEANTIME, I WENT ABOUT MY EVERYDAY LIFE. Graduating from college freed up more time than I knew what to do with; however, each month, Sallie Mae reminded me. Therefore, I continued working at Walgreens to pay off student loans.

Also, I hung out with Dan. The pool hall and bowling alley had become additions to our routine. However, MMA was still the super-glue that bonded our friendship. Dan, a much more socially inclined person than me, would invite other people along on outings. Eventually, our following grew as we watched UFC events at Hooters, shot pool, and bowled. Yet, the road trips persisted.

Each year, Dan went on a big camping trip. Late spring of 2010, he invited me to go camping at Shenandoah Valley, which encompasses part of the Blue Ridge Mountains. After a year and a half, I was only weeks away from heading to Paraguay, which is in South America, to begin my Peace Corps Service. This would be our final trip together, at least for a while.

Dan joked, "When you go to Paraguay, you're going to be living in a bamboo hut in the middle of nowhere. So, a tent is a perfect way to prepare for it."

I laughed and responded, "Maybe, but I might survive in the middle of nowhere. I've seen the movies where the Black guy goes camping in the woods. It never turns out well for him." I knew if all the White people could die in the *Blair Witch Project* movie, I didn't stand a chance. I was twenty-three years old and had never hiked a mountain in my life, let alone done camping.

Walking through the woods and sleeping outside seemed intense to me. I was an amateur. I would have been satisfied with an hour hike, taking photos for proof, and Pizza Hut. But Dan packed tents, walking sticks, and Meals Ready to Eat (MREs)[8].

From Norfolk, Dan drove for four hours to Shenandoah Valley. We trailed along narrowly inclined roads that wrapped around the mountain. The spectacular views of natural scenery captured my attention. It was like being alive in a photograph inside a *National Geographic* magazine. The mountains lived in the clouds, the trees reached for the heavens, the colors brought everything to life, and the vast cloud-filled skies made it all seem so endless. As Dan continued driving, the only thing that could have possibly removed me from such an intimate state of tranquility instantly brought me back to reality.

"Dan, you see that?" I exclaimed.

As he slowed down, we both gazed at what was undoubtedly watching us as well. A bear lumbered along the side of the road. Granted, it was a small black bear, but a bear was a bear. Dan drove closer to the furry little creature so we could take photos. We hadn't even begun camping, and terror oozed through my veins. Getting ripped into pieces by Yogi Bear's[9] distant cousin was the last thing I wanted. Actually, I didn't want that at all; I would have chosen a fate at the Blair Witch's hands over getting mauled by a bear.

After parking, we grabbed the camping equipment from the vehicle. It grew dark and began to rain. Paranoid that the bears were plotting an attack, I didn't want to go deep into the woods. I

---

8   During the Revolutionary War, the Continental Congress issued each soldier rations of beef, rice, and peas. One ration was intended to last a soldier for a full day. MREs were introduced in 1981. Unlike the Revolutionary War rations, MREs come with candy and sometimes, cake.

9   Yogi Bear is likely a grizzly bear.

convinced Dan to set up the tent near the parking lot. Although the chances of becoming bear food decreased, getting run over by parking vehicles slightly increased. That night, it rained so much that water entered the tent and soaked my sleeping bag. It was a terrible feeling having to pee but not leaving the tent because of rain and bears.

The following day brought pleasant weather. The sky cleared up, and we could see a lot farther. We had granola for breakfast, packed up, grabbed the equipment, and started hiking.

We walked the mountains along the edges of cliffs and treaded through beds of water. We gazed at breathtaking views. One of the trails extended along the steep sides. The ground was composed of massive silvery stones that ran down the side of the mountain. We walked over the rock scrambles while observing the valleys and mountains filled with lush green trees in the distance. We hiked for hours.

Finally, Dan decided it was best to head back to his vehicle. We walked back to where we thought he'd parked. Apparently, we had thought wrong. So, we walked the main road but couldn't tell whether we were walking up or down the mountain. We walked approximately four miles in one direction before turning around and trying the other way. Suddenly, it began to rain.

Dan and I decided that one of us would carry the equipment, and the other would run to locate the car. Being a runner in high school, I was like an Ethiopian version of Usain Bolt compared to Dan. Dan passed me his car keys like a baton and I took off. I had to have run two miles in the rain when a car pulled up beside me and stopped.

The driver was an African American guy like me. *Black people do camp*, I thought and felt a wisp of inspiration. He asked where I was going. I told him that I was lost and looking for my car. He smirked and asked, "If I offer you a ride, you won't kill me. Will you?" I thought, *Did he really just ask me that*? But then I understood ... a brother could never be too cautious in horror movies. I laughed and silently agreed not to hurt him.

Turns out, the guy was a photographer from Pennsylvania. He had gone to Shenandoah Valley to take photos of the landscapes; indeed, he had chosen a great place to do so. We drove for a few miles. Then I recognized Dan's car in a parking lot. The driver let me out. I thanked him, and we said our goodbyes.

I drove the car and found Dan walking along the road. We went to a rest area in the park, ate our last MREs, and headed home. It becomes terrifyingly apparent how big the world can be when you're lost only a few miles from your car.

Weeks later, I was in Paraguay, about four thousand five hundred miles from where we thought we'd parked.

CHAPTER 5
SOUTHERN HOSPITALITY

I wonder if things can happen too early or too late or if everything happens at exactly the right time. If so, how sad and beautiful. —*Simon Van Booy*

In June 2010, I arrived in the South American country with twenty other volunteers who were part of the Community Economic Development sector. Our group was identified as G-33.

Before becoming actual Peace Corps[10] Volunteers, we had to complete three months of intensive training in a small community called Guarambaré, located on the outskirts of the nation's capital Asunción. The training consisted of intensive language classes, including Spanish and Guaraní (Paraguay's indigenous language). Also, we took cultural training that helped us understand cultural differences and acclimatize to the way of life in our new country. Lastly, there was technical training; my group learned to design and implement projects based on the pillars of our sector: entrepreneurship, personal finance, civic education/ leadership, and computer literacy.

---

10   The Peace Corps was created by President John F. Kennedy in 1961. By 2020, Peace Corps Volunteers have served in over a hundred and forty countries.

Long Field incorporated the most hands-on training we received. During Long Field, new volunteers were paired together and then sent to spend a week in communities with experienced volunteers. We would learn first-hand what it was like to live and work as volunteers by shadowing seasoned warriors. Since there were twenty-one members in G-33, one group had three people while the rest were in groups of two. My partner was a charming young lady from North Carolina named Emily.

Emily spoke with one of the heaviest southern accents that I'd ever heard. Occasionally, I teased her for being one of those "country North Carolina people," but it was always in good taste. Besides, I had grown up in Virginia, the southern state directly above North Carolina. Anyone could tell that Emily came from a loving family by how she expressed the same affection toward others. She personified *Southern Hospitality*. Emily's personality was sweet like pecan pie, especially those made in the South. Because there, people add more sugar. Furthermore, she was friendly and respectful toward everyone, including me.

Her personality made her such a wonderful and pleasant person to be around. Even when the crickets chirped at my jokes, my terrible humor always seemed to entertain Emily.

One time, our group held a talent show. We quickly learned that G-33's volunteers possessed some serious talent. I'm talking about artists, actors, and singers. "We Are the World," the Peace Corps edition, was coming. My peers were going to bring art and music to the world through their volunteer work. Then there was me. I stood in front of everyone ... and in the most monotone voice, I read a humorous poem that made fun of everyone's cultural struggles and difficult training experiences. It would've been the perfect performance to boo; however, Emily couldn't stop laughing. Her laughter spread like an infection and filled everyone with exuberance. Because of Emily, I won the talent show. The prize was a cup and a metal straw.

Then there was the time G-33 made a five-hour trip to a youth camp organized by our sister group of volunteers. Riding in a cramped van, I had my music for comfort. Everyone seemed to be chatting except "old anti-social" me. Emily noticed that I wore headphones while listening to music on my iPod.

"Hey Mike, what are you listening to?" she asked.

I replied, "Whitney Houston."

"I love Whitney Houston! What music do you have by her?" Emily asked.

I unplugged my headphones and handed her my iPod. She went through the songs until she found what she wanted. She used an auxiliary cable to connect the iPod to the vehicle's stereo. Then she played the hit, "I Wanna Dance With Somebody." She transformed the passenger van into a choir. The Church of Whitney Houston sang in harmony, "Ohhh! I wanna dance with somebody!"

Emily always knew how to make the best of any moment. Luckily for me, she was my Long Field partner. Together, we would learn the ins and outs of being a Peace Corps Volunteer.

Emily and I boarded a flamboyantly colorful bus and traveled to Ayolas, a town located in Misiones, the most southern department of the country. We'd have seven hours to burn on "The Magical 'Cool Bus." We spent the time playing Hangman on my iPod Touch. I'd choose words like "irk" and "lucky" to make it difficult for her to guess. Unluckily for me, my word choices irked her, and I lost an opponent. After a while, we both took naps only to wake up at a rest stop. Then, vendors boarded the bus with all kinds of products.

"That lady is selling *chipa*," Emily said. "Our instructor recommended we try it, remember?"

"No. What is it?" I asked.

"It's a traditional Paraguayan bread with bits of cheese baked inside," she said.

"Cool. Let's get it!" I agreed. The fresh *chipa* was warm, and crunchy on the outside and gooey inside. I ate two of them. Afterward, my belly poked out like a pregnant woman's.

When we finally arrived at the bus stop in Ayolas, two volunteers awaited us. They were Theresa and Liam, who were both serving there. They lived close to one another; therefore, Emily and I spent most of our time together doing the same activities. Since my trainer Liam lived at the town's fire station, Emily and I stayed at Theresa's home. We even shared the same room. She slept on the sofa while I slept on a thin floor mattress, also known as a yoga mat.

We had a blast in Misiones. One of the highlights occurred on June 29, after Paraguay had beaten Japan to advance in the 2010 FIFA World Cup[11]. We watched the victory from a small, boxed television at the fire station. Everyone stood in excitement and started screaming and hugging each other. I wasn't even a soccer fan, and I embraced strangers wearing firefighting gear. Next, the celebration moved outside, where the firefighters turned on the truck's loud sirens.

Shortly after, Liam, Theresa, Emily, and I sat on top of the fire engine. Suddenly, the truck started to drive off; it was unexpected. I was too new to the country to understand how crazy Paraguayans were about *fútbol* and how it was acceptable to use public resources for celebratory purposes. Then again, this was

---

[11] Paraguay was eliminated in the quarterfinals after a loss to Spain. The Spanish National Team went on to win their first World Cup.

the same fire station that was taking rent money from a volunteer. I prayed no one's house caught on fire and enjoyed the moment. While riding on the fire truck, cars and motorcycles began following us. Large crowds formed on the sidewalks. Paraguayans wore their national team jerseys and waved their country's flag. Emily and I yelled as loud as we could while waving at the crowds from the top of the fire truck.

Not long ago, I had been a stranger in a foreign country, and today I was in solidarity with the country's achievement. Later that night, the firefighters made a special dinner, barbecued cow's head. It was a first for both Emily and me. U.S. citizens don't typically like to see the faces of the meat we eat.

We picked off the meaty cheeks. We both seemed to enjoy the peculiar delicacy.

One of the firemen said, "Try the brain. It tastes like scrambled eggs." Emily and I looked at one another, disgusted by what we had just heard. At least, he didn't say it tasted like chicken as everything else seems to do. So, I gave it a go. It didn't taste like eggs or chicken. It tasted exactly how I imagined "brain" would. It tasted like something I never wanted to eat again. I washed it down with Paraguay's most sophisticated cocktail, red wine mixed with Coca-Cola.

After spending a week in Ayolas, Emily and I returned to Guarambaré with once-in-a-lifetime experiences and great insight into what it was like to be Peace Corps Volunteers.

Three months in Guarambaré provided us with enough experience to understand and face the new reality we had recently entered. After training, studying, and practicing for our assignments. After three months of developing beautiful relationships with each other, the trainers, and the host families. After what seemed like an eternity, we swore in (by repeating the same oath as government officials and armed forces members) as Peace Corps Volunteers in mid-August 2010. Finally, we went our separate ways to different communities throughout the country where we would serve for the next two years. My town was Juan E. O'Leary, located in the department of Alto Paraná[12].

***

IT HAD BEEN OVER A YEAR SINCE I HAD ARRIVED IN PARAGUAY.

After swearing-in, each volunteer received a small, black, indestructible Nokia cell phone. I had always kept mine on vibrate. I'd never been a fan of any ringtones. A short vibration let me know that I had gotten a text when receiving a message. When someone called, the shaking lasted until the caller hung up or I answered the phone.

On the evening of November 28, 2011, my phone began to vibrate and didn't stop. *This is weird*, I thought. Typically, I received text messages. However, after looking at the caller ID, I saw Kevin's name. Kevin was another volunteer in the group and lived an hour from me, closer than anyone else from our G-33 clique.

After seeing Kevin's name, I answered the phone. "Kevin! What's up, bro?"

"Hey Mike," Kevin replied.

There was a short pause before he continued, "Last night, Emily and her boyfriend were involved in a car accident. Their vehicle drove over a pothole, causing Emily's boyfriend to lose control ... and, *um*, they crashed head-on into a truck."

Within the next second, my mind had gone haywire as it was trying to process what it had just heard. The suddenness and the

---

12   Juan Emiliano O'Leary, born in 1880, was a Paraguayan poet and historian. He is most known for work chronicling the War of the Triple Alliance, a war Paraguay fought against Brazil, Uruguay, and Argentina.

finality of it can't be understood all at once. Moments earlier, Emily had been living in my head as a memory and an assumption; I remembered how she had been and assumed she was all right.

My heart sank, and the only thing I could say was, "What do you mean? How is she?"

"I'm sorry for having to be the one to tell you this ..." Kevin took a deep breath. Then, with his voice hoarse, "Emily passed away. Everyone is heading to Asunción now," Kevin said.

That was all I could bear to hear. "All right, man. I'm on my way." But I really didn't want to be on my way. I just wanted it to be a bad dream. I lay across my bed. Maybe I could wake up from the nightmare and Emily would be alive in the morning.

Emily, Kevin, eighteen others, and I had sworn in as Peace Corps Volunteers at the U.S. Embassy in Asunción. That was the last time all of us had been together. A year later, we reunited in Asunción for a different reason, to mourn the loss of an incredible person.

Once a passionate Peace Corps Volunteer dedicated to helping others, she was gone. Once the *country* girl from North Carolina and my delightful Long Field partner, she had been called home. Once a cherished friend, sister, and daughter, she was no longer with us.

***

ONE OF MY MOST VIVID MEMORIES OF EMILY IS THAT SHE ALWAYS RECEIVED SO MUCH MAIL. During our trainee days, mail shipments would come in. Most of it was for Emily. There were always stacks of letters, magazines, and care packages addressed to Emily with each shipment that arrived. Out of the twenty-one volunteers in our group, she received more mail than everyone else combined. Once I asked her, "Who sends you all of this mail?" She let out a big chuckle and, speaking with her solid southern accent, replied, "It's my mum!"

Emily's mother, father, brother, and uncle arrived in Asunción two days after Emily's passing. They visited to know the country their daughter had served in and grown to love during her time as a Peace Corps Volunteer. The two-day memorial was more of a celebration of Emily's life. It took place at the Peace Corps headquarters in Asunción. On the morning of day one, volunteers and Emily's family created colorful mosaics in her remembrance. Later, the mosaics were placed on the wall inside the Peace Corps Paraguay's headquarters. After lunch, we [volunteers] spent time introducing ourselves to Emily's family and talking about our experiences. The morning and evening times were set aside so that volunteers, primarily from group G-33, could spend time with the family. In the evening, volunteers serving all over the country had come to pay their respects to Emily's family. At the headquarters was a beautiful outdoor patio and garden, where everyone joined to share their experiences with Emily. Volunteers told stories that made guests cry, while others' stories brought laughter and joy. The first day's event concluded after Emily's family emotionally shared stories honoring their daughter.

Day two was much more relaxed. Approximately two hundred Peace Corps Volunteers served in Paraguay during my service. Many had come to pay their respects. I'd never seen so many volunteers at the office before. I got to know volunteers from several other sectors, including health and sanitation, education, and agriculture. Additionally, I met volunteers who were a part of my sector, community economic development, but were part of different groups. We spent most of the day resting and supporting one another because of the circumstance and emotional night before.

On the evening of day two, Emily's family invited volunteers to dinner. At dinner, Emily's parents gave us two gifts. The first was a silver heart-shaped keychain with "Peace Corps G-33" inscribed on one side, and the other side read "With Love, Emily's Family" engraved beautifully in cursive. There were twenty keychains for twenty volunteers. The second gift was an address book. Emily's parents passed it around. They told everyone, including me, to write our names, phone numbers, and addresses in the book. After we had written our information in the book, Emily's parents collected it. Then came the third gift.

Mango was Emily's favorite fruit. That's why Emily's closest friends quickly obtained enough small mango trees to give to everyone who attended the memorial. Volunteers would plant the third gift all around the country.

CHAPTER 6

SEEDS OF NEW LIFE

Plant the garden of your life with friendship's lovely flowers.
—Anonymous

Paraguay is a small country with approximately six million people (as in 2011). The death of a Peace Corps Volunteer constituted major news in the media. I left my community on a Monday, and by Wednesday, the entire country knew Emily's story. I was not emotionally ready to answer the question that I knew everyone would ask me: "Did you know her?"

Before I could talk to anyone about it, there was something I had to do. I spent Wednesday night writing a letter. I spent the next day proofreading it and making minor changes. My Spanish was decent but not perfect. The letter had to be clear and concise. It had to be right before presenting it to Gloria.

***

WHEN I FIRST ARRIVED AT MY NEW COMMUNITY, JUAN E. O'LEARY, THE FIRST ASSIGNMENT WAS TO COMPLETE A COMMUNITY ASSESSMENT ADMINISTERED BY THE PEACE CORPS OFFICE. The thick packet included dozens of forms that would allow me to gather and learn general information about the city and the community's needs to assist me in developing projects. To make completing the packet easier, I extracted vital information and created a survey. Then, for weeks, I went door to door talking to people and asking residents to complete surveys.

Coming from a business background, professionalism was the name of the game. I wore collared shirts neatly tucked into my pressed slacks. I walked up and introduced myself to strangers, sitting on their front porches, with the intent of handing them surveys. Many people thought I was a missionary sent to convert them. Others suspected I was a spy.

Before leaving for Paraguay, I visited relatives in Missouri. After telling my family I would be a Peace Corps Volunteer, Grandpa Tommy said, "Peace Corps Volunteer, huh?" Then he snickered and continued, "You know them people over there are gonna think you're a spy." And I clearly remember thinking, *A spy? Yeah, right. You're crazy, old man!*

Turns out, Grandpa Tommy wasn't crazy. As Gramps predicted, I had become a CIA operative sent by the United States Government to Paraguay to steal their source of *agua dulce* or freshwater. At least, that's what a few Paraguayan conspiracy theorists believed.

Unsurprisingly, many believed that I had moved to Paraguay from South Africa. At first, I didn't understand why they thought a random African had immigrated to Paraguay. Then, I remembered that Paraguayans were soccer fanatics, and the 2010 World Cup had taken place in South Africa. *Where else would a Black guy come from*? That's right, Paraguay's neighboring country—Brazil. People constantly approached me and spoke to me in Portuguese upon our first encounters. Then when I'd say, "I'm from the United States," they'd have a look of bewilderment and respond, "What? There are Black people in the United States?" I'd respond, "Of course.

49

You know that Barack Obama is the President." This unsurprising news amazed them and left them perplexed[13].

That wasn't the only thing that amazed them. Paraguayans were all kinds of curious about me. They wanted to touch my hair. After one little girl got a feel, she laughed and questioned why it felt like a 3M Scotch-Brite cleaning pad. They inquired why my skin was dark and whether my parents were Black as well. Not to mention, I supposedly looked like every Black person they'd seen on television, from Eddie Murphy to Will Smith. People often asked me if I was related to those celebrities. Had I been related to *The Fresh Prince*, my black ass would've been trying to get a role in a movie instead of passing out surveys in rural Paraguay. That's for sure.

On one of the dreadful "community assessment" days, I passed by a field where a dozen kids were playing soccer. After noticing me, one of the boys left his prepubescent buddies and ran toward me. He was a short, skinny, well-mannered kid, no more than ten years old.

He politely asked, "Do you want to play soccer with us?"

As someone who had never been a fan of the sport, I politely declined by saying, "Hey, my friend. Maybe next time." I walked away carrying my folder filled with surveys.

A few days later, I walked by the same field while the kids were playing soccer. Again, the same boy invited me to play a game with him and his friends. I responded, "Next time, little buddy. I'm working right now."

Every time I saw the kid, he inquired about my interest in playing soccer. The interest always stayed low, but eventually, I began to feel guilty for dismissing him.

---

13 Paraguay is one of the most racially homogenous countries in South America. Roughly ninety-five percent of the population is mestizo, mixed Spanish, and Native American. The other five percent is largely White.

One evening, I dressed in my usual collared shirt and slacks. I picked up the folder housing the surveys, but then I sat it back on the desk. I replaced my trousers with athletic shorts and my collared shirt with a black, sleeveless Under Armour compression top. I went to the soccer field where the children were playing. The kid approached me. Before he could open his mouth, I said, "Let's play, *amigo*."

A week after our soccer match, I was walking on a cobblestone road a couple of blocks from my home when I heard someone calling me. I quickly turned around to catch a flash of someone going inside their home. One person went inside, but five came out, and they stared me down. I only recognized one of them, the tenacious little guy from the soccer game, and he was pointing at me. I figured the other people were his family. I approached everyone and introduced myself. They invited me inside their home, where we conversed for a short while. They seemed thrilled to meet me and invited me to return anytime I pleased. The kid's name was Luis, and his mother was Gloria.

***

FIVE YEARS MY ELDER, GLORIA WAS THE BEST FRIEND WHOM I HAD WAITED MY ENTIRE LIFE TO MEET. She made me feel what it was like to have a true friend or *amigo de alma* (friend of the soul), as she called it; she also taught me how to be a better friend to those who were important to me. When Gloria asked, "How are you?" it meant, "Tell me how you're feeling, I really care." More than her words, her facial expressions, and body language spoke volumes. When she invited me to visit her home any time I pleased, she absolutely meant it.

She lived in a small, three-bedroom house. The house held Gloria, her husband, their three young children, and Gloria's two younger sisters; seven people lived in a three-bedroom. They only locked their door when no one was home and at night when everyone was asleep. Every other time, I didn't even have to knock to go inside. I'd just walk in, say "Hi," sit on the sofa, and watch Spanish episodes of *The Simpsons* with the family. If I barged into their home when they were eating, they offered me a plate.

Gloria loved to offer me *sopa de mondongo,* a soup made of tripe (cow intestines), and whatever other organs she decided to put in the soup. Sometimes, she even added bulls' testicles. I tried it once and have hated it ever since then. If you're keeping track, by this point, I had eaten a bull's head, a bull's testicles, and a bull's intestines. It turned my stomach to think what other parts of a cow Paraguayans would feed me next. She laughed every time anyone mentioned *mondongo*, and I gave her a look of disgust.

She would proudly laugh and say, "The people in your country don't eat this?"

I would correct her, "A lot of older Black people and people from the South eat *sopa de mondongo*. It's called chitterlings[14]." I shared the stories about how my grandma cleaned them, and it made the entire house smell bad. "As a kid, I would go outside and play with my friends until my grandma finished cooking."

Gloria was a fantastic cook. Sometimes, I'd go over and just pick from her food while she was cooking.

No matter how much effort I made to wear out my welcome, I always failed. I visited Gloria and her family whenever I pleased, whenever I needed someone to talk to, whenever I missed my family back home, and anytime I passed by her home. I passed

---

14 Typically pronounced "chitlins," chitterlings are usually made from pig intestines. The dish is eaten all over the world, but in the United States, the tradition is believed to originate from slavery before the Civil War. When pigs were slaughtered, the best cuts were reserved for the master's household or for market. Undesirable cuts, such as ears and intestines, were given to slaves.

by her house almost every day. She and her family accepted me as their own.

We could talk about anything. For example, there's a concept that especially irks people throughout the Americas. It annoyed Gloria as well.

"Michael, why do people from the United States call themselves Americans? We're American, too," Gloria said.

After discussions with dozens of Latin American people, I arrived at an answer. It was in the language.

"Gloria, you're from Paraguay, so you can say you're Paraguayan. I'm from the United States of America. In Spanish, the word "*Estadounidense*" describes a person from my country. We don't have a word like that in English. So instead of saying, we're "citizens of the United States of America" or "*United States of Americans*," we say we're Americans for short. America is in the name of our country."

Gloria and I had a plethora of conversations like this, which allowed us to understand one another's countries on a more profound level. I knew that I could trust Gloria to give me real and honest answers. She trusted me to do the same. She even trusted me with her son Luis.

Luis and I became terrific friends. He was ten years old, fourteen years younger than me. I converted him into a hardcore MMA fan. Luis' favorite fighters became Anderson Silva and Jose Aldo, and I was proud because they were mine as well. In Paraguay, the live UFC events showed on basic television. The same Pay-Per-View events that Dan and I had to go to Hooters to watch, Luis and I watched them at my house for free. I'd fry chicken or make pizza, and the only things missing were the Hooters' girls and celery sticks.

In one year, I developed the closest relationship that I'd ever developed with anyone outside of my family. Gloria was the oldest of four siblings and a mother of three children. I don't know exactly where it came from, but her instinct to show people that she genuinely cared for them made her one of the most beautiful people I'd ever met in my life. Gloria was the only one who knew how I felt before I even said a word. Although I knew she would understand how I felt, I had to tell her anyway. That's why I wrote the letter for her after Emily's death.

Handwritten on lined paper, I carefully removed the letter from the notebook. I proofread it one final time before folding it into thirds. Before leaving to deliver the letter to Gloria, I grabbed the small mango tree that I received from Emily's close friends.

Everyone was home on the Thursday evening that I visited the family's home: Gloria, her husband Michel, her daughter Milena, her sons Luis and Alejandro, and both sisters Fatima and Nallma. I stood in front of them with the letter in my hand and read:

Dear Gloria,
Emily was a Peace Corps Volunteer like me. We met in Miami and arrived in Paraguay on the same flight. We spent two months training together in Guaramabé. During Emily's short time here, she was able to help so many people and make so many friends. Her friends thought of her the same as I think of you and as you think of me—like family.

There's no single day or moment that's promised to any of us. One instance, we're here, and the next, we are not. While we're still here and I have the opportunity, I want you to know that I'm thankful for all you and your family have done for me. I want you to know that you are my best friend.

Emily's best friends gave me this small mango tree because mango was Emily's favorite fruit. I'm giving it to you in remembrance of Emily.

May it grow into a tree that produces the sweetest mangoes and be an everlasting symbol of our friendship.

Love always,

Michael

***

MY EARLY INTERACTIONS WITH GLORIA TAUGHT ME THAT IF I WAS GOING TO BE A SUCCESSFUL VOLUNTEER, I NEEDED TO BUILD MEANINGFUL RELATIONSHIPS WITH PEOPLE IN THE COMMUNITY. Eventually, I left the surveys at home. Instead, I spent time mastering the art of walking up to residents and starting conversations. It wasn't that hard. Being the only foreigner in town, people stared at me curiously and wanted to know who I was anyway; and I definitely wasn't Don Cheadle, Samuel L. Jackson or any other Black person they'd seen on television. It was the perfect opportunity to introduce myself.

Through the conversations, I learned about the residents and what was important to them. I was building an endless network of contacts and subconsciously planting the seeds for some of the most amazing friendships that I would ever have. Early on, I spent more time getting to know people than working. After a while, people invited me to lunches, dinners, festivals, holiday parties, birthday celebrations, *Quinceañeras*, graduations, barbecues, community events, social gatherings, weddings, funerals, and soccer tournaments. I accepted every invitation I received. Not only did people know who I was, but now they were willing to work with me. After a year or so of knowing and working with me, these same people reached out to see how I was doing after Emily's passing.

Over time, the relations grew more robust, and my new community had fully embraced me. I realized this about halfway into my service. Together, community members and I worked passionately to accomplish dozens of projects that made a lasting impact on the lives of everyone involved.

CHAPTER 7
HEART OF SOUTH AMERICA

~~~~~~

The ornament of a house is the friends who frequent it.
—*Ralph Waldo Emerson*

Yerba maté, similar to loose-leaf tea, is packed into a small wooden or metallic cup called a *guampa*. A metal straw with a filter at its bottom sits inside of the cup of *yerba maté*. The ritual also includes a pitcher of cold water or a thermos of hot water. Various plants and herbs are crushed with a mortar and steeped in water. The plants serve as refreshments, natural remedies, or dietary supplements, or add flavor to the drink. Now mixed with plants, the water is poured over the dried *yerba* and sipped through the metal straw. The filter at the bottom of the straw prevents the *yerba* from entering the straw while drinking. Served with cold water, the drink is called *tereré*. Served with hot water, the drink is called *maté*.

The server has one of the most critical responsibilities in this tradition. The server pours the water into the *yerba*-filled cup and hands it to the first drinker. Once the first drinker consumes the liquid, the server refills the cup, passes it to the next drinker, and the process continues.

Even if you are a stranger, you would be welcomed to consume from the same straw as everyone else in the *tereré* circle. It could be just a few guests or an entire family. Paraguayans are nice and inclusive people. Friendship in Paraguay is held in very high regard. *Tereré* symbolizes the epitome of friendship in the heart of South America.

Drinking *tereré* or *maté* is the most common pastime in the country[15].

A curious person could likely find some version of *yerba maté* at their local grocery store. Throughout the United States, it is available in canned form and dried leaf form. However, the drink itself is only a fraction of the ritual. One would need to pass the *guampa* in Paraguay to get the whole experience.

❋❋❋

A FEW WEEKS BEFORE TRAINING WAS COMPLETE, OUR PEACE CORPS TRAINERS IDENTIFIED CONTACTS IN THE COMMUNITIES WHERE VOLUNTEERS WOULD SERVE. We'd spend three days with the advisors, getting to know the community and learning about the work we'd be doing.

I first visited Juan E. O'Leary on July 30, 2010, the same date as International Friendship Day. I stayed with an English teacher who taught at the local high school. It was a small house, but big enough for her, her niece, and barely me. We were still in our training days. I was supposed to spend the days meeting community leaders and getting to know the community. However, it rained

---

15   Maté has been long been consumed by the indigenous Guaraní native to modern-day Paraguay and surrounding areas. The practice and the herb spread with Spanish colonization. Presently, Brazil is the largest producer and exporter of yerba maté in the world.

almost nonstop for the entire duration of my visit. I passed the time getting to know the family and drinking *tereré* with them.

On the final day before returning to my training community, the English teacher introduced me to a business teacher at the high school. His name was Señor Luis. I didn't even care what I would be doing at that point. I just wanted to know where I could stay upon returning. Señor Luis informed me that he had an extra room at his home. He agreed to take me to his residence and show me the room.

First, he introduced me to his family. The professor was a serious man and not very talkative. He mumbled his words whenever he spoke, and I could barely understand him. His wife Gladys was charming and outgoing. She made me feel the most comfortable. The youngest daughter Adri looked like Wednesday Addams from the Addams Family and creepily stared at me. The older daughter Lili was like the teenager you'd see sitting at the "cool table" at a high school cafeteria in a Disney Channel show. Then there would be me, the newest addition to the family and the only Black person in the entire town or any surrounding city. I would fit in perfectly.

***

PEACE CORPS VOLUNTEERS RECEIVED A MODEST STIPEND TO COVER BASIC LIVING EXPENSES. To put things into perspective, first, there was the starving artist. A step up from him stood the broke college student, surviving off of packs of ramen and peanut butter sandwiches. Next on the economic ladder of prosperity was the resourceful volunteer.

When I lived in Paraguay, I must admit that my living situation was not typical for Peace Corps Volunteers. In fact, I probably lived better than ninety-five percent of my peers. Some volunteers wanted to get the full "third world" Peace Corps experience and ended up living in worse conditions than their host nation counterparts. Most of those volunteers chose to live like that, while a few had little choice in the matter. My buddy Kevin was in the unfortunate few.

Kevin was a tall and skinny guy with swag like John Travolta from *Saturday Night Fever*. He loved to dance, and his taste for music was like a bottle of Cabernet Sauvignon sitting on top of a jukebox; fine wine, that is. Back when the only Spanish music I listened to consisted of artists from Caribbean Islands, Kevin put me on to dozens of others. My favorite ended up being a band from Mexico known as Maná. Not only were Kevin and I big fans of Maná, but Gloria was as well. When the band toured in Paraguay, all three of us had the best time imaginable. Apart from swaying his hips while dancing the *paso doble*, Mr. Dirty Dancing was living like a contestant on the show *Survivor*.

Kevin lived in Tembiapora[16]. He spent time at my home more than almost any other volunteer. I didn't blame him. I visited his place on a few occasions, and a few was all I could stand. A trip to his house went like this: a ten-minute bus ride on the highway, a fifteen-minute bus ride on a dirt road, a forty-minute boat ride across Lake Iguassu, and a twenty-five-minute walk. The trek took ninety minutes, and every minute of it was a different kind of uncomfortable. His rural community reminded me of a level from *Donkey Kong Country*—dirt roads, thousands of banana trees, and enough animals to consider his community one gigantic farm.

Kevin lived in a house two miles away from the nearest anything. His house was composed of uneven slabs of wood. Although the Big Bad Wolf may not have been able to huff and puff and blow Kevin's house down, he could damn sure see through it because

---

16   Tembiapora is in the Caaguazú Department of Paraguay. Caaguazú in Guaraní means "great herb."

of all the cracks. There was a water well in Kevin's front yard. Unlike the pretty brick wells in Disney movies, Kevin's well was just a hole in the ground covered up by a wooden board. That was where Kevin fetched his water. One day, a cow walked over the board. The board broke under the animal's weight. The cow fell into the well and drowned, contaminating Kevin's only source of barely fresh water. Kevin resorted to carrying a five-gallon bottle for miles. Sometimes, he would go days without bathing. Even if it was only to take a hot shower and rehydrate, Kevin enjoyed making the long journey to my house. Where I lived, I was far from resembling a contestant performing dangerous feats for the luxury of a hot shower and rehydration. I lived about as differently from Kevin as one could.

I stayed with a host family the entire duration of my time in Juan E. O'Leary. We didn't live in just a house; it was more like a compound. They owned a pharmacy as well as a small office supply store. Their businesses were side by side and located on the main avenue; their home was directly behind their businesses. It consisted of several rooms, a bathroom, a kitchen, and a living area. I shared the kitchen and living room area with the family.

In the living room was a door that led to the backyard. On the left side, there was a small yard with clean-cut grass, two mango trees, a custard apple tree[17], and a garden area past the trees. The marble floor patio area on the right side of the yard had high ceilings to protect from the elements. It was big enough to use as a classroom. Like a motel set-up, there were two small rooms behind the patio area. The bathroom separated my room and the guest room.

---

17   Custard apples are native to the New World. They can be eaten raw or cooked. They're closely related to more popular fruits such as cherimoya, sugar apple, and soursop. In the United States, soursop is often called "pawpaw."

I had come almost full circle. In a past life, guests would come to my hotel and tell me about their world travels. Now, I was the world traveler staying in something of a motel.

All I had to do was leave the house, make a left turn, take about forty steps, and I would be standing in the middle of an international highway. That would place me approximately eighty miles east of Foz do Iguaçu, Brazil. In fact, I crossed the road almost daily to either go to the supermarket or go for a run. Before crossing the highway, there was a bus stop at the end of the avenue, which made my site highly accessible.

Having nice living accommodations and an accessible site made my residence a hub for Kevin, fellow volunteers and a few *Couch Surfers* passing by.

***

ONE EVENING, I RECEIVED A RANDOM PHONE CALL.

"Hey Mike, my name is Rachel, and I live in Ka' Jovái. We've never met before. I hope you don't mind that I got your number from a friend. A volunteer is coming to train with me for Long Field. She will arrive at the bus station in Juan E. O'Leary before I get there. Can you pick her up?"

As quickly as I could say, "Sure, I'll pick her up," Rachel hung up the phone.

Right after lunch, I waited outside of my house because I could see the buses arrive at the terminal from there. When I saw a bus arrive, I went to the terminal to pick up the volunteer that would be training with Rachel, whoever that was. The volunteer was the only foreigner to get off the bus. She was also one of the most beautiful people to exit the vehicle. My day was looking up. I approached her.

"Hi, my name is Mike. Rachel asked me to pick you up," I said.

She replied, "My name is Alejandra." Beautiful, and she had an exotic accent. Thank you, Rachel!

"How was the bus ride?" I asked.

"It was long, but not too bad," Alejandra answered.

"Did you eat yet?" I asked.

Alejandra replied, "Not yet, but I really have to use the bathroom."

It took a minute to walk to my place. First, I led Alejandra to drop off her bags in the living room. Then, I directed her to the bathroom.

When Alejandra returned to the living room, I politely told her to grab a seat at the dining table. Due to my host family's busy schedules, they hired a housekeeper named Feli. Feli was in her late thirties and had worked with the family for years. Monday through Saturday, Feli cleaned the house, washed clothes, and cooked lunch. And she was an outstanding cook. I prepared Alejandra a plate of pasta with tomato sauce topped with beef strips called *tallarín*, *mandioca* (cassava), and served her fresh banana juice.

As Alejandra enjoyed Feli's cooking, she asked questions about what it was like to be a volunteer. I had been in site for less than a year. I explained as much as I could about Paraguayan culture, work, and the overall Peace Corps experience. I enjoyed the conversation with the lovely Alejandra. I would have liked to continue getting to know her.

No more than ten minutes after Alejandra finished her meal, a stranger appeared in my living room. She was a slim, blue-eyed brunette with puffy cheeks. Her voice sounded very animated, and she spoke quickly.

"Hi Mike, I'm Rachel. Thank you so much for picking up Alejandra from the bus station."

Then she introduced herself to Alejandra before turning back to me.

"Sorry I can't stay longer. Our bus is leaving soon. Alejandra, let's go."

That was my first encounter with Rachel. Like a tornado, she blew in the door, snatched up Alejandra, and blew out.

Weeks later, I received a second phone call from Rachel.

"Hey Mike, I'm heading to Asunción tomorrow. Is it okay if I spend the night at your place tonight? It'll shorten tomorrow's journey. I just want to wake up and go in the morning."

"Sure, just let me know what time you're coming by," I said. Of course, living in a handy location upped my social game.

"It'll be later in the evening," Rachel responded.

"Oh yeah, and I'll make dinner for you," Rachel added.

In Paraguay, lunch is the heaviest meal. Breakfast and dinner are lighter meals, usually consisting of bread, crackers, or cake served with Paraguayan milk tea known as *cocido con leche*. Paraguayans would barbecue or serve larger meals if there was a party or festival. But that was only on special occasions. Therefore, it was nice to eat an actual dinner. Although a guest, Rachel cooked dinner to thank me for letting her spend the night. She made a Chinese dish of shredded chicken with a peanut butter sauce, served with rice and salad. Rachel's cooking was divine.

It was my first time tasting anything like that combination of flavors. The peanut butter sauce was not overwhelming and complemented the chicken perfectly. My tastebuds were going wild with the contradictions. In Paraguay, an American made me a Chinese dish that I'd never tasted before. Wild indeed.

"Rachel, you gotta give me this recipe!" I told her.

That night, Rachel and I got to know each other personally. Rachel had a crazy energetic personality and spoke with great enthusiasm. She was a fellow Midwesterner from Illinois, the state that borders my birthplace. Rachel grew up on an apple orchard two hundred miles from St. Louis, Missouri. Curtis Orchard & Pumpkin Patch was where she developed an interest in agriculture. Her fiancé was in the United States Marine Corps. After her Peace Corps service, she planned to get married and take over the family's orchard business.

Also, I learned about her work as an Agriculture Volunteer.

I listened as Rachel explained, "I work with children in schools, as well as families throughout the community. I teach them how to plant gardens and grow vegetables. Part of this is for dietary reasons. Paraguayans, especially in the rural areas, have meat- and starch-heavy diets. This provides them energy as they work arduously in the fields and tend to their farm animals; however, they miss out on essential nutrients. By teaching the importance of a well-balanced diet and helping them to grow food, they can live healthier lives. Economics is another reason. People can sell their fresh vegetables as a source of income."

Additionally, she worked with a cooperative on beekeeping projects. In Paraguay, a cooperative is an association in which people come together for social and economic purposes. Being a part of a legally recognized organization makes it easier to achieve everyone's interests. Rachel worked with a cooperative, teaching women how to maintain bee colonies and collect honey that members could sell.

I shared with her some of my experiences as a volunteer.

"A week after arriving in Juan O'Leary, I was playing chess with my host mom's nephew Rodney. Rodney and I connected instantly because we were the same age. He lived right across the street, and he owned a chessboard. We discussed the types of projects he believed were important in the community. Every time Rodney and I played chess on the front porch, kids always came over to watch. So, I began to teach these stragglers the rules of chess. No matter how many kids I taught how to play, more wanted to learn. I got an idea.

I visited the schools in my community and spoke with the administrators about starting a chess club. Once they were on board, I advertised it to the students from first grade to high school. The elementary school's administrators let us borrow a classroom. I purchased twelve chess boards. After school, dozens of kids showed up to learn chess, play against other students, and eat snacks. I was the chess master. In the beginning, challenging me was a death sentence. I'd lure kids into a false sense of winning, and then, 'Checkmate!' After months of studying and practicing, several kids became impressively good, and I had to pretend that I let them win."

Rachel smiled as I continued.

"Eventually, the chess club became English classes on the weekends. There's an Education Volunteer named Kristin who lives in the area. She has a reading program on the local radio station. So sometimes I'll take kids from the chess club or English class, and we'll co-host Kristin's radio show."

"That's so cool!" Rachel exclaimed.

"I know, right! Then the kids wanted to learn about American football. We left the classrooms and started playing football. People took notice of how much the kids enjoyed hanging out with me. The high school then gave me permission to teach business classes throughout the semester. The students started talking about me to their parents. Once that happened, parents wanted to learn about improving their personal finances. I collaborated with local banks and hosted personal finance workshops. Kristin helped me execute some of these activities. One thing just keeps leading to another.

Eventually, I became very popular in my community. All the students and teachers know me. Their parents and relatives know me. The mayor knows me. It's not all work. People invite me to gatherings, festivals, and all kinds of events. I'm more popular than I've ever been in my life. And, at times, it's overwhelming."

Rachel headed out early the following morning. Before leaving, she thanked me again and said, "If you ever need to escape the celebrity life or need a place to relax, just let me know."

Then, she smiled and gave me a warm hug. Paraguayans kiss the opposite sex on the cheek upon meeting and departing. So, it was the first hug I had received in months. It felt nostalgic and familiar.

A few weeks later, I received a text from Rachel.

"Hey, Mike. If you're not busy this weekend, you're invited to my place. Alejandra will be here."

I must admit that I was just as happy to see Alejandra again as I was to indulge in Rachel's home-cooked meal. I had only seen Alejandra when I picked her up from the bus station. From what I remembered, she was gorgeous. My Afro-Peruvian crush had almond brown skin with small hints of red and amber. Her thick, wavy, brown hair flowed around her face and stopped just above her shoulders. Although she didn't have an athletic build, her physique was healthy. Alejandra's accent was the icing on the cake. Accepting Rachel's invitation was a no-brainer.

Rachel lived in a rural community called Ka' Jovái. Like Kevin, Rachel lived in the middle of nowhere. She lived an hour's bus ride by dirt road from me. The rocky, red dirt path made the journey seem even longer. If it was even questionable that one would have to use the restroom (especially poop) during the trip, then it was best to call off the trip. It was bumpy and uncomfortable for the entire bus ride to Rachel's house. The bus driving over the red dirt road spun up thick clouds of red dust that stained whatever it touched. The dirt turned to mud on rainy days, and Rachel's community became inaccessible until the dirt re-solidified. Small communities in the rural areas were something like islands. Instead of being cut off by oceans, these rural Paraguayans were separated by mud seas.

After arriving at her place and settling in, Rachel gave Alejandra and me a tour of her community. Her community was located on one main dirt road. It was like Paraguay's version of a wild west town. The town consisted of three bold primary colors: red, green, and blue[18].

The dirt was red. The unkempt grass and the palm trees were green. The sky was blue. Scattered over the land were decently sized wooden houses with sheet-metal roofs. Rachel lived in one of those houses.

Generally, great cooks are great hosts, and Rachel was no different. She was a great conversationalist. She knew when to speak and asked the right questions at the right time to keep everyone engaged in the conversation. When Alejandra and I were no longer strangers and felt relaxed around each other, Rachel stepped away.

"Hey guys, I'm going to cook. Let me know if you need anything," Rachel said.

Like a great host, she came back within minutes with what became my favorite drink, *caipirinha*. It was a Brazilian cocktail

---

18   James Clerk Maxwell, a Scottish scientist, theorized in the 1860s that human beings used three colors to see every color—red, green, and blue. His theory was proven by early photography that used red, green, and blue filters to produce colored photos as early as 1861. Red, green, and blue are still used to produce color in several types of televisions and computer monitors.

made from *chachaca* (liquor made from sugarcane). The drink was made by mashing lime and sugar together in a glass. Crushed ice was added, and the *chachaca* drowned it all. It was an otherworldly and satisfying drink. Rachel handed a glass to Alejandra and then to me. She returned to the kitchen, where I could see her cooking and sipping her own *caipirinha*.

Then the music started playing in the background.

Alejandra was a sight to behold. She was naturally and mysteriously beautiful. She didn't wear any makeup, style her hair, or dress provocatively, but God was she stunning. And that accent was my weakness. She was brains and beauty and possessed a great sense of humor. I was kind of smart; Alejandra was an intellectual. She built her conversations on foundations of meaning and critical thinking. Meanwhile, I was just looking for someone who wanted to analyze UFC fights and talk about people punching each other in the face. Alejandra made me think.

The more time Alejandra and I would spend together, I'd learn that we disagreed heavily with one another on almost everything. She was passionate about the causes she believed in. I admired her passion and respected her beliefs; however, I was unyieldingly stubborn. When it came to my beliefs and ideologies, they belonged to me, and no one could change them, not even Alejandra.

Alejandra was an Environmental Volunteer, and in another world, she would have been a Planeteer with the power to summon Captain Planet. She would probably wield the power of Earth, or maybe she'd be Captain Planet herself. And I was a Community Economic Development Volunteer. Like the boy in the book *The Giving Tree*, I just wanted to sell some apples, build a house, and make a decent living—plus have a little fun, every once in a while.

No matter how politely our conversations started, we found ways to disagree with one another.

"That selfish little bastard from *The Giving Tree*! How could you ever identify with him?" I can imagine Alejandra saying.

Thank goodness for Rachel. Although she never got involved or took sides in our quarrels, Rachel always found them entertaining.

The arguments stopped as soon as Rachel brought the drinks and food. The one thing we both agreed on was Rachel being an amazing chef. On the night of our first get-together, Rachel prepared homemade pizza, which tasted delicious. Since I had been in Paraguay, it was my first time eating pizza that reminded me of home.

Rachel wasn't a person to boast, but she was well aware of her cooking abilities. After taking one particularly delectable bite, she proclaimed, "This is so goooood!"

"This is so goooood!" became my favorite Rachel quote.

That is how it went when Rachel, Alejandra, and I hung out. Sometimes I visited them at Rachel's place. Other times, they would visit my site. Anytime we got together, several things were certain: delicious food, good music, and tasty cocktails.

Despite our conflicting personalities, Alejandra and I tolerated one another pretty well. If she hated me, I would have never guessed it. For me, it was hard to hate someone that I had a crush on. Nonetheless, our relationship was anything but romantic. Honestly, I enjoyed listening to Alejandra speak and seeing her pretty smile. She was so smart and hummed with conviction in every word she spoke.

I believe most people join the Peace Corps to make a difference, and most do. Most travel to remote towns in Africa and teach kids how to read. In contrast, others get assignments in South America and work with women in rural communities. Only a few are willing to stand up for what they believe in, even if it means putting their lives in danger, and Alejandra was one of the few.

One night she arrived at my house. She didn't seem her usual fired-up self. She just looked tired and drained. I wanted to cook dinner together, watch television, and talk with her like we had always done. She was not very talkative, which was a red flag. I didn't push the matter. I knew she'd tell me when she felt better. She just wanted to go take a shower and get some rest. The next morning, she left my place early. That was the last time I saw Alejandra.

Later, I learned from Rachel that Alejandra had to be immediately moved out of her community. Some farmers in the community where Alejandra served were using unhealthy environmental practices. Alejandra confronted them, and they didn't like it. They ignored her and went about their usual ways. Alejandra reported them to an environmental agency. These *machista* farmers didn't like this foreign woman getting involved in their business and would not back down. Alejandra started receiving threats and was eventually moved out of the community by Peace Corps officials.

It saddened me to know what happened to Alejandra and that she had to leave her community. I was even more downhearted when my messages to her went unanswered. I didn't know what she had gone through and wanted to hear it from her. That never happened.

Rachel and I continued to hang out. Even before meeting Rachel, I considered myself a pretty good cook. My grandma taught me how to cook when I was a kid. Soul food was my specialty. I specialized in macaroni and cheese, collard greens with ham hocks, cornbread, fried fish or chicken, and stews. Almost everything I was good at cooking, I could not make. They weren't common foods in Paraguay; therefore, the supermarkets didn't carry the ingredients.

The recipes Rachel put together weren't common, though. She knew how to make it work; I didn't. Rachel became one of my heroes when she taught me how to bake. It all started when I told her, "I miss cookies." In Paraguay, a cookie meant sweet cracker. That's not exactly what a Paraguayan cookie was. Still, it sure wasn't the sweet, crisp, gooey, chocolate-chip snack that I grew up eating. One day Rachel made "real" cookies and shared a batch with me. They tasted like fireworks, bald eagles, and refined sugar—finally, a real American cookie. They were just like the ones my grandma used to make.

"Please, Rachel, you have to tell me how you made these," I begged.

Rachel taught me all about baking. I learned the purposes of leavening agents like baking soda, baking powder, and yeast. Rachel taught me to make not only cookies but also pizza dough, pancakes, and cakes.

One piece of advice from Rachel transcended my cooking abilities to the next level. She told me, "You have to mix all of the dry ingredients in one bowl and mix the liquid ingredients in a separate bowl. Then, you combine the dry and the liquid ingredients." Of course, every baker with any skill knows that. That's Baking 101: An Introduction to Everything. I wasn't a baker with any skill, though, not until I learned from Rachel. Now, fully equipped with my grandmother's fundamentals and Rachel's advice, I could be unstoppable.

It was great having Rachel as a friend, and I wanted to place her cooking skills on full display. One night, I took her to Gloria's house and introduced Rachel to Gloria's family. That night, Rachel made three pizzas. Everything was homemade from the crust to the sauce. Everybody loved it!

Paraguay has traditional dishes such as *vori vori* (soup with balls made of cornmeal, corn flour, and cheese), *sopa Paraguaya* (like a buttery, cheesy cornbread), and different kinds of *caldos* or stews. Normally, any Paraguayan who had some culinary ability could do a decent job making their traditional cuisines.

Besides the traditional dishes, rural Paraguayan palates were generally bland. For example, meat is a staple in Paraguay. Every week I spent in the country, there was guaranteed to be a family barbecue at somebody's house. Paraguayans didn't season the meat before grilling it. They just threw it on the grill. For flavor, they would mix lemon juice and salt together. Then they'd dip their meat in it.

Paraguayans ate *mandioca*, or cassava, with every meal. Imagine peeling a potato, cutting it into thick strips, and boiling it until it is almost tender but not quite. That's Paraguayan *mandioca*. It is eaten without butter, salt, or pepper.

Lastly, there was the vaguely pizza-like concoction that Paraguayans called pizza. All the dough was prepackaged. Normally, the sauce was a thin coat of tomato sauce. Next, they covered the sauce with strips of sandwich cheese and lunch meat, such as ham. Then, they'd top it with canned corn and canned green olives. Toast it. Finally, the pizza maker would squirt some ketchup on top, and that's a Paraguayan pizza.

I'm a pizza lover, and I give every pizza a chance. The first time I bit into a Paraguayan pizza, I nearly cracked my tooth. It felt like I had bitten down on a marble ball. Come to find out, the green olives still had the pits inside. That was Paraguayan pizza.

Rachel changed the game. And now it was time for me to take over.

For one of my projects, I formed a youth group at the high school, and we did a lot of community service, but we needed cash.

Selling homemade pizzas became an instant moneymaker. One day, I heard a customer say, *"Es rica la Yanki pizza!"* (This Yankee's pizza is good!). Yankee is a slang term used to refer to people from the United States. "Yankee Pizza" became a brand for the youth group and me.

Everybody loved Yankee Pizza. We were taking orders from people all over the community—delivery by foot. Not only were our dough and sauce homemade, but the kids and I also topped our pizzas with more than just corn and ham. Our toppings included ground beef, chorizo, chicken, and others that only this North American could introduce to a small town in eastern Paraguay. They had the ingredients, but they had very bland tastes and lacked the spirit of culinary adventure that makes the U.S. population so obese.

We used the money we raised from pizza sales to fund field trips. We toured dairy factories, wheat-product factories, cheese factories, and other businesses. The students learned about different industries, production, and business management. Also, we visited national attractions such as Itaipu Dam and *Saltos del Monday* (Monday's Waterfall)[19]. We used the money to fund transportation and fees for youth camps and leadership workshops. In addition, our pizzas funded trips that allowed the youth to participate in a national business plan competition where our team placed fourth out of twenty teams. Also, the team placed second in a national business case study competition. It was a very exciting time for the kids and me.

I owed a great amount of my success to Rachel. Eventually, Rachel's service was cut short due to personal obligations back home, and she returned to Illinois. However, it wasn't the end of our friendship. After returning to the United States, I visited Rachel's

---

19   The waterfall is approximately 45 meters high.

hometown on several occasions. Like many of my Paraguayan friends, Rachel and I would remain in contact long after the Peace Corps.

CHAPTER 8
AN AMERICAN DREAMING

~~~~~~

You cannot change your destination overnight, but you can change your direction overnight. —*Jim Rohn*

After my Peace Corps service, I felt very optimistic about the future. There were many education and employment benefits that volunteers were eligible to receive. For example, the non-competitive eligibility benefit allowed qualified volunteers to circumvent the hiring process for employment at certain federal agencies. I took advantage of this benefit by applying to many federal jobs all around the country.

I started the job-hunting process six months before leaving Paraguay. Not hearing anything except unfavorable responses from most employers, I began to worry. I believed that maybe I would be more successful once I returned to the United States but quickly learned that was not the case. I visited companies to apply for jobs in person. They all referred me to their company websites to complete electronic applications; the job search landscape had changed entirely. When I called employers to follow up, they told me they would contact me.

My hope diminished after a few months. Job hunting was a soul-crushing process, especially after months of unemployment.

The optimism that I once felt had fallen into the pits of despair. All my experience and accomplishments meant nothing. The life I believed I was working for was just a product of my imagination. Employers say they are looking for real-world experience and creative thinkers, but I learned that's just something they say. I had experience working with Fortune 100 Companies, and I had used limited resources to solve problems daily in Paraguay, but it amounted to very little. At that moment, I felt I had no purpose. I felt the rudimentary drive for survival, the desire to only exist. I placed my dreams aside, complacency set in, and I had to cope with the current situation.

Instead of making progress toward a long-term career, I found a job working at a call center managing the health and pension plan benefits for employees of third-party companies. Part of my job involved listening to people making six-figure salaries complain about why they were paying $200 monthly in medical costs on an after-tax instead of a pre-tax basis: typical rich people problems. Then there was me, considering dropping my medical coverage so that I'd have more income.

Although grateful to be employed, I was sitting on the bottom step of Maslow's hierarchy pyramid. I felt like I was not good enough because I failed at securing a profession I really wanted. The problem was that I had so many skills that I was not using. I felt useless waiting thirty to forty-five minutes for the phone to even ring and then answering the call at my cubicle. I wasn't living the life I wanted. I wasn't making a difference or any real connections. There wasn't any adventure.

While sitting at my desk one evening, I decided to plan a two-week backpacking trip through Central America. It would start in Panama and end in Belize. *Or maybe the other way around,* I thought. Two weeks seemed too short for such an ambitious adventure; five countries separated Panama and Belize. Maybe I could visit just two or three countries. Whatever I decided, I felt the trip needed to be done to cure me of feeling complacent and worthless.

While planning the trip, I thought about working abroad again. However, working abroad really wasn't in my heart or my best interests. I had returned from Paraguay only eight months earlier; three of those months, I had spent unemployed. I used my skills to help others in other countries. Now I wanted to be a productive citizen by working and helping people in my own country. Instead, I felt like a failure because I couldn't even help myself toward any real progress. Unfortunately, at the moment, my life did not reflect anything close to the meaningfulness that I was searching for.

Finally, I swallowed my pride and began looking for work opportunities in Central America. While searching jobs on the website Idealist.org, I came across a job post that caught my attention: Program Coordinator in Nicaragua[20] for a cultural exchange organization called Global Glimpse. The job description explained that primary responsibilities included designing itineraries and planning activities for American high school students visiting Nicaragua during the summer. That sounded exciting. The only problem was that the job post expired three days earlier.

I figured, *What the hell?* and applied anyway. A day later, I received an email that said my resume and essays looked good. The organization would consider me for the position. Two weeks later, I passed the interview process and received the job offer.

---

20   From 1912 to 1933, the United States occupied Nicaragua and supported an unpopular regime. General Augusto Sandino fought against American forces from 1927 to 1933. His guerilla war partially inspired the Nicaraguan Revolution in the 1970s.

One month later, my old cubicle was thousands of miles behind me. I was in Nicaragua.

***

ON MARCH 7, 2013, I ARRIVED IN MANAGUA, THE CAPITAL OF NICARAGUA. After going through customs and getting my luggage, I took a taxi to a nearby hotel. Observing the surroundings from the taxi's window, nothing looked familiar. Unfamiliarity was my comfort zone. I had pressed the reset button on my frozen, despondent life. I had another chance to play and win the game. Better yet, the world was new, and I was where I needed to be.

After checking into the hotel, I dropped off my belongings inside the room. I asked the desk clerk if he could recommend a restaurant. He told me about a mall with a food court within walking distance. I asked him, "How much money should I take for lunch?"

He replied, "40 *córdobas*[21]," the equivalent of $1.50.

Whoa! I like this place already, I thought.

I took 120 *córdobas* because I needed to purchase shower shoes as well.

Ten minutes later, I found a Nicaraguan restaurant at the food court and ordered. I craved the grilled chicken, *gallo pinto* (rice and beans), mixed vegetables, corn tortilla, and a twenty-ounce bottled Coca-Cola.

I asked, "How much?"

"140 *córdobas*," the cashier replied.

She even pointed up at the menu so I could see the combo I ordered. I reached into my pocket, pulled out 120 *córdobas*, and held it up. It was all the money I brought along.

21   The currency is named for Spanish Conquistador Francisco Hernandez de Cordoba. In 1524, he led an expedition in modern-day Nicaragua.

The cashier took the twenty-ounce bottle of Coke, opened it, and poured some into a small plastic cup. She handed me the cup and said, "Now you have enough."

I ate my lunch feeling like my credit card had just been declined on a date. After finishing my lunch, I went back to the hotel to get more money. I returned to the food joint and offered to pay for the bottle of soda. The cashier politely smiled and declined to accept the 20 *córdobas*.

***

THE FOLLOWING DAY, I LEFT THE CAPITAL FOR LEÓN[22], NICARAGUA'S SECOND-LARGEST CITY. Global Glimpse's office was located in León. The first day of training was several days away, but I wanted to get there early to explore the area. After checking into the hostel, I went into the lobby. I chatted with the receptionist, Yadira, and her visiting friend Angela. There are two types of people "who talk too much": the one you want to shut up and the one you can listen to all day. Angela was the latter and everything that a reserved person like me could ask for. She was kind, sociable, and animated. Angela invited Yadira and me for lunch and the beach the following day.

Two of my coworkers, Denis and Skarleth, arrived in the morning. Shortly after introducing ourselves, I told them that I was headed to lunch and the beach. And I invited them on an outing that someone invited me on; I have a bad habit of doing that. Angela warmly welcomed the additional guests.

She took us to her family's home. There, we joined her sisters and parents for a traditional Nicaraguan dish called *vaho*—tender beef brisket and plantain cooked in banana leaf and topped with

---

22   One of two cities founded by Cordoba in the 1500s.

ensalada de repollo or cabbage. I looked down at the mountain on top of my plate.

"*Hay tenedores*?" I asked. (Are there any forks?)

Angela looked at me and said, "*Cómelo así.*" (Eat it like this.)

She grabbed the food with her hands and placed it into her mouth. And I did the same. The beef brisket melted in my mouth like warm butter. It was a miracle that food could be so delicious.

After lunch, Angela's two sisters joined our group, and we headed to Poneloya Beach, where we spent the entire day playing in the surf.

Before the day ended, Angela said, "Isn't it strange that we met yesterday? And yet, here we are sharing a moment together that either of us will probably remember years from now. Do you think you'll remember me?"

I pulled out my camera and began to record us. I said, "If I don't remember you, I'll at least have evidence that we shared this day together. One day, I'll send it to you to remind you as well." How could I ever forget someone as pleasant as Angela?

She holds a special place in my memory as remarkable as my first time experiencing the Pacific Ocean. The constant flow of the ocean symbolized that I had the power to change my situation by having the right attitude and taking action. Paulo Coelho wrote, "When you want something, all the universe conspires in helping you achieve it." Satisfaction had accompanied me at that moment. *But damn ... I wished the universe knew how much I wanted that six-figure annual salary.* A little over a month had passed since I applied for the coordinator position. Less than a week after leaving the call center, I was enjoying life on a Central American beach with new friends.

Training began the next day. That's when I met the rest of the coordinators. We were a group of fourteen; half of us came from foreign places. We arrived from the United States, United

Kingdom, Spain, and the Netherlands. Our supervisors paired each foreigner with a Nicaraguan counterpart and assigned each group to a specific city where we'd work for six months. We spent one week learning how to design cultural exchange programs for the U.S. high school students who would arrive in a few months. As fate would have it, Denis and I were partners, and assigned to a city named Jinotega in the north-central region of Nicaragua.

***

JINOTEGA IS A SMALL, BEAUTIFUL TOWN WITH COBBLESTONE ROADS. The city lies in a valley completely surrounded by forested green mountains. The clouds frequently hovered in the hills and often draped the town, which is how it inherited the nickname "City of Mists." Many of those mountains are home to coffee plantations that export some of the best coffee[23] worldwide. At night, the 360-degree silhouette of the mountains could make a person forget that anything exists beyond those spectacular natural giants.

The week-long training ended on a Friday, and I wasn't sure what to do next. While Denis returned to his hometown, Matagalpa, to spend the weekend with his family, I took a bus directly to Jinotega so I could find a place to live. It was Global Glimpse's first time running a cultural exchange program in Jinotega. Therefore, all other foreigners received community contacts and hotel information except me. It would be my job to figure out everything on the fly. Not even Denis could help me. The *boonies* is a place in the middle of nowhere, and Jinotega was in the boonies[24], albeit very picturesque boonies.

---

23   Nearly seventy percent of Nicaragua's coffee comes from the north-central part of the country.
24   Due to its remote location, Jinotega was a hideout for the leftist group Sandinistas who were fighting against the U.S. Marines and Dictator Anastasio

Upon arriving at Jinotega's bus station, I had never felt so lonely in my life. It was the first time I had ever blindly arrived at a destination, and it wasn't exactly by choice. No one at the bus terminal knew where I could find a hotel. Not even Google could help me; I had traveled beyond the all-seeing eye of Google. I walked around town, pulling my luggage behind, and asking random strangers if they knew of any hotels. Most people didn't know, and others gave me "Nicaraguan" directions. "Go two blocks east, three blocks south, and it's the fifth building across from the hair salon." Who can reliably say at any moment which direction is east?

In Hemingway's novel *The Sun Also Rises*, a character says he went bankrupt "[...]two ways. Gradually, then suddenly." Getting lost is something like that. For a while, I pulled my luggage around, pretty sure I would find a hotel or a helpful stranger around the next corner. There's an element of disbelief in being lost. At first, you don't really believe it's happening to you. I had been walking around for nearly an hour. That was the gradual part, a dawning realization I was alone and homeless in an unfamiliar valley. Then, suddenly, I came to accept that I could be sleeping on the streets in a couple of hours.

Finally, I came across a young lady of my age, and I asked her about hotels. She went inside her home and returned with her mother, who became my guide. My guide said, "Follow me." Soon, I'd learn my guide's name was Señora Lucia. We walked half a block south, two blocks east, and a block down was Hostel Doña Maria. Señora Lucia could reliably say at any moment which direction is east. Señora Lucia called for Doña Maria and inquired about vacancies. Fortunately, the hostel had an available room. Señora Lucia said, "After you check into your room, come back to my house," and she left.

Somoza's National Guard during the Nicaragua Revolution.

After getting situated, which equated to putting down my luggage and then pooping, I navigated back to Señora Lucia's home. She invited me inside and asked if I had eaten anything. My stomach was in the process of consuming itself. I said, "No."

She sat me at a table, gave me the remote to watch television, and left the room. Fifteen minutes later, she returned and served a traditional Nicaraguan dish called *nacatamal*, a corn tamale stuffed with pork and vegetables. We conversed for a brief moment, and then she politely left me to enjoy my meal. Before leaving, she said, "My son David speaks English. Tomorrow, come back so you can meet him."

The following day, I returned to meet David, who gave me my first tour of Jinotega. David was twenty-one years old and in college. He attended school in León and returned home on the weekends. He spoke English effortlessly, and even more impressively, he taught himself by watching movies and listening to music. I was sure those movies were Rated-R, and the music had Parental Advisory labels. Every phrase that came out of his mouth was followed by, "Man, you know this fucking shit...."

"This is the main street. And man, you know this fucking shit has a bunch of stores. You'll be able to buy everything you need. Do you understand my English because man you know this fucking shit I learned by myself. I'm not sure if I speak properly because I don't have people to practice with. You know what the fuck I'm saying, right?"

I nodded my head and said, "Yeah, I understand perfectly."

After a week of paying $15 a night for a hotel room, I finally found a place to rent. My only furniture included a cot and a flimsy nightstand. I slept in a room that looked like a jail cell without the bars.

Denis and I hired Señora Lucia as our personal chef, primarily because I didn't have cooking appliances at my place. Almost every day, Denis and I went to Señora Lucia's house for lunch. As soon as she entered the kitchen, she transformed into the Nicaraguan Martha Stewart. This woman cooked like her life depended on it. I spared no crumb.

Nicaraguans have this thing, where they put salt in lemonade or passionfruit juices to nullify the acidity. As a kid, I put salt in my cousins' drinks to prank them. It wasn't supposed to be a real thing, but it was in Nicaragua. I hated anytime I received lemonade with salt at a restaurant. Denis would laugh at how much juice with salt pissed me off. Nonetheless, Señora Lucia aimed to appease my tastebuds.

The first student group would arrive months later. I would take them on the same community tour that David had given me. During the tour, I stopped by Señora Lucia's house to introduce the students to her. For the first time, I told the story of how we met. "I got off the bus and didn't know where to go. I just walked around, worried that I wouldn't find a place to stay. Then I found Señora Lucia. She helped me find a hotel. She didn't even know me, but she asked if I was hungry. And she invited me ..."

Somewhere while telling the story, I lost my voice. The words just vanished into thin air. After a glance at Señora Lucia, I tried to speak again but my voice cracked. As I attempted to continue the story, tears ran down my face, and I began to experience an emotional meltdown. I heard a student ask, "Seriously, is he really crying? Is he for real?" I covered my face with my hands to hide the tears. At first, I felt embarrassed about whimpering in front of a bunch of American teenagers. Señora Lucia came over and embraced me in her arms. Then I realized the power of small acts of kindness.

Before the first delegation of students arrived, Denis and I spent three months preparing the entire summer exchange program for three separate groups of students. We planned activities, organized field trips, and built itineraries from sunup to sundown. Each group of students would stay in Nicaragua for three weeks. Therefore, we had to create a detailed hourly itinerary for every day of the three weeks. Each day had a different theme: culture, history, education, poverty, aid and development, global business, and politics.

We also designed "Reality Challenge Days." One challenge involved the U.S. students accompanying Nicaraguan high school students for an entire day of school to learn about their educational experiences. It took numerous trips and meetings with school administrators to set up days when the U.S. students could visit their schools. One day, we stopped by a high school during recess. This was when that "Harlem Shake" song by Baauer was awfully popular. Somehow, Denis and I convinced the principal of a private Catholic school to let us make a Harlem Shake video with his students. Later we posted the video on our team's Facebook page. Reps from Global Glimpse went into full damage-control mode and told us to immediately take it down. At the time, it seemed funny: male students running around shirtless and everyone else jumping around like punk rockers at a mosh pit. It didn't take long to understand why the organization may not have wanted to use the video to promote its image.

The second reality activity challenged students to spend a day with families living in impoverished rural communities along the outskirts of Jinotega. The students would gain an understanding of poverty in the developing world; in addition, the students would assist the families with their daily chores. Lastly, for the "working like a local" challenge, we took students to a farm area called *La*

Bastilla. They worked at various stations, including milking cows, cleaning pigs, gardening, baking bread, and feeding chickens.

Finally, each group of students had community service projects that they had to do while in Jinotega. One of the activities was teaching English classes to community members. The students taught three nights per week. Also, each group of students worked with a local community organization to realize a project that benefitted the organization or community.

The first delegation arrived in June, and the last group left in late August. Each group had approximately twenty students and again stayed in Nicaragua for three weeks. Denis and I served as facilitators and tour guides for each program.

Most of the students came from Northern California, which made *hella* sense; Global Glimpse's headquarters was located there. The majority of the students were Asian and Hispanic. Additionally, they were first- and second-generation Americans. For many of the students, it was their first time outside of the United States.

At the end of each delegation, most students expressed how the program changed their perspectives on life and inspired them. I thought back to my first time traveling abroad to study in the Dominican Republic and its effect on me. I had never been the same afterward. Therefore, it was gratifying to see growth in the students and know their time in Nicaragua was worthwhile.

Personally, my time in Nicaragua reinforced the idea that I find great happiness in traveling, no matter the reason behind the journey. I met so many incredible people, from my coworkers and students to my Nicaraguan friends. As the second poorest country in the Americas, the culture, spirit of its people, and nature were wealth in their own. My life had once felt like a ball of purposefulness that slipped from my hands onto the ground. Like a kind stranger, Nicaragua picked up that ball and handed it back to me.

As I reflect, I can't help but say how blessed I am for receiving the opportunity, from Global Glimpse, to go to Nicaragua. Meeting Denis was perhaps the greatest blessing.

***

MEETING A PERSON IS MORE THAN JUST ENCOUNTERING A PHYSICAL BEING WHO CAN SPEAK, MAKE US LAUGH, AND KEEP US COMPANY. It's coming into contact with someone made from millions of experiences, someone who feels and exists, and someone who is more than what we see on the outside—and definitely more than what they show us.

Denis had a profound knowledge of his country. He helped me deeply understand Nicaraguan culture and the strength of its people. Denis was born at the end of a twelve-year civil war that had a devastating impact on his country. In 1979, a leftist-revolutionary group known as the Sandinistas overthrew an autocratic dictatorship that ruled the country for more than forty years. The Sandinistas were primarily poor farmers and students turned militants. To ensure communism did not spread in its backyard, the United States backed the Contras, who fought against the Sandinistas in a bloody conflict that ended in 1990, the same year Denis was born. The *Nicas*, as the Nicaraguans refer to themselves, take pride in their history and the role that ordinary people took in toppling a corrupt government, and shaping their future.

During the seven months I worked in Nicaragua, the relationship between Denis and me transcended far beyond coworkers.

Before the students arrived, we spent countless hours traveling the country and building cultural exchange programs. We stood at the edge of an active volcano in Masaya. We decided, "This will be an awesome spot to bring the students to." Conversely, we visited *los vertederos*, communities built on landfills. People lived in tents made of plastic bags and collected recyclable trash that they could sell; that's how they earned a living. Unsure of whether or not to take the students on such a raw trip, Denis told me, "This is what real poverty looks like. It's not pretty." It embarrassed me to express my discomfort, in front of the residents, as I waved away the flies that scurried around the garbage (and my face). From our visits to impoverished communities, I have images in my mind of Denis just sitting down and chatting with the residents like he would anyone else. Everyone deserved respect in Denis' eyes, and he treated everyone accordingly.

Once the students arrived, Denis and I worked six days for months executing our programs. We worked together, dined together, and in our free time, we hung out together.

Denis had incredible social skills. Because of Denis, we received the opportunity to work with many well-known figures in Nicaragua, including the eccentric sculptor Alberto Gutierrez, business owner and historian, Eddy Kühl, and one of Nicaragua's former Vice Presidents, Jose Rizo.

Mr. Rizo owned a house, much like a museum that displayed gifts from leaders all over the world. On numerous occasions, I visited his home decorated with elegant statues and colorful paintings. What caught my attention was a framed newspaper with a story of a failed assassination plot to kill the bloodied Mr. Rizo. And there I was, sitting on his sofa, drinking freshly squeezed pomelo juice. It's almost unbelievable to think that I had a country's former Vice President's cellphone number on my contact list. "Good afternoon. Sir, we would like to bring the students to your house and coffee farm next week." Each couple of weeks, he gave the students a tour of his properties. He discussed his coffee business as well as politics. And Denis made it happen.

Despite his limited travels outside of Nicaragua, Denis was hip to the world outside of his borders. One afternoon, while waiting for Señora Lucia to serve a bomb-ass lunch, we sat at the dining table with our eyes glued to the television screen. A musician, with dreaded hair, stood alone as she played her guitar and sang. The performer appeared reserved, and her voice sounded calm. It mystified me how simple, but powerful the song played.

I could tell by the video's production quality that it was not a modern performance; however, I could not turn away from the screen.

"Hey Denis, you know who this is?" I asked.

Denis mumbled a name, but I didn't catch it.

"Who?" I asked again.

"Tracy Chapman! You don't know who Tracy Chapman is?" Denis shouted, surprised that I didn't.

In time, Ms. Chapman's music would take me on an awe-inspiring journey as well as provide a fond source of consolation throughout challenging moments. As Denis and I watched her performance of "Fast Car," the lyrics resonated with me. Deep down, *I had a feeling that I belonged*; likewise, I shared the sentiment that *I could be someone*, as well. That's what kept me going.

When I looked at Denis, I saw pieces of myself. Three years my junior, he was the oldest of his siblings. We connected greatly via our similar taste in authentic music. We hungered for adventure. Both of us agreed that the best part of traveling was the people encountered along the way. Denis loved meeting people, especially foreigners. Due to the high cost associated with traveling internationally, it was difficult. This was why he took advantage of his encounters with foreigners. He wanted to know about their countries, cultures, and experiences. That was part of his reason for working as a Program Coordinator for Global Glimpse. Now, he had a foreign brother in me.

As coordinators, we worked with several NGOs—non-governmental organizations. A gorgeous young lady from the Netherlands worked at one particular organization. Denis had miraculously found the love of his life. We often visited her office for "work" related reasons.

One day as Denis and I were leaving her office, I told the beautiful Hollander, "We're in Nicaragua. You know kissing is common etiquette when departing?"

I looked at Denis and said, "Right?"

He blushed as she walked toward him. Until then, I had never seen a brown-skinned guy turn pink. She didn't do the typical "cheek-to-cheek" kiss. Instead, she puckered her lips and placed them on the side of Denis' face. I could basically see the butterflies flapping around the inside of Denis' stomach.

After we left the office, Denis said, "Thank you so much! I owe you big time. I'm going to find you a girlfriend." I thought he was joking. Three days later, Denis introduced me to a friend in his hometown. We dated during my time in Nicaragua.

***

AS HUMANS, I BELIEVE THAT OUR INABILITY TO INDIVIDUALLY SEE OURSELVES FOR WHO WE TRULY ARE IS A COMMON VULNERABILITY. I believe this to be especially true regarding our most positive traits and strengths. Time after time, we face challenging situations and overcome even the most difficult circumstances. It's a clear reminder of who we are, but we ignore it. Since we constantly aspire to accomplish more, we overlook and undervalue our own achievements. We shouldn't underestimate those achievements, especially when they include the remarkable friendships we made along the way or the people we helped. For a while, I'd forgotten who I was. Denis helped me remember.

It's a beautiful feeling to know that someone admires and believes in you. They respect the work you've done, the places you've been, the experience you've had, but most importantly, they admire who you are.

Although I wasn't living the American Dream as advertised in the twenty-first century, I was satisfied with many of my decisions and lived with few regrets. In Nicaragua, my white picket fence was a brown wooden fence built to keep the animals away. My milk and honey was milk in coffee. My salary was less than the minimum wage in the poorest U.S. state. Nonetheless, I was living in the moment and satisfied.

Weeks before leaving Nicaragua, Denis and I decided to take a trip to celebrate our last few days together. We packed our belongings and headed to Ometepe, a double volcanic island that stands above Lake Nicaragua. We spent several days biking the island, relaxing on the uninhabited beaches, and appreciating the last moments we'd spend together. Leaving family and friends behind is one of the most challenging aspects of traveling—especially when you know you'll probably never see them again.

My brother Denis continued his passion for cultural exchange and tourism. Years later, he would start his own tour guide company called NicasDetour. He's shown hundreds of locals and foreigners around his beautiful country.

***

BEFORE RETURNING TO THE UNITED STATES, THERE WAS STILL ONE MORE MISSION TO COMPLETE. There had been a time when I was sitting at a cubicle daydreaming about backpacking Central America. Now the time had arrived.

I packed a backpack. It was a regular bag that any fifth-grader would own. I took a bus from Managua and traveled through Costa Rica, all the way down to the country home to the Panama Canal.

Before going to Panama, I scanned a map, looking at the names of cities until a place finally grabbed my attention. The site was *Las Islas de San Blas*—Saint Blas Islands. I decided to go there for one specific reason. It reminded me of a song. "*El Muelle de San Blas*" was my Paraguayan friend Gloria's favorite song by Maná[25].

It tells the story of a woman who goes to a dock to watch her lover sail away. He swears that he will return, and she promises to wait at the pier until he returns. She wears the same clothes so that her lover will easily recognize her once he returns. Translated, one line says, "Thousands of moons passed by, and she waited at the dock." The woman spends her entire life waiting for a lover who never returns. The people in her town just see her as a crazy, old hag staring into the distance of the sea. One day, town members attempt to remove her from the dock to take her to an insane asylum; however, they can't move her. The woman spent so much time at the dock that she became rooted in it.

Once the dock had been a cubicle, the sea had been the world, and the lover was my dream. I could've ended up like the woman except I decided to go and search for my lover.

And Central America was beautiful.

---

25   Maná is a Mexican band formed in 1986. They've sold over forty million records worldwide.

CHAPTER 9
ANCHORS AWEIGH

It's not a sin to get knocked down; it's a sin to stay down.
—Carl Brashear

After leaving Nicaragua, I returned to Virginia. I found myself in the same situation I had been in after leaving the Peace Corps: unemployed and without any prospective employers. Again, I was in a desperate situation. I began applying to jobs all over the country. Unlike last time, employers were reaching out to me. "Are you available for an interview?"

From Virginia, I had driven to Washington, D.C., Maryland, Pennsylvania, and Georgia for interviews. The road trips didn't come without costs. Paying for gas and staying at hotels were expensive. Georgia is nearly eight hundred miles from Pennsylvania. No matter how great I thought the interviews had gone, no one called back.

In addition to applying for jobs, I applied for an MBA program at a university near Atlanta, Georgia. Being a Returned Peace Corps Volunteer (RPCV), the school offered me a Fellowship that covered nearly one hundred percent of the tuition. I only had to pay small out-of-state fees, medical insurance, books, and room and board. Everything was going according to plan, except for one thing: I didn't have the funds to cover those costs. Surprisingly, working in the poorest country in Latin America didn't pay very well.

Months after applying for jobs in Georgia, I had no luck. The MBA was nearly free, but I would've had to take out loans to support my living situation. I was not ready to go into debt again, especially after working like an indentured servant to pay off my undergrad loans. The more unlikely it seemed that I would be finding a job in Georgia, the more I began looking into other options.

While searching for job opportunities in Asia, I came across a university in California that had a study-abroad Master of Arts in International Studies program focusing on International Business. After a summer semester at the university, the rest of the program would be in China. While in China, graduate students would study and receive a salary to teach English at local schools. I applied to the program and got accepted.

The more I thought about it, the less it made sense. I had just turned down a fellowship worth $30,000 because I did not want to take out a loan to move to Georgia. However, I was willing to take out a $30,000 loan to attend a school in California. The program in California was slightly different than the Fellowship because of the paid internship in China. I predicted that I'd study in China, work, and save a little money; furthermore, I'd return to the United States in debt looking for employment. I would be repeating the same damn mistake. It was a cycle, and I'd finally grown tired of it.

Fortunately, I knew what I wanted and had an idea of obtaining it. I wanted to work, travel, and go to school. Importantly, I didn't want to keep getting rejected. In December 2013, I went to the Navy Recruiting Office in Chesapeake, Virginia. I told the recruiter, "I want to serve my country by joining the Navy." A couple of weeks later, I went to Fort Lee Army Base to the Navy's Military Entrance

Processing Station (MEPS) to select a job. Mid-June of 2014, I was on a flight heading to Great Lakes, Illinois, where I would complete basic training, also known as boot camp.

***

THE FEELING WAS SURREAL. I couldn't believe what I had gotten myself into. But I just knew that if I played my cards right and did what was expected of me, the reward would be sailing the deep blue seas and visiting foreign places[26] I never imagined I'd go.

Until then, I was cut off from the rest of the world for eight weeks. I had to go through intense training designed to transform civilians into military men and women. The training introduced me and my fellow recruits to how the Navy operates and taught us the skills we needed to successfully perform in the fleet. In other words, we had drill instructors telling us what to do and how to do it. If our performances didn't meet their standards, they yelled and "beat" us.

The first "beating" came when approximately ninety recruits were given thirty minutes to shower in one big shower room and dress into our uniforms. As expected, we failed to finish in time. A lot of boot camp is like this; the instructors give you tasks that are just barely impossible. They're well-designed tasks that almost seem doable, and when you fail, the instructors blow up on you.

One of the drill instructors yelled, "We gave everyone a simple task, and you couldn't do it! All you had to do was take a quick shower and get dressed. You all chose to take long-ass *Hollywood showers.*"

Some of the stuff that came out of the drill instructors' mouths was comical, but I wouldn't dare laugh at them.

---

26   There are more than forty U.S. Navy bases across the United States. Also, there are bases in countries including Bahrain, Italy, Spain, Japan, and Korea.

"If you can't follow simple instructions, we'll "beat" it into you. Drop down and get into a push-up position. Up, down, up, down, up, down!"

Time slowed as I looked around the room.

"Up, down, up, down, up, down!"

I thought about how the pain meant something different to everyone. Everyone was there to defend the idea of freedom at the possible expense of our own lives. For some of us, the military provided job opportunities that seemed unobtainable in the outside world. I saw the faces of those who joined to pursue a better life for themselves and their families. Also, some wanted the opportunity to travel or go to college.

Then I returned to reality. "Up, down, up, down, up, down!"

We showered and put on clean uniforms, only to be told to drop down on the floor and do push-ups until we were drenched in sweat. That's how we remained, and that's how we went to bed.

After the beating, we [the recruits] developed a motto for taking a shower, "Pits, sac, and crack." That meant when you were in the shower, you washed and rinsed your armpits, balls, and butt; then you got the hell out.

Push-ups weren't the only thing we did. Just when a drill instructor noticed we were struggling with push-ups, he'd tell us to stand up. There would be an instant of relief before the instructor would say, "Squat position. Bend your knees and stay there."

It didn't feel bad for about the first thirty seconds, but then my leg muscles started to burn. Like an actual fire, the burning starts small and grows. Some of us stood up for a quick second to relax our thigh muscles. "Stop fucking cheating!" one of the drill instructors yelled.

Afterwhile, everyone was hurting. "Okay, I see, you don't want to do this. Get back down into push-up position. Up, down, up, down!"

Sweaty and exhausted, some recruits started to grunt. "Stop making those moaning noises! That shit sounds weird!" But unfortunately, some continued to verbally express their pain.

"Oh, so no one wants to listen. You know what, just push up and hold the position. You better not go down!"

No longer able to support our weight with our arms, we began to drop one at a time. Recruits fell in sporadic bursts like the first raindrops that signal a coming storm.

Then came the thunderous roar, "Get up! Does anyone give up? Who wants to go home?"

There were a few who couldn't handle it. Those recruits stood and a Drill Instructor directed them to the office.

Then the other instructor said, "Those guys didn't want to be here and that's ok. But if anyone else wants to leave, there are two ways. You can graduate. Or you can pretend you're crazy and get sent to the psych ward, where you'll end up like that little fucking man in *The Hobbit*!" I knew which option I desired and ending up like Smeagol[27] wasn't it.

Boot camp wasn't terribly bad, but it was not a jolly happy place to make friends either—at least while there. I kept to myself and barely spoke. As time passed, things became routine and simpler, although the beatings never stopped. The beatings were designed to develop physical and mental toughness. We attended dozens of classes covering military training, weapons familiarization, naval history, swim lessons, firefighting, and financial responsibility (to name a few). Finally, we began to understand that everything was to prepare us for working in stressful situations; therefore, the

---

27   In J. R. R. Tolkien's middle-earth mythology, Smeagol is a Stoor Hobbit, which is a type of hobbit similar to Frodo and Bilbo Baggins. Smeagol's longtime possession of the One Ring transforms him into a bestial creature named Gollum.

Navy designed it to be stressful. Also, it was to teach discipline, accountability, and introduce us to military life.

Although I had many experiences to look forward to, it would take time to manifest. W. B. Yeats once wrote, "But I, being poor, have only my dreams." Similarly, all I had to keep me sane were memories. Fortunately, I had enough from previous adventures to keep my mind occupied, to help me persevere until the day arrived.

***

AFTER BOOT CAMP, I HAD TO COMPLETE APPRENTICESHIP TECHNICAL TRAINING AND SCHOOLS THAT WOULD PREPARE ME FOR THE JOB. The schoolhouse was located on a different base right across the street from boot camp. Unlike in boot camp, I was able to leave the base when I wasn't in class or attending mandatory training, though that was hardly ever. The schedule was very demanding, and I was required to be in my barracks room at specific times. I remained in Great Lakes for over a year, where I experienced the most brutal winter ever; likewise, the winds of change inevitably brought more pleasant conditions.

One day while passing through the lobby to exit the barracks, I noticed what seemed to be a feast. I saw aluminum foil pans filled with food, desserts, and drinks. I figured that someone was celebrating their birthday, and I exited the building.

Soon the feasts began to occur weekly. One evening, I was heading to the mess hall to grab dinner when I glanced at the banquet across the lobby. Again, there were giant pans filled with food. What really caught my attention was the pile of Chick-fil-A sandwiches stacked on the table. I asked the yeoman sitting at the front desk, "What's the deal with all this food?"

He replied, "It's free to grab for anyone who wants it."

He didn't have to tell me twice. I walked over to the lobby to join the small group, already scavenging through the food like vultures. I lifted the foil covers to see what was in each pan. Pancit in this one. Salad in the other. Roasted chicken in another. There were even chips and granola bars. I grabbed a paper plate and began loading it to the brim with everything. Pancit dangled from the side. I was in deep thought, *Damn, where can this Chick-fil-A sandwich go?*

Then, a friendly-looking Asian gentleman spoke, and my thought bubble popped. He had a medium-sized build. I'd never seen him in the barracks before, and he didn't have the "Navy fade" haircut that everyone else got at the barbershop on base.

"Hey, I'm Danny," he said.

With the plate of food in my left hand, I extended my right for a handshake, "I'm Mike. Nice to meet you!"

Danny asked, "Did you go to church growing up?"

"Yes, I used to go with my family," I answered.

Danny continued to size me up, "You seem old-fashioned. As a kid, did you spend a lot of time with your grandparents?"

I answered, "I lived with my grandma when I was younger."

Danny said, "Yeah, I can tell. Do you mind if I pray for you?"

He got me! He wants to convert me, I thought.

I said, "Sure."

"Dear Lord, thank you for introducing us and bringing us together. I pray that you bless this food that Mike is getting ready to receive. Lord, please continue to watch over Mike and protect his family. In Jesus' name, we pray. Amen."

"Amen," I repeated.

Before heading off, Danny took me over to meet a woman. She was petite and seemed to be older than Danny. The first thing I noticed was her inviting monolid eyes and warm, gentle smile.

Danny introduced both of us to one another. We spoke briefly. Shortly after learning the woman's name, I had forgotten it. Turns out, when I asked my fellow barracks buddies if they knew the woman's name, no one could tell me her name. They just called her Navy Mom.

Years before I even thought about joining the Navy, Danny had gone to the YMCA to play basketball. While shooting around, a guy approached Danny and asked if he could join him. The guy was a young sailor at the beginning of his Navy career. Both would constantly run into one another on the basketball court and shoot hoops. Over time, Danny and the sailor developed a great relationship. Danny learned a great deal about the sailor. Like many sailors at the barracks, the young sailor felt lonely because he was far from his family. Not fully accustomed to military life, he found comfort at the YMCA. Danny, after hearing this, thought it would be a great idea to visit the barracks where the young sailor and his shipmates lived and socialize with them. Then, he started bringing food and snacks to the barracks. Even after his buddy left, Danny continued to visit the barracks. Years later, I met Danny because of my appetite for a Chick-fil-A sandwich.

Every Wednesday, Danny and Navy Mom brought food and snacks to the barracks. I didn't know how I missed it before, but I never missed a Wednesday after meeting them. They brought food, socialized, and counseled those who asked for guidance.

Later they began inviting us to join them in events outside the base. We were fresh out of boot camp and only temporarily living in Great Lakes; therefore, no one had cars. No matter how many sailors from the barracks wanted to go on the excursions, Navy Mom always had enough friends who transported us to different events. One Saturday, they picked up fifteen of us and took us to Lincoln Park Zoo[28] in Chicago.

What I found strange about Danny and Navy Mom was that I didn't know who they were. Yes, they brought food, took us places, and engaged in thoughtful conversations with us, but they were still mysterious to me. They were not affiliated with the military in any way. The base had chaplains and counselors for sailors who needed their services. Navy Mom and Danny were just friendly people.

No one is as nice as they are without any particular reason, I thought. *They want something. I just can't figure out what it is.*

One weekend, Navy Mom and Danny invited us to an outdoor cookout at a park located in the outskirts of Chicago. There were many people there, including my peers from the barracks. We engaged in sports, games, live music, and a ton of food.

Three important things happened at the cookout. First, I devoured Korean barbecue for the first-time in my life, and it tasted amazing. Secondly, I learned Navy Mom was a Korean American who came to the States at a young age. Later, everyone crowded in front of Navy Mom because she was getting ready to speak. Finally, I learned that the sweet lady everyone called Navy Mom was a pastor as she gave a sermon. Danny was an assistant pastor.

Next, they invited us to church. Well, they had been inviting sailors from the barracks to church the entire time. They never pushed us or overtly advertised it. For months, I spent my Wednesday evenings eating their goodies and Saturdays going on excursions, not knowing they were ministers. Their prayers were brief and sincere enough that I thought they were blessing

---

28   Founded in 1868, Lincoln Park Zoo is one of the oldest in the United States.

the meals; nonetheless, there was comfort in their prayers and visits. Any Sunday I was free of military duties, I spent it at church.

Honestly, I can only think of a few moments in my life when I enjoyed going to church. The moments with Navy Mom, Danny, their congregation, and my barrack mates were some of those times.

Navy Mom borrowed a church for her sermons. To not interfere with the owner's ministry, Navy Mom's ministry began at 1 PM. Therefore, no one had to wake up too early. We'd listen to beautiful gospel songs. Danny played the guitar, and Navy Mom was a soul singer.

Anytime anyone new attended the church, she would say, "Don't be shy here. Sing and dance for the Lord!" She wore her soul and passion on her sleeve as she preached.

After the sermons, we would have lunch in a dining area. Lunch also allowed the sailors to converse among one another and with the church members. We'd spend hours socializing. Then, we'd clean up, and there were always tons of leftovers from lunch to take back to the barracks. Instead of going straight to the barracks, we'd always stop by a coffee shop. There, we discussed what we had learned at church. In addition, we discussed personal experiences and our relationship with God. That was the most close-knit spiritual community and fellowship I'd ever been a part of.

Navy Mom possessed a kind and caring heart. She brought together sailors who were going through challenging times in their lives or needed guidance, and she embraced us without ever asking for anything in return. Every Sunday, the church members picked us up using their personal vehicles to take us to church. They never asked anything in return—no gas money, no tithes, and Navy Mom never allowed us to contribute to food or coffee. Her only concern was our spiritual well-being.

Her kindness made me feel guilty because she was so selfless. It bothered me so much that I could not do anything to express my gratitude for what they were doing. They would not let me, or my peers, reciprocate their generosity.

During one of the discussions, one of the sailors mentioned that he wasn't a Christian but believed in a higher power. Although he wasn't a Christian, he enjoyed coming to the church because it was an environment where he could connect with God. Navy Mom made clear that she was Christian and had accepted Jesus as her Lord and Savior, but she never turned anyone away.

During my fellowship experience, I learned three simple prayers that I carry with me everywhere. The first is "Thank you." I thank God for life, family, friends, and health.

The second prayer is a request. "God, give me strength" to endure life's challenges. That strength is needed in different ways. Sometimes, it's in the area of compassion, patience, courage, wisdom, and so many others.

The last prayer is simply "God, I love you."

As much as I despised Great Lakes and its nightmarish winter[29], leaving there was difficult. Navy Mom and Danny were the first people I'd considered spiritual mentors. They gave me something that I didn't get from school, any of my travels, or the Navy. They helped me find purpose and comfort in my beliefs.

---

29   January 20, 1985 is the coldest day recorded at Chicago O'Hare International Airport. The temperature was –27°F.

CHAPTER 10
LIBERTY BUDDIES

To become a good man, one must have faithful friends, or outright enemies. —*Napoleon Bonaparte*

While going through my apprenticeship and technical job training in Great Lakes, classes were long. Many days, they ended as late as 11 PM. Midnight rations, also known as *midrats*, were available at the base galley[30]. *Midrats* comprised food, normally leftovers, served to personnel either going on or being relieved from the late shifts. After the late classes, many students went to the galley to grab a bite to eat before bed.

One Friday night, my classmate Anderson and I had recently finished class and went to the galley to get some grub. While enjoying our meal, two of Anderson's associates came to our table. Their class schedule was different from ours. So they'd gone out, had some drinks, and returned to base with the munchies. One of the guys, whom I'd never seen before, was noticeably more intoxicated than the other.

He looked at me and said, "What the hell are you staring at?" and laughed before continuing. "You guys see this? Doesn't this motherfucker look like John Wall from the Washington Wizards?"

---

30   The kitchen and/or cafeteria on a train, plane, ship, or Navy base.

He pointed his finger at me while yelling, "Look at him! This motherfucker looks like John Wall." I did not watch basketball, so I had no idea whom he was talking about. He continued spewing out other indecipherable gibberish. I was getting annoyed but remained calm.

He spoke loud enough that people at nearby tables heard and focused their attention on the commotion taking place at my table. What irritated me the most was that I didn't even know this guy. I had never wanted to karate chop someone in the throat so badly. However, we were sailors at the galley, so I just sat there trying to stay collected and keep my eyes fixed on the guy who was making a fool of not only me but also of himself. The buddy who accompanied him finally grabbed his clown friend and took him away.

After they left, I asked Anderson, "Do you know that son of a bitch?"

Anderson laughed and said, "Yeah, that's Lane."

"Lane," I repeated. "I really don't like that guy."

***

AFTER FINISHING MY TRAININGS IN GREAT LAKES, I NEEDED TO COMPLETE ONE MORE SCHOOL BEFORE HEADING TO THE FLEET. The schoolhouse was in San Diego, California. On the first day of class, my peers and I waited outside the locked classroom. Once the instructors arrived, they directed us to locate and sit at the desks with our nameplates. The classroom was shared between morning, evening, and night classes. Therefore, each desk had multiple nameplates. While searching for my name, I saw a nameplate that read "Lane." Below his name was his future ship, USS *Shiloh*. Finally, I found my nameplate, and below it read USS *Shiloh*. Lane and I were going to the same ship. Since our jobs were the same, we'd work in the same division.

Lane had morning classes, and I had night classes, so we never knowingly crossed paths in San Diego. However, we had several mutual friends.

One night, one of those mutual friends invited a group of us out to a restaurant called Dick's Last Resort in downtown San Diego. Dick's Last Resort was a restaurant with obnoxious staff that insulted and acted purposely rude toward the customers. We were a decently sized group. Naturally, I engaged with the people I knew; therefore, I didn't even notice Lane was there.

I would never have known Lane was there if it weren't for an incident that occurred. It was an occurrence even more ridiculous than dining at a restaurant where employees got paid to be rude to customers.

Here's the story:

Our party had already received our food. We were close to finishing when an older woman walked into the restaurant. Based on her slim, fragile body and wrinkly skin, she had to have been in her late fifties. If I were to guess, I'd say she was homeless as well.

She walked straight toward our table and started hitting on my friend Karl. Karl and I were classmates back in Great Lakes and reconnected in San Diego. He was a handsome gentleman, tailor-made for the ladies. Karl was dark-skinned, muscular, bald-by-choice, and had an appealing smile—a Morris Chestnut-looking brother. This was probably why the old lady chose to stand behind him and massage his shoulders. She whispered in his ear, "You're sexy, aren't you?" Everyone laughed at what was happening.

While rubbing her veiny hands over Karl's physique, she began making conversation with others at the table.

Then, observing the food on the table, the old woman asked, "Can I have a French fry?"

One of the guys at the table handed her a plate of leftover fries.

Then she asked Karl, "Can you give me the ketchup?" As he reached for the bottle of ketchup, the lady said, "You can see my titties for some ketchup."

The woman pulled down her tank-top, exposing her pale and saggy breasts.

"Look at my tits!" she said as she wiggled her breasts around at Dick's Last Resort.

It was the kind of image that haunts a person throughout their entire life. Obviously, it was the kind of experience you never forget because it would later become a turning point for me and Lane.

In three months, San Diego had come and gone. After San Diego, I received orders to serve onboard the USS *Shiloh* located in Yokosuka, Japan[31].

***

I DON'T REMEMBER HOW MANY MONTHS HAD PASSED SINCE I CHECKED ONBOARD THE USS *SHILOH*. However, enough time had gone by to miss American food. The guys in my division and I were talking about random restaurants. I remembered and shared the story of Dick's Last Resort. When I brought up the "tits and ketchup" part of the story, Lane shouted, "Oh man, I was there too! My fiancée and I were both there. That shit was hilarious!" Then he let out his outrageously contagious burst of laughter.

---

31   The United States has maintained a base in Yokosuka since the end of World War II. Commodore Matthew Perry established the first U.S. Navy presence in Yokosuka in 1853 when he arrived to force the Japanese to open up trade.

By then, Lane had redeemed his image of the drunken idiot from the base galley in Great Lakes. He and I had become agreeable shipmates; in fact, he was my best friend on the boat. Lane had never been one to make a good first impression.

I enjoyed telling the story of how Lane and I met because it embarrassed him. I'd tell anyone who listened, "I didn't even know who this motherfucka [Lane] was, and he walked up to my table talking shit. He's lucky I didn't kick his punk ass!"

He'd respond, "Man, I had way too many drinks that night. Why do you have to make me seem like an asshole?"

On countless occasions, I witnessed him look at guys twice his size and say, "Yo, what are you staring at, fool?"

I'd ask Lane, "You know that person?"

His response would be, "No." Then he'd laugh.

Lane was one brain cell short and a few pigments off from being the White Steve Urkel. And he thought he was tough. Actually, he didn't think that. He just had a goofy personality, and no one took his theatrics seriously, except for me on our first encounter. Now that I had the opportunity to punch him in the throat, I couldn't stop laughing at his jokes; and I enjoyed being around him.

Ironically, the only person to physically assault Lane was an intoxicated guy who mistakenly accused Lane of urinating into his beer bottle. Then the accuser punched Lane in the chest, knocking the wind out of him. When I heard the story, I laughed so much. For one, only Lane could tell an enthusiastic story about getting beat up. Two, even though Lane didn't do it, he still deserved the ass-kicking.

For some odd reason, he excelled at making friends. I envied him for his people skills. He was the asshole who had all the friends. I was the nice guy who looked unapproachable, so my circle remained small. I understood why people liked him, though.

He possessed a wide range of interests that never stopped expanding, making him exceptionally relatable. Plus, he was authentic.

The Floridian loved astronomy, video games, and basketball. He could talk about Lebron James and Steve Nash as much as he could speak about Pikachu and Bulbasaur. Lane prided himself on knowing how to make the sounds of all the first-generation Pokémon. Anytime I heard him and other guys talking about Pokémon, I'd try my best to offend them.

"What the fuck is wrong with you guys? You're a bunch of grown-ass men talking about Pokémon. Let me take you nerds out and help you find some girlfriends," I'd tease.

Lane fired back, "Your old boring-ass is just jealous that you're out of touch."

I replied, "Dude, I may be three years older than you. At least I look younger." In the Navy, people age in dog years. An eighteen-year-old kid joins. After two years, he looks like a thirty-five-year-old man after two divorces and a midlife crisis. I had gray hairs and a bald spot, but Lane had wrinkles. I had witnessed other sailors go from looking like Chris Hemsworth to looking like Chris Farley.

I didn't enjoy basketball or video games, and I hadn't watched Pokémon since middle school. Lane didn't watch the UFC, but he knew I loved MMA. Therefore, he'd watch events just so that he could discuss the fights with me. "You see Conor McGregor knock out that Brazilian fighter? He fucked him up!"

I'm thinking, *The Brazilian is Jose Aldo, and he's my favorite fighter.* His charisma didn't end there.

My shipmate was an anomaly. Lane was the first person, especially a White person, I met who could bump Tupac Shakur and contrastingly serenade the environment with Sade Adu.

I remember the first time he played Tupac's music.

"Hey man, what do you know about Pac?" I inquired.

"Before the Navy, I worked in the kitchen of a restaurant. And there was this cook, who listened religiously to Tupac. At first, I didn't like the music. But the chef was this huge *Green Mile*-looking Black dude, and I didn't have the balls to tell him to turn off his music. Eventually, I started listening to Tupac's lyrics, and the songs grew on me."

When Lane said I couldn't name a Tupac song, he didn't know, he wasn't lying.

On the contrary, no one loved Sade as much as I did.

"Lane, what about Sade?" I asked.

"My mom loves Sade. When I was younger, that's all she played. Sade is amazing. I know all her songs, too," he said.

"Really?" I asked curiously.

"Try me," Lane challenged.

I sang, "*Coast to coast. LA to Chicago ...*"

"Smooth Operator," Lane quickly answered like a contestant on *Family Feud.*

I continued throwing out different lyrics, and he named the correct song each time.

Lane also introduced me to different musicians and different genres. One day, I entered the space and heard country music playing. Once I realized it was Lane's music, I just wanted to rile him up.

"Turn that trash off," I shouted.

His response didn't disappoint, "Trash? Dude, I bet this song is more profound than any of that bullshit that's in your playlist!"

"Listen to it," he replied as he restarted the song.

I bobbed my head to the rhythm and listened to the words. The artist sang about fried chicken, beer, and freedom—all things Black people enjoy as well.

I smiled at Lane, and said, "Ok, I'm feeling this. Who sings it?"

He smiled back and said, "Zac Brown Band."

Working on a warship was not the most stress-free environment. In the Navy, chaplains serve on vessels and provide counseling, advice, and spiritual services for crew members in need of them. I've witnessed instances where chaplains have carried the morale of the crew on their backs. Likewise, my division had brothers (and a sister) who looked out for one another. If someone appeared down and needed to vent, we listened. We encouraged and helped one another to get back up. No matter how tough the situation seemed, Lane would always say, "Things always get better." If he was dealing with the hothead that I could sometimes be, he'd say, "Cooler minds always prevail."

The only time cooler minds didn't prevail was when Lane would pass gas. His farts caused agonizing reactions. I witnessed people gag and nearly vomit from Lane's hydrogen sulfide anus bombs. Peers in our division pleaded with desperation, "Could you please step outside of the space next time?"

"You think I'm going to hold in my farts and experience discomfort for your convenience? Get the fuck out of here!" was Lane's self-justifying response. Then he laughed. Lane was a scrawny, tell-it-like-is, confident little bastard. Admirable, but Lane failed to realize that there are some people who you just don't fuck with.

I watched the guy as he impolitely removed Lane from his seat and unkindly placed him on the floor for causing a stench.

"You lost your seating privileges!" said his assailant.

Lane just laughed and farted again. The other guy got so upset that he stormed out of the space slamming the door behind himself. Lane remained on the floor—laughing hysterically—like the Joker after getting the Batman beatdown.

At first, I found Lane's antics disgusting and immature. But, then the entertainment value of pissing people off far exceeded the disgust.

***

THE THING ABOUT THE NAVY, ESPECIALLY ON SMALLER SHIPS, IS THAT YOU CAN'T ESCAPE PEOPLE. In port, those people are your coworkers. At sea, they become your roommates as you're stuck together in the middle of the ocean and sleep in the same berthing. Likewise, when visiting foreign ports, shipmates become friends because you'll need a liberty buddy to accompany you if you want to leave the ship and explore the local area.

During a port visit to Singapore, Lane and I were liberty buddies. A liberty buddy is someone you sign out with to leave the ship. Commands implement the liberty policy so that sailors can help each other out if anything goes wrong. For some, a liberty buddy was the designated sober babysitter. As much of a pain that Lane could be on the boat, he was a fun person to hang around and quite polite. However, there was one area of his indecency on which he never compromised.

Singapore has some of the strictest laws[32]. Even caning is legal on the small Asian island. We stood up inside of the crowded train as I looked at the signs posted around: "Smoking Onboard $1,000 fine," "Durian Fruit $500 fine," and "Eating and Drinking $500 fine." Those signs did not deter Lane from releasing his toxic gases. *Sssss* ... It was a silent killer. Thank God because no one could pin it on him. Otherwise, we'd have been sitting in a Singaporean prison, sharing a cell with murderers.

---

32   Walking around naked in your own house is a crime punishable by a fine. Connecting to someone else's Wi-Fi can be punishable by three years in prison.

On a port visit in Subic Bay, the Philippines, my division had gone out on the town. We spent the day checking out the local food scene. Pineapple fried rice with chicken ... Banging!

Shrimp spring rolls with chili sauce ... Banging! "*I don't know what this is,*" but ... Banging! We could've chilled on the beach or gone on excursions and taken photos with drug-addicted tigers; however, the blistering heat kept us inside of authentic Filipino restaurants. When the night arrived, the weather was still hot, although complemented by a merciful breeze. We passed the time visiting bars on the waterfront.

It was late at night when we decided to head back to the ship. We laughed aloud as we told jokes, still in good spirits from all the drinks. As we walked, everyone in the group noticed a suspicious wooden board lying across the sidewalk. Something about it screamed, "Do Not Walk Across Me." Without much thought, everyone except Lane walked around the board. He walked over the board. It tilted like a seesaw, sending Lane sliding toward the sewer. Luckily, Mr. Florida Man was able to grab onto the sidewalk. One second, he was by my side, talking and laughing. The next second, he was hanging onto the sidewalk for dear life.

"Help!" Lane shouted.

It was a powerful feeling —looking down and seeing fear in the eyes of a person, I once despised. It resembled the scene from *The Lion King*—the part when Mufasa is hanging from the cliff.

I imagined Lane pleading, "Brother, help me!"

Like Scar, I could've crushed Lane's fingers, sending him plunging into the wildebeests of human waste. Instead, the guys and I grabbed and pulled him up.

There was never a dull moment with Lane. I enjoyed spending time with him at work or during port visits: in the Philippines,

Singapore, and Australia. He was great company and had a five-star sense of humor.

His personality was tailor-made for entertaining. He'd have a huge audience if he had his own television show or YouTube channel. However, he spent his free time playing Pokémon on his Nintendo D.S. and drinking beer.

Although he became one of my best friends, he didn't share my love for traveling. During holiday stand-downs or vacation periods, Lane would either stay in Japan or visit his family in Florida. Meanwhile, I had a lady friend, and we were taking trips to places like Thailand and Cambodia. I often tried my best to convince Lane to join us in our endeavors across Asia. Some activities are more fun to do with the boys than with the girlfriend (and vice versa). I imagined Lane and me filming videos of each other eating scorpions at night markets on Khaosan Road in Bangkok.

"My girl and I are going to Malaysia this year. Why don't you and your lady come along?" I asked.

He'd tell me, "That sounds like a good idea. My fiancée wants to travel. I'll talk to her."

It would always fall through. I didn't take it to heart.

For a long time, traveling had seemed like a lonely hobby, and at times, I wished my loved ones were around to share the experiences. I remember the first time it hit me. I was living in Paraguay at the time and took a solo trip to Rio de Janeiro, Brazil, during the week of my birthday. I visited the famous Christ the Redeemer statue[33]. It was my first time seeing a Wonder of the World. As I looked around, it seemed that all the other tourists had family and friends accompanying them. They had people to share the experience with, and they looked so happy together. Then there was me, alone with a statue.

---

33   Construction lasted from 1922 to 1931. The statue is ninety-eight-feet tall.

I learned a world of valuable lessons from Lane. I realized that not everyone, including best friends or family, would share the things (ideas, beliefs, hobbies) that I am most passionate about in life. I used to find excuses why I was traveling alone. "Maybe they didn't have the money or time." It was as simple as they just didn't want to go, and they didn't want to disappoint me by mentioning it. I used to believe that having similar interests and aspirations brought people together. That obviously wasn't the case.

Lane was the perfect reminder. I knew he had the time and money. He enjoyed living in Japan. Together we discovered local eateries such as ramen shops, *yakiniku* (grilled meat) spots, and Japanese curry restaurants. We visited many of the infinite temples and shrines. It would have been nice to do similar activities in other countries, but that wasn't what he was interested in doing.

At the end of 2018, Lane left the *Shiloh*. He departed a few months before I did. I believe most people experience what it's like to have a best friend at least once in their life, even if the friendship fades away as all things do due to time. It was a sad feeling seeing one of my best friends go. This was the guy who approached and insulted me when we were strangers. Now, he was leaving Japan to return to the United States. I was happy for him. For much of his time on the *Shiloh*, he had been engaged to a woman in San Diego.

***

MONTHS LATER, I RECONNECTED WITH HIM WHEN I RETURNED TO SAN DIEGO FOR MORE TRAINING. I got the opportunity to meet Lane's fiancée, who was also a Pokémon fanatic. They took me around the city, visiting their favorite Mexican restaurants. I became a loyal customer at California Burritos and Tacos El Gordo. Additionally, Lane had discovered an area in San Diego with many Japanese shops and restaurants.

"I really miss Japan's ramen and sushi. I want to take you to a Japanese restaurant and know what you think," he said.

After dining out with Lane and his fiancée, I told him. "It's decent, but it's definitely not Japanese food as we've experienced it."

We visited Hooters on several occasions to watch UFC events and basketball games.

Lane had been living with his fiancée for several months, and it was magical how a woman could transform a man such as Lane. The guy who once couldn't hold in a fart was now talking about getting married and having kids.

Months after leaving San Diego and returning to Japan, I received a message from Lane.

He told me that he and his fiancée had finally gotten married, and a kid was on the way.

"Oh no! She got you, man. How do you feel about having a kid?" I wrote.

"Bro, I'm nervous as hell," he responded.

"Don't worry. I know you'll do just fine. I'll pray that the kid doesn't smell like you," I teased.

I joked with Lane about his family life. But I was delighted to see my goofy friend transform into a husband and father. It gave me the feeling that I was long overdue for settling down. My heart had belonged to many throughout the years, but travel was a possessive and satisfying paramour. She removed the diffident young man I once was from behind a hotel desk and gave me a new life. It seemed like no one could have transformed me more than the experiences I gained from being abroad.

For me, traveling has always been about exploring new places, learning, and self-improvement. Along the way, I got torn between travel and everything else that existed in my world. Whenever there was tension between seeking greater financial opportunities or traversing through foreign lands, I had always looked for a way to incorporate travel into my plans. Sometimes, this meant limiting my earning potential. When it came to relationships and travel, I chose the latter. There wasn't anything even remotely close to it. Therefore, I couldn't produce any reason to justify choosing anything over traveling. I had become obsessed.

Every time I chose travel, it created another rift. Anything that provided the opportunity to travel, I went for it. It began with studying abroad, then the Peace Corps, next a nonprofit organization in Nicaragua, and now the military. Twelve years later, there still wasn't anything that I wasn't willing to do to travel. There had to be an ending somewhere nearby.

CHAPTER 11
UNDERWAY REPLENISHMENT

To send a letter is a good way to go somewhere without moving anything but your heart. —Phyllis Theroux

In late 2014, not too long after graduating boot camp, I purchased my first smartphone, a Galaxy 4. Honestly, I didn't know the difference between Android and iOS. A few months earlier, I had a Nokia flip phone. I was long overdue for an upgrade. The Galaxy was cheaper, so that was all that mattered.

When I got to my barracks room, I fiddled around with the phone. I could not figure it out. I thought, *This thing is complicated. I should've stuck with the flip phone.* I remembered the time when I was a kid and had to teach my mom how to use the videocassette recorder, most often referred to as the VCR. Damn, I feel old writing the previous sentence. Trying to operate the Galaxy 4 must have been how my mom felt trying to work the VCR.

Speaking of my mom, I had some downtime and needed to call her. I was smart enough to at least figure that out. During our conversation, my mom asked, "Do you know a Susan?"

I replied, "Yes."

My mom continued, "She's been sending you a lot of mail. Recently she sent a letter addressed to Mrs. Nixon, so I opened it.

She wanted to know if you were okay, and she wants your current address. Is it ok if I give it to her?"

"Sure, go ahead," I told my mom. She gave Susan my P.O. Box.

Susan was a retired schoolteacher with eloquent and beautiful cursive handwriting. She loved to cook and could have easily succeeded as the executive chef of a luxurious restaurant. She had a heavenly voice and sang gracefully in the choir at her church in Burlington, North Carolina. Additionally, Susan was a lifelong Tar Heel fan and possessed tons of the teams' paraphernalia to prove it. In time, I would learn that Susan was a lot of wonderful things.

I knew her because she was Emily's mother. Emily was my friend and former Peace Corps Volunteer who had passed away in Paraguay.

The last time I had seen Susan was three years prior (in 2011), at the dinner on the final night of Emily's memorial. That was the night she passed around her book and collected all the volunteers' addresses, including mine. After my Peace Corps service, I received holiday cards from her. I replied to a couple but assumed she'd stop writing; therefore, I stopped writing.

I definitely dropped the ball by not responding to her never-ending arrival of cards. When Susan didn't receive anything from me, she sent a letter addressed to my mother. That's when I realized that I better respond to this lady because she was concerned about me.

After boot camp, Susan's holiday cards turned into letters. They were open-ended letters, so I had to respond to them. Eventually, the envelopes multiplied when I began receiving letters from Susan's congregation as well. The paper envelopes transformed into boxes or care packages, to be specific. In their letters, strangers wrote, "I hope you're doing well" and "Thank you for your service."

I always responded to Susan's letters. Eventually, I became pen pals with members of Susan's church.

I went from Great Lakes to Japan, and the mail followed. At sea, the Navy employs "underway replenishment." Underway replenishment is when a ship receives parts, fuel, food, and everything else that allows commands to execute their missions. Also, this is when sailors' personal mail arrives. And every time we received mail, I always had letters and care packages.

My shipmates would say things such as, "I didn't know people still write letters." One time, my buddy Finn said, "Damn, Mike. You're lucky to receive mail."

I replied, "What are you talking about? You always get packages too!"

"Yeah, but I order my stuff from online. I don't get thoughtful handwritten letters and postcards from Europe," Finn responded with a smile on his face.

Finn had a point. The letters I received were thoughtful and comforting, especially during difficult times.

In the late spring of 2016, tensions escalated between the United States and North Korea. As North Korea fired missiles into the ocean, U.S. ships were on high alert. We were prepared to shoot down any projectiles headed toward the United States, Japan, or any other ally nation. It was my first time at sea. And God knows, I felt like our countries were going to war. At first, these provocations of war seemed terrifying as armed conflict seemed inevitable. Then I got used to it. It's a peculiar feeling, accepting the possibility of going to war. While my family and friends had no clue where I was or what I was doing, the only people I had were those serving with me. We spent months at sea with no timetable for returning to land. As the crew's morale began to diminish, I received letters from Susan.

Again, I had Susan's letters asking me if I was ok after the USS *Fitzgerald* and USS *John S. McCain* (both stationed in Japan) were involved in separate deadly collisions in 2017. The accidents left me shaken, knowing that I could've easily been stationed on either ship. As the metal bed frame folded around me and the water rose to drown me, I awoke from my nightmare. It was one of the most terrifying dreams I'd ever had. It wasn't a dream for everyone. It was real for my shipmates who lost their lives including my former classmate Petty Officer Aaron Smith from Apprenticeship School. In an article I read, his father said that Aaron would be missed, and he was thankful for their twenty-two years together. If anyone could relate to losing a young child, it was Susan. And so, she sent me letters.

Sometimes, those letters came from places around the world. Susan and her husband Steve enjoyed traveling. They sent me postcards from cities all over the United States. Even during their international trips, they always thought of me. I received postcards depicting castles in Spain, cathedrals in France, and museums in England.

Susan inspired me to write letters and send care packages with Japanese products to family and friends back home. Out of all the letters I've handwritten throughout my entire life, I'd estimate that seventy percent of those letters went to Susan. Writing Susan taught me how to express myself and helped me understand that it's okay to share my story, feelings, and experiences with others. I had always believed that it was best to be modest, ask questions, listen, and avoid talking about myself.

Susan wrote essays talking about what was going on in her life. "Steve [Susan's husband] and I are taking care of the grandkids today." "Steve and I are news junkies. Last night, we saw that North Korea launched a missile over Japan. We pray that you're ok."

"Tonight, I'm making homemade chicken potpie, sweet potatoes, asparagus, and macaroni salad with ham." "Last night, I tried a new recipe." "Last weekend, I had a Civitan meeting and sung in the choir on Sunday." "Next month, we're going to Paris." At the bottom of her letters, she'd write, "Now, tell me EVERYTHING that's happening in your life. Don't leave out any details."

Then I'd write, "It's cherry blossom season in Japan. Japanese people are crazy about these trees." "My ship just came back from a two-month deployment. We spent a couple of days in the Philippines. The weather was so hot!" "My holiday leave begins in a couple of weeks. This year, I'm going to vacation in China and Thailand." "I have a Japanese girlfriend. Her name is Kaori."

Traveling was part of my reason for joining the Navy. Fortunately, I ended up in Japan. In six years, between two ships, I had six port visits outside of Japan—two in Singapore, one in Australia, one in Guam, and one in the Philippines. The other fifteen countries I visited were during the holiday periods and on my dime. Being stationed in Japan made traveling around Asia inexpensive.

No matter where I visited, I always found cool postcards and special treats to send to Susan and members of her church. I sent them care packages, including snacks such as Salted Egg Crispy Fish Skins from Malaysia, Durian Wafers from Thailand, and Kangaroo Jerky[34] from Australia. In hindsight, I don't know what I was thinking by sending them so many peculiar edibles. Nonetheless, I wasn't even disappointed when Susan wrote, "I shared the snacks with members from the church and Civitan group. Many of them weren't brave enough to try most of it but, they loved the postcards!"

---

34   Kangaroos are protected species in Australia. However, certain licenses are granted to harvest and process the animals.

By 2018, I had only met Susan and Steve during their daughter's memorial ceremony in 2011 in Asunción, Paraguay. Seven years later, we knew a great deal about each other's lives through the constant letters we sent. Also, I learned a great deal about the church members because of the letters we wrote to one another; however, I'd never met them.

After my three-year contract was complete onboard the USS *Shiloh*, I received orders to the USS *Curtis D. Wilbur*, located a pier across from the USS *Shiloh*. I had some downtime between assignments. Instead of going on another wild adventure in Asia, I decided to go to Virginia to visit my family for the holidays. It was my first time home in three years.

On December 22, 2018, my family and I drove to Burlington, North Carolina, to visit Susan and her family. Susan prepared a three-course meal and dessert for my family and me on that evening. The next day, we went to church. I was able to take part in the marvelous Christmas ceremony. In addition, I was finally able to meet the strangers who had become my pen pals over the years.

***

I ONCE SENT SUSAN A NEW YEAR POSTCARD THAT READ, "WHAT'S YOUR NEW YEAR'S RESOLUTION?"

She responded, "I haven't made any New Year resolutions. Long ago, I figured out I could not stay on that diet. The resolution I made that I'm still working on is 'love unconditionally.' It is challenging, especially in traffic. I remind myself, 'This is a child of God, and you may be the only connection they feel today.' I really try to be kind and grateful."

CHAPTER 12
NEW YEAR FESTIVAL

~~~~~~

Fitting in allows you to blend in with everyone else, but being different allows you to be yourself, to be unique and to be more creative. —Sonya Parker

"My father worked for an international company. His position required him to relocate to the People's Republic of China. So, he moved my mom and older brother from the United States to China. But me ... I was born and raised in China." Hannah said.

"Say something in Chinese," I ordered.

"Do you mean Mandarin?" she asked.

I smiled at her and replied, "You know what I mean."

I listened as she spoke the language so effortlessly.

"Damn, that's impressive! You even have the accent down pat. I'm convinced," I replied and winked.

"Did you think I was lying to you? I may be White, but I'm the whitest Chinese person you'll ever meet. I speak perfect Mandarin as well as some Cantonese." Hannah said.

I remembered I had a friend who was from China. I had always had a hard time pronouncing her name. So, I pulled up an email and showed Hannah my friend's name in Chinese characters.

Hannah looked over the characters and said, "Huifen."

I squinted and raised an eyebrow to show I didn't understand. Hannah pronounced slowly, "Huì-Fēn."

"Way-fin," I tried.

"There's an 'H' sound at the beginning. Less emphasis on the 'W' sound. Then you'll get it," Hannah said.

"Huifen, that's a girl's name," Hannah said, implying there was romance involved. Then she asked, "Where is she from?"

"Shenzhen[35]," I told her.

Hannah replied, "Ah, that's near Hong Kong. I've never been there. I grew up in Wuhan."

Hannah explained that when she was a child, her blue eyes and blonde hair had given natives the impression that she was from somewhere far away like the United States or somewhere in Europe. Despite receiving unwanted attention for looking different, Hannah was born on the same soil as everyone around her. Sometimes, she overheard people say hurtful things about her. The culprits didn't realize Hannah understood the language. As she got older and started interacting with others, she built relationships with her peers, improving the situation.

Then she experienced a significant life event: she moved to the United States for college.

She explained, "When I first came to the United States for college, it was terrifying. It was an absolute culture shock, and I had difficulty adjusting. There were many things about American culture that I did not understand. Truthfully speaking, I feel more Chinese than White or American. Even now, I still identify strongly with Chinese culture. But here in the States, I don't exactly fit into the Chinese American community. It's weird. Does any of this even make sense to you?"

---

35   Shenzhen is the fifth-largest city in China and one of the busiest container ports in the world. It's home to the Shenzhen Stock Exchange.

"Yes, it makes perfect sense," I said.

There was something I didn't say. I had spent most of the past decade outside of the United States. I stood out everywhere in every country I had visited. Each time I returned to my homeland, things were different: the culture, values, economy, technology, and political atmosphere. The United States, as I remembered it, was a thing of the past. I had friends all over Latin America and Asia. *But did I really fit into the Hispanic or Asian community in the United States?* Not really. I didn't know where I particularly belonged anymore, but I'd grown to accept myself. I knew precisely how Hannah felt.

"So, how did you end up at this Chinese New Year's Festival?" she asked.

I went into what brought me to this moment. Here's the story:

It was January 2019, and my three-year tour on the USS *Shiloh* was coming to an end. Before transferring to my new command, which was also in Yokosuka, Japan, I had to attend a three-month school in San Diego, California. I had morning classes Monday through Friday. Since the barracks on base didn't have any rooms available, I stayed at a hotel. After class, I'd go back to my hotel room and sit around bored out of my mind. The only thing I did was study, read novels, and go for jogs. For weeks, I passed most of my time inside the hotel room. I was going insane.

Finally, I came up with a plan to get me out of the cycle. I went online and found a volunteer website. I signed up for any volunteer event that fit into my schedule. The sole purpose was to get me out of the hotel room. On the last week of February[36], the Chinese New Year Festival just happened to be one of the

---

36   The traditional Chinese calendar is lunisolar, determining dates based on lunar cycles and the position of the sun. Thus, the date of the New Year fluctuates on the Gregorian calendar. Typically, it is between mid-January and mid-February.

events I signed up for. It was a two-day event that took place over the weekend. There were specific time slots that volunteers could sign up for. I put my name in all the spaces. I was there from 10 AM to 8 PM for both days. As you can see, I very badly did not want to be in that hotel room. My duties at the Chinese New Year Festival were simple: walk the area and pick up trash. The bonus was that volunteers received free food and free t-shirts. Also, I could take breaks anytime and enjoy the shows, which included karate demonstrations, musical performances, art shows, and dancing dragons.

I met Hannah on the second day of volunteering. I had been promoted from the trash crew to traffic guard on the final night of the event. Hannah was assigned to the traffic guard post with me. That's when we started conversing. I learned about her life in China, college experiences in the United States, and her reason for being at the Chinese New Year Festival. She just wanted to experience Chinese culture and find someone to speak Mandarin with.

After two days, the festival had ended, and it was time to go. Hannah was getting ready to call an Uber, but I stopped her. I was in no rush to get back to the hotel room, so I offered her a ride to campus.

Before leaving, Dennis-Michael, the Event Coordinator, approached me and said, "Mike, thanks for volunteering and being here both days of this event. You worked your ass off. I appreciate it. You know ... next week, the local Association of Asian Americans is holding a networking event, and I would love for you to come."

"I'll be there," I said without hesitation.

I was thinking, *I'm going to be the only Black person there. It's going to be so weird*. Most of my travels, especially in Asia, whether on the flights or walking the streets of Ulaanbaatar[37], ninety-eight

37   The capital and largest city in Mongolia, founded in 1639.

percent of the time, I was the only Black person present. It was normal to stand out in places like Mongolia. I was supposed to be out of place when I was in foreign countries. Now I was back home, in one of the most diverse countries in the world. I received an invitation to an event where the guests would be predominantly Asian American. Nonetheless, we were born in the same country, spoke the same language, and possibly shared some of the same experiences. I had grown so accustomed to being out of my comfort zone that it made me feel uneasy when placed into an environment of familiarity.

***

IT WAS CLOUDY AND RAINY THE NIGHT I ARRIVED AT THE FILIPINO RESTAURANT, THE LOCATION OF THE NETWORKING EVENT. I parked my car near the door to avoid getting soaked. After entering the restaurant, I recognized the gentleman at the entrance. It was Dennis-Michael, the Event Coordinator of the Chinese New Year's Festival, and the one who invited me to the event. He had a guest list in his hand. It was the first time my name had ever appeared on a guest list.

"Hey Mike, I'm glad you could make it. Go grab a drink. Once the event begins, I'll come to find you, and we'll chat," Dennis-Michael said.

Then he handed me a Bingo card and a pen. The game was an icebreaker. Inside of the blocks were descriptions. I had to find guests who met the criteria, such as those who enjoyed reading, owned a business, had an introverted personality, traveled abroad, and so forth. If I met someone who identified with the description, I had to write their name inside the block. To win, a person had to complete two rows.

As time went on, more guests began to show up. Although I was one of the few non-Asians there, it didn't stop me from approaching groups of people. After becoming acquainted with my fellow guests, I felt a part of the group. I realized that although almost everyone was Asian American, they were still strangers to one another. Therefore, everyone was a bit shy in the beginning. There's a strange quality to familiarity and foreignness. In a foreign country, simply sharing a nationality with someone can create familiarity. In your own home country, you're more strangers than if you were halfway across the world. The Bingo icebreaker made it easier for us to converse.

It did not take long for the restaurant to flood with people. There were guests everywhere. By that time, I had already devoured a plate of lumpia and rice with pork adobo and made it through the buffet line for the second round. I was sitting at a table with the DJ and a couple of people I met at the Chinese New Year's Festival. We conversed as everyone stared at the pancit hanging from my mouth.

Those who were keeping me company began to leave the table. I watched as they disappeared into the forest of people. Soon, I was alone with an empty plate. I scoped out the room. Then, I turned around and caught a glimpse of an Asian man and a woman sitting at the table behind me. The man's eyes, wide-opened, focused on me. His eyes said what his mouth didn't, *"What the hell are you doing here?"* I sat frozen in disbelief. Then, suddenly, he rose from his seat and walked toward me. Without thinking, I stood up quickly.

As predicted, he asked, *"What the hell are you doing here?"* I felt tears begin to form in my eyes like I wanted to cry.

Immediately the man grabbed me and pulled me toward him. I patted his back over and over with my right hand so loud that it sounded like I was hitting a bass drum.

"Holy shit!" I shouted.

Then I pushed him away and said, "Me? What are you doing here?" Then we embraced again.

Andrei said, "Fool, I saw you when I first arrived. That's why I sat behind you. I've been waiting for you to turn around!"

I laughed and could not believe that it was really Andrei! It was really him. Three years had passed since the last time I saw him.

Andrei turned toward the lady sitting at his table. "Maribel, this is Mike!"

As we politely waved at one another, Andrei said, "Mike, have a seat. Tell Maribel how we met. Maribel, you have to hear this! This shit is so crazy!"

CHAPTER 13
THE HAND IN THE SAND

We don't meet people by accident. They are meant to cross our path for a reason. —Anonymous

In mid-October of 2011, I was a year into my Peace Corps Paraguay service and needed a break. So, I took a vacation. It was about a month before Emily's accident.

A couple of weeks earlier, I had been reminiscing about a *Lonely Planet* travel guide that I used to have. I would flip through the pages when dreaming of travels to stunning and exotic locations. I remembered vividly a statue of a hand reaching through the sand on Uruguay's page. The image of the "Hand in the Sand"[38] had never left my mind.

After a quick Google search, I learned that the statue was in Punta del Este, Uruguay. That's why I purchased a $30 bus ticket that would travel twenty-two hours from Ciudad del Este in Paraguay through Argentina to Uruguay's capital, Montevideo.

Once the bus arrived at the southern border of Paraguay and Argentina, passengers had to wait outside of the vehicle. At the

---

38   La Mano (The Hand) was built in 1982 by Mario Irarrázabal, a Chilean artist. The sculpture is made from concrete and plastic reinforced with metal. It was conceived as a drowning hand to warn swimmers about dangerous waters.

same time, a border patrol agent inspected the bus for weapons, drugs, signs of human trafficking, and everything else that may have been on the checklist. Also, we had to get our passports stamped since we were leaving Paraguay and entering Argentina. Besides me, two other passengers shared the double-decker bus. One was an elderly Uruguayan woman, and the other was her young granddaughter.

Waiting for the bus to complete the inspection, a foreign-looking gentleman walked over. He wore one of those big jetpack-looking travel backpacks that gives you the feeling he was getting ready to launch off into space; he looked more like an astronaut than a tourist. First, Buzz Lightyear began speaking Spanish to the Uruguayan woman. Then he started a conversation in Spanish with me. Soon, we realized that we were both English speakers.

The guy's name was Andrei! He was a slim, brown-skinned fellow with a "Bruno Mars" smile. He was the kind of guy who smiled as he spoke, so everything he said seemed more interesting.

Andrei wanted to go to Montevideo, Uruguay; however, he was on a bus headed to Buenos Aires, Argentina. From Buenos Aires, he planned to travel directly to Montevideo. Our bus company was the same, so I suggested he speak with the drivers to see if he could switch buses. After all, there were only three people on my sixty-passenger bus headed to Montevideo. For whatever reason, the drivers did not allow the swap.

Andrei asked for my email address and the hostel I would be staying in. He seemed so excited about meeting up and hanging out in Uruguay. I gave him my information to be courteous, knowing that I would never see this guy again. I could not have been more wrong.

The following night, Andrei showed up at the hostel where I was staying.

The next day, we rented bikes and toured the city. First, we visited a huge outdoor market known as *Feria de Tristan Narvaja*. Hundreds of people strolled along the sidewalks on that beautiful day. We chained our bikes to a pole on some random street. Then we walked around, bought souvenirs, and enjoyed flavorful Uruguayan burgers. Later, we rode through different neighborhoods, up and down busy streets, and along the coast. We made pit stops at museums, local shops, and restaurants.

I'll never forget the time while riding along the coast, we saw a bunch of girls holding a sign that read "Free Hugs." *What guy, in his right mind, would pass on the opportunity to hug cute Uruguayan girls?* Not Andrei and me. We hopped off the bikes to get those hugs and take pictures. Then we were on our way again. We spent the evening chilling on the beach.

Andrei served as the beacon that allowed me to see how close-knit the travel community can be. He was the first backpacker I had ever met. We had known each other for a day. And a day later, we were sharing new experiences, roaming unknown land, ending up on the beach, and engaging in intimate conversation.

While spending the day with Andrei, I learned quite a bit about him. He was born in the Philippines. He moved to the United States when he was a teenager. Later he served five years in the United States Navy, which allowed him to gain U.S. citizenship. After the military, Andrei moved to Australia where he lived for over a year. Not too long after departing Australia, he decided to backpack South America until he reached the tip of Argentina. His next destination was Antarctica, which he would reach by a cruise ship. After the cruise, he planned to go to Egypt. That would complete his goal of visiting all seven continents by the age of thirty.

Andrei intrigued me. As much as I wanted to travel like Andrei did, the idea had still frightened me. It wasn't the physical dangers that scared me. Instead, it was constantly traveling into the unknown of countries, the unfamiliar cultures, and not having a soul to rely on. It was 2011, and the only countries I'd been to were the Dominican Republic, Paraguay, and a piece of Brazil that borders Paraguay. Uruguay was the fourth. Uruguay was special because it was my first solo trip.

"Backpacking South America must be a dream come true," I said.

Andrei responded, "It is a dream come true, brother! I always wanted to travel solo, but I was hesitant. By serving in the United States Navy, I was able to get my feet wet because the ship would make port visits in other countries. It helped me build a lot of confidence to do this."

He paused and looked away as if he had lost track of his words. Then, he continued, "Mike, you're in a unique position and able to experience travel much different than me. You're a Peace Corps Volunteer living in Paraguay. You have the opportunity to travel around South America in ways that I can't. I wish I was like you when I was younger."

It was weird to hear this from a guy four years older than me.

I didn't want to pry too much into his background. I knew he'd at least lived in the Philippines and the United States by the time I was in high school. He traveled the world through the Navy, and he lived in Australia. Now, he was adventuring through South America. I had been to four countries, and Andrei was five continents deep in the game. How could I live up to that?

"Tell me about a highlight of your trip," I said.

"Peru!" he said with excitement in his voice.

"What did you do there?" I asked.

"Have you ever heard of Machu Picchu[39]?" he wanted to know.

I couldn't even pronounce what he had just said. *Macha Peek-a-who? Sounded like a character from Pokémon. Is that what a Pikachu evolves into?* I thought.

Instead of saying something stupid, I just shook my head to indicate I hadn't heard of Machu Picchu.

"Bro, you gotta look it up. The site is unworldly. It's the type of creation that makes you question whether humans had extraterrestrial assistance. I traveled by hiking the Incan Trail to Machu Picchu. It took a week, but it was worth every step," Andrei said.

I thought, *This guy might be nuts.* I understood the possibility of humans and aliens working together to build *Machu Pikachu*. For some reason, it made sense. But he hiked for five days; that was the crazy part. At the time, my hiking experience included a few trails with Dan at Shenandoah. As Andrei spoke of the Incan trail, I had no idea what he was talking about. Some years later, I would visit and see the wonder he described.

That was Andrei's niche. Some people enjoy luxury travel, while others are foodies or hedonists. Andrei explored ancient sites, looking for clues on whether ancient people had extraterrestrial visitors in the past. Later, he would brand his adventures as P-Day Pursuit.

After a busy day of getting to know Montevideo and hanging out with Andrei on the beach, we returned to the hostel.

We arrived at the front desk and inquired about any events that may have been taking place on that night. The staff recommended that we check out an Afro-Uruguayan event called

---

39   Incas likely built Machu Picchu around 1450 as an estate for Emperor Pachacuti. Often mistakenly referred to as the "Lost City of the Incas," it is the most familiar icon of Inca civilization.

Candombe. Candombe[40] is a style of music and dance that immigrated to Uruguay with enslaved Africans. An Australian lady checking into the hostel overheard our plans and wanted to join Andrei and me. Why not?

The three of us arrived at the location of the event. The celebration began with a few people beating on drums and shaking tambourines in the middle of a street. Before we knew it, many people were drumming their hearts away while others danced. The spectacle attracted a large crowd of local people. Spectators became participants in the celebration. Anyone who wanted could join the dancing parade. Although we witnessed this in one community, the same thing was happening simultaneously in nearby neighborhoods. Eventually, all parades and their audiences started moving toward a central location. It turned into one massive celebration and beautiful display of culture.

After the parade, we headed back to the hostel. Andrei and I stayed up and formulated a plan. We spent the next couple of days traveling together. We ended up in Punta del Diablo, a small fishing town located on the eastern side of Uruguay. As far as the journey had taken Andrei and me, I really didn't want to leave him. He was the first traveler I met on my first solo trip. He inspired me and made my trip worthwhile. However, the purpose of the trip to Uruguay was to visit Punta del Este to see the "Hand in the Sand." So, after meeting a new brother, I had to leave Andrei behind and journey to Punta del Este.

***

---

40   "Candombe" means "pertaining to Blacks" in Kikongo, a language spoken in and around the Democratic Republic of the Congo.

THE DAY WAS BEAUTIFUL, ALTHOUGH SOME-
WHAT WINDY. The sky was light blue, and the perfect white
clouds billowed like cotton balls as they floated across the sky.
As I approached the beach, I saw it from a distance: *The Hand* or
the *Monument to the Drowning*. Chilean artist Mario Irarrázabal
designed the statue as a warning to swimmers that the beach had
strong waves.

It possessed a different significance to me. I reflected on years
back when I looked through that *Lonely Planet* travel book. That
was the first time I saw the hand in the sand. Although an image in
a book, it was almost like the hand was physically signaling me to
come to it. Maybe I was drowning years before. I remembered the
burning urges of wanting to be in a foreign place and not knowing
where to start to make the trip possible. I thought back to when
I used to work forty-five-hour weeks for Corporate America, and
how my earnings would flow through me into Sallie Mae's pocket.
I recalled waiting almost two years since I applied to Peace Corps
to leave for my assignment in Paraguay. I remembered not having
many friends. Now I was on my first solo trip and meeting people
from other walks of life.

Once a picture in a book, now the *Monument to the Drowning*
grasped the sand in front of me. It was an accomplishment, a
fulfillment of a dream. Waves of contentment rushed over me,
maybe even pride. Those feelings washed away as swiftly as the
currents in the ocean. One thing remained intact. That was my
connection to Andrei.

***

AS IRONIC AS IT WAS, TWO YEARS AFTER COM-
PLETING MY PEACE CORPS SERVICE, I JOINED
THE MILITARY.

After spending eight weeks in boot camp (in 2014), I graduated and spent a year in Great Lakes on the base right across from boot camp. After completing my apprenticeship schools in Great Lakes, I had another three-month school in San Diego.

In early September 2015, life would take me to the west coast for the first time in my life. I was heading into unfamiliar territory. Everything I knew about the Golden State I had learned from Tupac's song "California Love", but I didn't recall Tupac mentioning San Diego. I went through the lyrics in my head. L.A., Watts, and Compton kept it rockin'. Just as I thought. Not one mention of San Diego.

Who did I know in San Diego? I logged into my Facebook account and searched to see if I had any friends or family in San Diego. I got one result, Andrei.

The last time I spoke with Andrei was four years earlier in Uruguay. Still, I decided to send him a message. I wrote him that I was coming to San Diego and wanted to see if he was interested in meeting up. A couple of hours later, I received a message from Andrei. It included his cellphone number.

It was good to hear from him even after so much time. He asked how I was doing and wanted to know about my plans for San Diego. I told him that I had joined the Navy and was in the area for training. Andrei was delighted and proud that I joined the Navy because that was how he gained his U.S. citizenship.

Andrei asked, "Are you going to be stationed in San Diego?"

I told Andrei that I was going to Yokosuka, Japan, in a few months.

Andrei laughed, "My boy Mike's always traveling. Which ship are you going to?"

"The USS *Shiloh*," I said.

He gasped, "Stop fucking with me!"

He had a serious tone in his voice, and his words caught me by surprise because they came out aggressive.

"What?" I said.

Andrei continued, "You're fucking with me, right?

"What are you talking about?" I asked, confused by his reaction.

Then he asked again, "You're going to the *Shiloh*?"

"Yeah," I confirmed.

Then he answered, "That was my ship when I was in the Navy. I was on it when it switched homeport to Japan."

***

FOR ME, ANDREI HAS REPRESENTED THE MIRA-CLES THAT ONLY TAKING CHANCES AND TRAV-ELING CAN MAKE HAPPEN. I've felt this way, ever since I met him at the border of Paraguay and Argentina back in 2011. A day after meeting, we traveled through Uruguay together. In 2015, we reconnected, and I learned that he served on my first ship in the Navy. In 2019, I returned to San Diego, and we coincidentally ran into one another at the Asian American networking event. It's strange the way life works. Little did I know that when I briefly met Andrei at the South American border town, he would end up being one of my best friends for life.

CHAPTER 14
WAR WITH CHINA

A ship in harbor is safe, but that is not what ships are built for.
—John A. Shedd

"Who's ready to go to war with China?" the Captain asked at an all-hands gathering as he stood in front of us, his men and women serving aboard the USS *Shiloh*.

We responded with a deafening roar of the Navy's battle cry, "Hooooyah!!!"

Four years earlier, I had raised my right hand and sworn to support and defend the Constitution of the United States against all enemies. I was prepared. My shipmates were prepared. That was the mission: be prepared.

***

TWO WEEKS BEFORE HEADING OFF TO BOOT CAMP, I VISITED MISSOURI TO SPEND TIME WITH MY RELATIVES BEFORE HEADING TO GREAT LAKES. So, I went there for a few days to visit my grandparents, aunts, uncles, and an ever-growing number of cousins.

This story begins on the trip back to Virginia. While returning to Virginia, I had an overnight layover at Chicago O'Hare

International Airport. It was almost midnight. The only people waiting at the gate were me and a young lady in her early twenties sitting in the row of seats directly behind me.

On any separate occasion, this woman would've ended up being one of the thousands of strangers I passed by at the airport like any other time. I would have gone through a badass playlist of Jon B., Alicia Keys, and Anthony Hamilton; and maybe a little Gloria Estefan. She would've read her book. The night would have passed, our flights would have arrived, and life would have gone by as it always does. But, this time, something inside encouraged me to challenge the inevitable, so I did.

I turned around and said, "If I had to guess, I would say you have an overnight layover."

The lady lifted her head. Then, realizing that I was speaking to her, she carefully replied, "Yes, I have a layover."

"Where are you coming from?" I asked.

"China," she responded.

"Is that where you're from?" I inquired.

She answered, "Yes, I'm from China."

I asked for her name.

She said, "Huifen."

"Way-fun," I pronounced.

"Huifen," she repeated. "But you can call me Sonia. It's the name my English teacher gave me."

"My name is Mike," I said and offered her my hand.

She looked at my hand before extending hers. Sonia shook my hand and repeated, "Mike. That's easy to remember."

Sonia and I bonded instantly after our brief introduction. Once we began talking, we didn't stop. First, we talked about common interests such as food. She was excited about being in the United States and couldn't wait to try Starbucks coffee. I told her that Chinese food[41] was one of my favorites.

"What kind of Chinese food do you like?" Sonia asked.

I said, "I love shrimp fried rice, sweet and sour chicken, and pork egg rolls[42]."

Her facial expression read, "I think I know what you're talking about." Then she explained how in China, the cuisine varies drastically depending on the region. She went into specifics, but I don't recall hearing anything about General Tso chicken or Crab Rangoon.

Next, the topic turned to music. I handed Sonia my headphones and let her listen. I played "Turn Your Lights Down Low" by Bob Marley and The Wailers.

Sonia said, "This sounds nice. Who sings this song?"

"Bob Marley. You don't know who Bob Marley is?"

"No," she replied.

Wide-eyed, I said, "Jamaica? One Love? Dreadlocks?"

Both embarrassed and amused, she covered her mouth and giggled. I had a lot to teach her about music. Next, we moved on to language.

"How do I say 'hello' in Chinese?" I asked.

"Nǐ hǎo," she enunciated.

I repeated, "'Knee-how.' I knew that. What about, 'My name is Mike.'?"

"Wǒ jiào Mike," Sonia said.

---

41   Chinese cuisine is often divided into the so-called "Eight Great Culinary Traditions." These are regional cuisines based on history, local culture, and traditional farming practices.

42   Americanized Chinese food is often significantly different from Chinese food in China. Available ingredients, ingredient prices, and American palates often determine how the food is prepared.

She repeated it several times, but I struggled to pronounce it. That's as far as the Chinese lesson went.

Overall, it was easy to converse with Sonia, and I could tell she felt just as comfortable interacting with me. Curiosity made it easy to discuss topics that most people avoid when talking with strangers, such as politics and religion.

"What's your religion?" Sonia asked.

"I'm Christian. What about you?"

"I don't practice religion, but I believe in God. In China, the government focuses more on science than religion. There are people that practice Buddhism, Christianity, and other religions," she explained.

Somewhere, I learned that religion was not something to bring up in and meet and greet conversation. So, I changed the conversation to something more intriguing.

"What is dating like in China?"

Sonia responded, "First, people are introduced to one another through a matchmaker such as a friend. Then they date like you Americans. They hang out, watch movies, and eat meals together. Soon, they get engaged, and the man gives money to the woman. In my hometown, it's 50,000 yuan. I think that's like $8,000. Then, they marry."

Sonia had a free and outspoken personality. No matter what kind of questions I asked her, she saw it as only a question that required a candid response. Sonia didn't wear much emotion on her face, nor did she express it in her voice. She had a pleasing smile that only appeared when it was well-deserved. We conversed the entire duration of the layover, and we talked about everything. By the time morning arrived, I felt like I had known her for years.

Sonia was from Shenzhen, China. She was participating in her university's study-abroad program, which allowed her to study English and work part-time in the United States. Sonia was waiting for her morning flight to Richmond, Virginia. Once she arrived in Richmond, she would take a shuttle to her residence in Williamsburg. I told her that I lived close to Williamsburg and informed her of some local attractions.

"If you're interested, I'll come to pick you up and show you around the area," I told her.

Sonia didn't have an American phone or phone number, so she gave me her email address.

A few hours later, I was standing in line at Starbucks to get Sonia her first real taste of America.

A few days later, I was on my way to visit Sonia at her hotel in Williamsburg. She waited for me inside the lobby. When I entered, I noticed that nine of her peers accompanied her. She introduced me to her fellow classmates and asked, "Is it okay if they join?"

The year was 2014, and I drove a 1994 Saturn SL2[43], not really a flashy or spacious vehicle. A decade earlier, it would have been the perfect candidate for MTV's *Pimp My Ride*. If the mechanics could have just fixed the air conditioner, that would have been satisfying enough for me. There probably wasn't enough space for a fish tank anyway. I agreed to take as many students as I could. This included Sonia and three of her friends. Definitely couldn't fit the fish tank.

We spent the morning touring Colonial Virginia. The first stop was the Colonial Williamsburg Historic area. Next, we visited the Jamestown Settlement and Native American villages. Then we embarked on the Jamestown-Scotland Ferry, where we took a ride down the Jamestown River and witnessed hundreds of seagulls trailing behind the ferry. After the tour, we grabbed lunch.

---

43   Saturn was dissolved in 2010.

Like Americans going to a foreign country only to eat McDonald's, these Chinese students wanted Chinese food. This was during my pre-smartphone era. I carried a Nokia flip phone. It may not have had Wi-Fi, but I could go two weeks without charging it. Not being able to search Yelp! for recommendations, I stopped at the first hole-in-the-wall restaurant we saw. Sonia and her friends told me that they would treat me to lunch. They spoke Mandarin with the restaurant's staff. I say Mandarin like I was sure. It could've been Cantonese or Swahili for all I knew. When the food arrived at our table, it wasn't the shrimp fried rice and egg rolls that I was used to eating. It was food that I'd never seen before.

"We spoke with the chef and asked if he could make us traditional Chinese food," Sonia said. Then, she prepared a serving and handed it to me. The first thing I noticed was the smaller portion size. I thought, *For real, this is all you're going to give me? No wonder y'all are so skinny*. But I was much too polite to say it. "Please enjoy," Sonia said. It was my first, but not last, time having egg drop soup. Although I found the texture somewhat slimy, I didn't mind the taste. Also, it was my introduction to Chinese dumplings, which I enjoyed.

Additionally, Sonia ordered the smaller, lighter, crispier spring rolls, whereas I'd always ordered egg rolls. I wasn't completely unfamiliar with Chinese food. I recognized the fried rice, sweet and sour pork, as well as chicken with vegetables.

We passed the evening at the Williamsburg Premium Outlets mall. Sonia and her comrades wanted to experience the American discount industry. I found it comical, considering most products probably came from their country.

The moon shined brightly as I pulled up to the hotel. Sonia invited me to come inside the lobby, where we talked and enjoyed one another's company. It was getting late, so I decided to head home. Before leaving, I opened my arms. At first, she looked confused by my cultural gesture. Then, she opened her arms, and we embraced. That was the last time I saw Sonia.

This was the closest I interacted with foreigners in my country outside of hotel guests I encountered. It was my first time giving someone a tour of my area. It was a beautiful experience as we spent the day together, learning about different aspects of one another's cultures.

Sonia knew I was joining the Navy and would be leaving for basic training the following week. I told her the first night we met at O'Hare Airport. While I was in Great Lakes, Illinois, she continued to work and study English in Williamsburg, Virginia. Two months later, I graduated from boot camp. I checked my email for the first time since leaving Virginia. There were several messages from Sonia.

She expressed the challenges of living and working in the United States. Apart from studying English, she worked at a restaurant. Sometimes, customers treated her rudely, and the unpleasant experiences had taken a toll on her. She developed friendships with her coworkers; however, she found it challenging to make American friends because of the cultural differences and her demanding schedule.

She was happy when I finally responded to her messages. If studying abroad in the Dominican Republic or being a Peace Corps Volunteer taught me anything, it was that being in a foreign country could be an overwhelming experience—and having friends helped. She was a guest in my country, and I wanted her to leave with a positive impression of the United States. So, from that moment forward, we became electronic pen-pals writing messages back and forth.

Once Sonia sent me some photos. In a lot of Asian countries, the ladies go for the "cute" as opposed to the "sexy" look. Sonia looked so pretty in her white dress as some old homeless guy had his arm wrapped around her waist. She wrote, "This guy is kinda weird but he's nice. I see him outside of my restaurant every night and I give him food. He says that he can help me get a visa to live in New York."

I was angry and jealous at the same time. Some bum was trying to run game on Sonia. I wrote, "You're so sweet. I know some people, whom you could hang out with."

I transferred some money to my brother DJ's bank account, and I told him, "I need a favor. I want you to pick up someone and take her to Busch Gardens Williamsburg theme park." DJ gathered a group of friends and carried out my request.

Sonia and I moved further and further apart. After Virginia, she went to New York to live with relatives for some months. Once her U.S. visa expired, she returned to China. After Illinois, I went to California and then Japan.

Life continued. I served onboard a warship conducting Freedom of Navigation Operations[44] in the South China Sea as Sonia's country was reinforcing its claim and demonstrating military strength in the region by building and militarizing artificial islands known as the Spratly Islands. While U.S. Naval vessels, including mine, were sailing close to these islands to challenge China's claims, Chinese warships were tailing us.

Sonia and I managed to keep in contact whenever I wasn't at sea, although not as frequent as before.

Sonia wrote,

---

44   Operations to ensure that civilian vessels are able to travel freely in international waters.

"Hey Mike, how have you been? It's been about six months since I finished my trip to America. I hope you are enjoying Japan. That's so fabulous that you're there! I am so jealous. America is the only country I've been to, but I plan to go to Thailand next year. I'm preparing for the postgraduate exam, which will allow me to teach English at colleges. It's going to be tough. English majors must choose a second language. I could have chosen French or Japanese, but I chose German. German is cool. And German women are really strong and independent."

I responded, "Sonia, it's great to hear from you! How come you're jealous that I'm in Japan? We're practically neighbors. Besides, you're welcome to visit me anytime.

That's impressive that you're learning German. That'll make it easier to find a German boyfriend. Good luck on the exam!"

Sonia responded, "A German boyfriend? You're so funny. Personally, I don't want to worry or disobey my parents. It may be difficult for them to accept any foreigner as their son-in-law."

I responded, "Do you think they would accept me as their son-in-law?"

"You really are funny," she replied.

In Japan, U.S. Naval ships are forward-deployed, meaning that they are the first responders if a conflict breaks out. Our ships constantly and sporadically deployed to project American sea power and protect trade routes in the region. Being at sea for months at a time gave me much time to think. I thought about my friends and family, the places I wanted to visit, and the work I was doing. There were incredible amounts of politics and conflict involved between the United States and nations including Russia, North Korea, and China. I had nightmares about world-ending conflicts between my country and Sonia's. Every time I thought of China, she came to mind.

I definitely could not email her from my ship. So I'd write her whenever I returned to Japan. Also, I couldn't write her as frequently as I did in the United States. We'd get random messages from one another a few times a year.

"Hey Mike, I haven't been doing so good lately. I'm having problems deciding what to do after I graduate from the university. Should I go with a small company, leading a different life than my friends? Or should I work for a big company like my classmates? If I do that, I don't think I'll be happy." Sonia emailed me.

"You sound down. Everything will be ok. You have options. That's a good thing. Where do you envision yourself two years from now?" I wrote.

She told me that she preferred to work for a small company; however, the salary would be low.

"Will you be able to live comfortably with the salary the company offers?" I asked her.

"It's hard to say. Please, define "comfortably." Everyone wants higher pay, right?" Sonia wrote.

She made a good point.

"Will you be able to buy everything you need? That's what I mean by comfortable. Higher pay is good. But do you prefer to work for the sake of making money or to have a career that makes you happy?" I asked.

"I think I know what to do. You're Philosopher Mike. Hahaha."

Over a year passed before I heard from Sonia again. I was excited to see her message in my inbox and open the message from her. She wrote to update me on her current situation, and things were going well for her. She had just gotten out of an abusive relationship. The guy she dated had treated her horribly, but she didn't want to leave because she was afraid of being alone. Finally, she mustered the courage to leave him. Also, she informed me of the career path she chose. She decided to teach English at a high school in her hometown. She seemed happy with her choices, and I was proud of her.

On the other hand, I couldn't tell her much about what my work involved. Instead, I told her more about my experiences living in Japan. Also, I told her that I had a Japanese girlfriend.

"A girlfriend? Japanese? That's nice! I'm happy to hear that. She's so lucky," Sonia messaged me.

Having Sonia's blessings meant a lot. Our communication was more friendly than flirtatious. However, I'd imagined that if I ever dated an Asian woman, it would be Sonia.

While in Japan, I took advantage of the inexpensive flights and traveled extensively around Asia during my vacation periods. Surprisingly, my command approved my request to vacation in Beijing, China, in December of 2017. I emailed Sonia to tell her the news.

"Sonia, how have you been? My girlfriend and I will be visiting Beijing in December!" I wrote.

Sonia emailed me, "That's so cool! If I can help, please let me know."

I responded, "It would be even cooler to visit you in Shenzhen."

Sonia wrote, "Yes, but Shenzhen is far from Beijing. Plus, I'll be visiting my brother around that time. It's a pity that we won't be able to hang out together. I'm sorry."

The three-day trip to China included exploring the Forbidden City and Tiananmen Square, visiting the Temple of Heaven and Summer Palace, and climbing The Great Wall. It was awesome witnessing China's Wonder of the World. The only thing that could have made the trip even more memorable was seeing Sonia. That didn't happen.

I wrote to Sonia and told her about my trip and how much I enjoyed my short time in her country.

"Hey Sonia,

I want to share a story from my trip to Beijing. My girlfriend and I were dining at a restaurant close to our hotel. There was a group of four guys sitting at the table next to ours. I felt them staring at me. Each time I looked their way, they turned away and started laughing. I began to feel uncomfortable because I thought they were being rude and making fun of me.

Finally, one guy asked, 'Where you from?' Then he showed me a map of China on his phone and pointed to one of the inland cities. 'We from here.' Next, he typed something into his phone and handed it to me. It was a translation that read, 'Can we take a photo with you?' After the photo, one of the guys poured me a glass of rice wine, which was intense.

He said, 'Tomorrow, Great Wall. I like you …' Then he started laughing. He pulled out his phone and began typing. Afterward, he handed it to me. 'Tomorrow, we're going to the Great Wall. We would like you to join us. It would be an honor.'

My girlfriend and I had already visited the Great Wall. I felt silly because I thought that they were making fun of me. Really, they were laughing at the crazy idea of inviting me to see the Great Wall with them."

Sonia responded,

"Mike,

That's a funny story. People from inland China don't see a lot of foreigners, especially like you. That's why they wanted to take photos. You should've gone again to the Great Wall! I'm glad you had fun on your trip."

In 2018, she sent a message, "I will be visiting Japan with my students in August!"

"Which part," I wrote with excitement.

"Tokyo, Kyoto, Nara, and Nagoya," she responded.

"Please let me know what days you'll visit Tokyo. I promise I'll make time to come and see you," I let her know.

It would have been a tremendous opportunity to catch up with her; however, I never received a response from Sonia.

At the end of 2018, she emailed me and explained that she was returning to the United States as part of a field trip with her students.

Over time, our communication dwindled until the candle's fire finally burned out. And I'm mostly to blame. We had always communicated via email, but Sonia wanted me to download a Chinese-owned messaging application called WeChat. Google and Facebook were prohibited in China. With WeChat, we could chat and make video calls. No matter how much she insisted that we do video calls, I didn't feel comfortable doing it, so I made up reasons why I couldn't download the app. Honestly, I knew that as long as I was in the military, constantly writing and video chatting with a Chinese national could have been interpreted as suspicious behavior. This was especially true due to our countries' strained relationship. Therefore, I had to tread the waters carefully.

In 2018, I wanted to write Sonia and see how she was doing when the trade war was declared between our countries. In 2019, I wanted to write and know that she was okay when the protests erupted in Hong Kong[45] since her hometown Shenzhen borders Hong Kong. In 2020, I wanted to make sure she was safe and healthy when the COVID-19 pandemic took millions of lives and brought the world to a halt. Although Sonia occupied my thoughts, I didn't write her during any of the aforementioned events.

---

45   Hong Kong was a British colony from 1842 to 1997. Protests erupted in 2019 due to concerns over the Chinese national government changing Hong Kong's special status within the country.

In another life or perhaps a less problematic world, she and I would have been closer friends. What I admired most about Sonia was her thoughtfulness and bluntness. People who are straight-forward and honest don't get the credit they deserve. Sonia always told me exactly how she felt and what she thought. She was one of the most genuine people I knew. Even during one of our first conversations at O'Hare International Airport, she asked me, "Do you want to know one of the things that my country resents most about the United States?"

"What is that?" I asked.

She continued, "You know, China is a country that has existed for thousands of years. We are very rich in history, culture, traditions, and resources. The United States hasn't been around half as long. In a shorter period, your country has managed to become more technologically advanced and economically prosperous."

I'll always remember her as the ingenious and kind-hearted young lady who I met at the airport. Over time, we became good friends. I lived with a double consciousness, though. As long as I was in the Navy, I had to be ready to go to war with Sonia's country.

CHAPTER 15
SHUTTER SPEED

~~~~~~

*Life is like a camera. Focus on what's important. Capture the
good times. And if things don't work out, just take another
shot. —Ziad K. Abdelnour*

My first Navy tour in Japan was two years with an additional
mandatory twelve months. This made me eligible for a benefit called Overseas Tour Extension Incentives Program or simply
OTEIP. OTEIP provides incentive options to sailors who volunteer
to extend their tour at a duty location outside of the continental
United States (OCONUS) by twelve months or more.

There were four options to choose from including a $2,000
lump sum payment. An extra $2000 sounded sexy, but then there
was Option B: Thirty days of paid leave.

Without hesitation, I chose Option B. I could receive a monthly
salary and take a thirty-day vacation. I submitted a travel request
for Mongolia, India, Nepal, Myanmar, and Laos. Honestly, I was
nervous about submitting the leave, thinking it would spark some
suspicion. I'd visited three countries in one leave period, but five
was a record. Thankfully, my command approved the request. I
purchased a multiple-destination ticket to those places for $1,500.

This would be an epic trip, and I wanted to make sure I captured it accordingly.

I spoke with my shipmate and buddy. I'll call him "Wiz." Wiz had a fancy camera and took stunning photos of Instagram models who requested his services. Once, he boasted that his Instagram following had reached four thousand. At the time, I didn't know what any of it meant. I just saw high-quality photos of half-naked women. I thought, "I have to get a better camera."

I upgraded from the iPhone 6 that I had purchased shortly after arriving in Japan in late 2015. Then, I ordered my first camera that wasn't a point-and-shoot, a GH4 Lumix Panasonic. The trip was months away; therefore, I had plenty of time to hone my videography and photography skills.

As soon as the camera arrived, I went out and started taking photos and videos. When I got home and reviewed my work, the videos looked nothing like the ones I saw on YouTube. The 4K made the videos appear washed out. No doubt, the camera took better photos than my iPhone 6; however, they didn't compare to the ones that Wiz was taking.

The next time I saw Wiz, I showed him my photos. Then I asked to see his. "Hey man, how come my photos don't have the same quality as yours."

Wiz asked, "What kind of camera do you have, DSLR or mirrorless?"

I had no clue.

He'd tell me things like, "I use the 85-mm F1.4 lens for portraits to get a nice bokeh."

"Bokeh[46]. Is that German?" I didn't know what any of it meant. It sounded like I was listening to Charlie Brown's teacher speaking, "Shutter speed wa wa wa. Aperture wa wa wa. ISO wa wa wa."

---

46   Bokeh is the quality of the blur in out-of-focus parts of a photograph. The

After purchasing and testing new lenses, I'd return to Wiz. "How come my photos look like this, but yours look like that?"

He responded, "Which format do you use, JPEG or RAW?"

"What? I don't know. Which one do you use?" I inquired

Wiz told me he always used RAW because it retained quality. I went online and learned how to adjust my camera settings to take photos using the RAW format. Wiz was right; the quality was better.

I was proud to show Wiz how far I had come. "Bro, I did what you said. Check these out and tell me what you think."

Wiz reviewed my work and said, "They look like they're straight from the camera."

"No shit, they are from my camera," I responded.

"Yeah, but what I mean is that you have to edit the photos so that you can manipulate the images and produce better results," Wiz explained.

Teaching myself to edit photos was a tedious process. I would spend hours lifting shadows, brightening the image, adjusting the contrast, and everything else. Not only did I learn to create quality photos, but I also learned how to edit videos.

I continued to use Wiz as a resource. He would show me his work in the form of photos of naked women with their boobs out and no bikinis. But I could only focus on the lighting and how he got rid of shadows underneath the model's chin.

There were no Instagram models DM'ing me; I didn't even have an Instagram account. I would go to cities like Kamakura, Yokohama, and Tokyo. There, I'd take photos of the landscapes and buildings. Also, I'd ask people if I could take pictures of them. Although it hurt me to hear "No," I could understand why people would not want a stranger taking their photo. Surprisingly, a lot of people allowed me to take their pictures. But there were no

---

word comes from boke, a Japanese word meaning "blur."

Victoria's Secret panties dropped in front of my lens. The images I captured, I'd go home and practice editing them.

Finally, I knew how to use my camera. In addition, I possessed amateur photo- and video-editing capabilities. I was ready to capture every moment of this epic trip and become a YouTube sensation. I was on my way to becoming a social media influencer, or so I thought.

CHAPTER 16
SIGHT, SOUND, AND MIND

~~~~~~

If the stars should appear one night in a thousand years,
how would men believe and adore; and preserve for many
generations the remembrance of the city of God which had
been shown! But every night come out these envoys of beauty,
and light the universe with their admonishing smile.
—*Ralph Waldo Emerson*

The birthplace of Genghis Khan and the first country on an adventure through Asia, I arrived in Mongolia via its capital Ulaanbaatar. Ulaanbaatar is one of the coolest sounding names of a city I've visited. It's also the coldest capital city in the world[47]. This is why I was freezing my buttocks off when I got there on the morning of September 5, 2018.

Besides Mongolia, the other countries in my itinerary showed a forecast of hot weather, so I didn't pack a jacket. *Mongolia shouldn't be too cold in October?* That was a terrible assumption. The afternoons weren't so bad. When nighttime arrived, it felt like the season had skipped to winter.

---

47   Temperatures in January can dip as low as –40°C.

I took a taxi from Chinggis Khaan International Airport to Golden Gobi Hostel. The hostel was named after the famous Gobi Desert[48], which sits between northern China and southern Mongolia. Although I wasn't staying at the Golden Gobi Hostel, I reserved a tour through their agency.

Upon arrival, I met with Gan; I had only known her through email preparations for the trip. She was the agent who assisted me in developing my itinerary for Mongolia. Initially, Gan sent me a pricier quote for the tour package. After inquiring about lower costs, I received an email from her asking, "Would you be interested in joining another group? This would bring down some of the cost."

I replied, "That'll be fine."

The entire time we spent emailing one another, I thought Gan was a man by the sound of the name. To my surprise, she was not only an attractive woman in her early middle age but also, she was the manager of the company.

Per her instructions, I followed her to an office where I checked in and paid for the tour package. As she escorted me outside, we passed by a closet with outdoor gear, including tents, backpacks, boots, gloves, and jackets. I did not miss the opportunity to ask Gan if I could borrow a jacket. She shuffled through some coats and grabbed a forest green Nike one. She held it up to my chest to ensure it was a good fit. Gan smiled and said, "Here you go."

After exiting the hostel, I met the driver at the van. The passengers included the tour guide and seven tourists, including me. There were two groups. The first consisted of two New Zealanders. The second was three Argentines and one Spaniard who were friends and traveling together. I wouldn't know until later that I

---

48   Deserts are classified as such due to their precipitation. Unlike the Sahara or the Mojave, the Gobi is very cold.

would be a part of the second group. That's why originally, I stuck with the native English-speaking Kiwis.

The driver took us on a ride around the capital. First, we visited the Zaisan Monument, a memorial that pays tribute to the Mongolian and Soviet soldiers killed during World War II. The monument is located on a site that rests above the city, providing an incredible panoramic view of the capital. Although striking, looking down, the capital felt somewhat incomplete. Maybe it had to do with the unique spacing between the buildings, or perhaps it was because some high-rises weren't fully constructed. Nevertheless, there was just something about it that felt a lot different than anything I'd seen.

Afterward, we left the capital. The scenes changed as fast as we drove. The tall office buildings and high-rise apartments turned into power plants that spewed smoke that hung like fog. By the way, Ulaanbaatar is also known as one of the most polluted capitals in the world.

Over forty percent of Mongolia's three million people (in 2018) live in the capital. This rural scarcity becomes obvious when leaving the city and seeing the country's iconic yurts, round, white tents, spread irregularly throughout the land. A yurt is often called a *ger*, although the two are slightly different; however, I will use the terms interchangeably. As the drive continued, eventually, everything just disappeared. There was only the road, uninhabited land, and an exceedingly blue sky. Somewhere along the journey, we came across the most isolated grocery store in the world. Surprisingly, it ended up being an immaculate and well-stocked store. I grabbed some snacks, Mongolia's versions of Frito-Lays and Snickers. Also, I purchased sweetbreads and crackers. When I got to the counter, I noticed the Spanish speakers had bottles of Mongolian vodka and red wine.

***

AFTER A TWO-HOUR DRIVE, WE ARRIVED AT GORKHI-TEREJL NATIONAL PARK, HOME OF TURTLE ROCK. It's exactly what it sounds like, except the rock is large enough to hike. The first course of action was to climb the rock. I'm no fan of heights, especially those with steep slopes; therefore, it presented somewhat of a challenge.

After the climb, the two groups split, and we went our separate ways. Again, I joined the group including the three Argentines and the Spaniard—all males. I'll call them the *Cuatro Amigos*. In the beginning, I was my usual not-very-social self. Since I had joined their group, I didn't want to intervene too much in their trip.

The tour guide came with us. He was a lanky and personable young fellow, no older than twenty-two. The young man was quite stylish. He wore blue jeans, brown lace-up boots, and a heavy blue coat. He was the reason I got some brown laced boots several months later.

When I first noticed him wearing the boots, I asked, "Where did you get those?"

His response was, "Russia."

"You ordered those from Russia?" I asked to be sure I heard correctly.

He said, "Not exactly. I study tourism at a university in Russia. During seasonal breaks, I return home [Mongolia] to work. I bought the boots when I was in Russia."

"Ok, I understand," I replied.

The driver chauffeured everyone to a campsite at the Gorkhi-Terejl National Park. Upon arrival, the tour guide led us into the yurt where the *Cuatro Amigos* and I would be staying for the night. There were five beds. In the center was a wood-burning furnace with a chimney to direct the smoke to the outside. Inside the yurt, I revealed my secret to the *Cuatro Amigos*. "*Yo hablo español*." They were shocked that I could speak their language—even if it was degraded from all the years of not speaking or practicing it. More so, the Argentines admired me after learning I visited their country during my service as a Peace Corps Volunteer.

"*De donde eres?*" the Spaniard asked.

"The United States," I responded but in Spanish.

"Yo, what up my nigga?" he said with excitement.

There goes that word, I thought. It didn't bother me that the Spanish guy said it. I knew exactly why he said it. He said it the same reason that every other person outside of the United States, who didn't know any better, said it. The short answer is the media and how it promotes American subculture through degrading rap music, stereotypical urban content, movies, and so forth. Those things glamorize the word. On the outside, looking in, it seems cool to say the word for someone like the Spaniard.

I've had conversations with numerous people who whole-heartedly wanted to understand the full context of the word and expressed my unfavorable opinion of it.

Some of my acquaintances deemed it necessary to correct others who are not supposed to use the word. I felt it would be a waste of time explaining why it is offensive. For one, I could count on one hand how many times I heard the word while traveling, and no one abroad had used it maliciously. Two, the term is a euphemism of a harsher word. It's confusing explaining to foreigners the history of the word and why it's acceptable to say between those offended by it the most. Lastly, I don't refer to myself or anyone I know in that manner. I could go on, but ultimately, I had more important battles to fight. In my mind, it was foolish for anyone to use the word so openly.

If I was in the United States and heard a foreigner say it, I'd warn them to be careful of their word choice.

However, we weren't in the United States. We were in Mongolia. So, I looked at the Spaniard and said, "What's up, man?" in English.

There is a world of people who have never encountered Black people[49]. Their only exposure to our culture (and many times the detrimental aspects) is through the media. After traveling and seeing how people like me were portrayed and misrepresented, I could no longer support certain music, television shows, and the like. So instead, I'd do my best to be a positive ambassador of myself, my culture, and my country.

After my roommates and I settled into our yurt, we went to have a traditional Mongolian lunch with a family who resided at the camp. The family included a wife, husband, adult daughter, and son. The lunch was rice with stewed beef, carrots, and potatoes mixed in one large pot. The chef prepared it well enough to encourage everyone to go for seconds. Juan from Argentina pulled a bottle from his backpack and said, "No meal is complete without this!" Then he offered it to everyone at the table. The glasses, previously filled with water, were now full of red wine.

After the hearty lunch, it was time to explore. We walked long distances across endless grass fields filled with tall pine trees. Like waves, we moved up and down the hills. Later, we crossed a rope bridge which provided an incredible view of the landscape. Our destination was Aryapala Temple Meditation Center, which sits below a rocky cliff. Along the final path, leading to the temple, there are dozens of wooden signs that include words of wisdom.

The *Cuatro Amigos* were a great group to be a part of. All of them were hardcore world travelers and photographers. Luis, Rico, and Juan were from Argentina. Luis was a veteran traveler.

---

49   In 2010, only six hundred and fifty-six Americans lived in Mongolia.

He had been traveling the world for over seven months when we met. Rico was the oldest and the most laid-back of the group. Juan had a fantastic sense of humor. No matter what joke anyone made, it was *Comedy Central* to Juan. I can't remember a time that he wasn't laughing or smiling. The Spaniard's name was Manuel, and he was the extreme adventurer. He was the rock climber, skydiver, and fighter. He studied mixed martial arts and owned a gym in Barcelona. That made it impossible for me not to like him.

At sunset, we made our way back to the campsite.

Around 10 PM, the sky had become dark enough to gracefully reveal the Milky Way. The nighttime sky is one of the most beautiful exhibits of nature that I've ever seen. The only other time I'd seen the sky so complete with stars was once upon a visit at Yosemite National Park in Central California. An honorable mention includes the night sky at sea.

Unlike my trip to Yosemite, I finally possessed a camera that could capture the dark heavens glittered with light. I brought out my Panasonic Lumix GH4. I pointed my camera at the sky and clicked. When I reviewed the image, it was just a black photo. Thank goodness for the *Cuatro Amigos*. They were Canon and Nikon users; nonetheless, these guys were way more experienced than me. Rico fiddled around with my camera. Like an expert, he scrolled through the settings until he figured it out. Then, he showed me how to place the camera in the correct mode to capture the galaxy.

The night's temperature was painfully cold. I had to remove my gloves to use my camera. It was impossible to remain outside without gloves; my fingers were numb. Nonetheless, the sky appeared too alluring to resist and was worth the agonizing cold. I'd spend ten minutes taking photos, and then warm up inside the yurt. I'd take a swig from the bottle of my roommate's Mongolian vodka, then head back out for more photos. With that, a beautiful closure was brought to my first night in Mongolia.

In the morning, we returned to the yurt of the Mongolian family for breakfast. We had a small selection of bread and crackers, served with jam. To wash it all down, we drank one of the most popular beverages in the world—coffee[50].

We spent the morning horseback riding through the Gorkhi-Terejl National Park. When I was a kid, I visited a farm with my family. My parents made me sit on a horse to take a photo. That was my only previous experience with horses. So yeah, *I'd kind of been horseback riding before. Right?* This was the first time in my adult life that I'd ridden a horse. As someone who has accidentally sat on his own balls once or twice this lifetime, horseback riding did not seem to decrease the risk of such an excruciating experience. Therefore, I avoided it. Also, I loved Christopher Reeve as Superman when I was a kid[51]. Horseback riding didn't turn out too well for him.

The *Cuatro Amigos* excelled at everything, including horseback riding. We arrived at the stable; they meticulously chose their horses like true *caballeros*. Meanwhile, I thought the gray horse looked cool, so that's why I selected it.

The hostler[52] was a short, old man who looked like he had never missed a day of hard labor in his life. If he had the ability to smile, I couldn't tell. In a post-apocalyptic world, he was the guy I'd want on my team. He was wise, serious, and tested.

He asked, "Who's been horseback riding before?"

---

50   Coffee is a fairly new addition to the Mongolian diet. Traditionally, Mongolians drink tea with milk.
51   Reeve was thrown from a horse during a competition in 1995 and was paralyzed from the shoulders down.
52   An employee who cares for horses at an inn.

Everyone raised their hand except me. Then, looking at me, the hostler said, "You'll have to be careful with that horse. She can be aggressive."

I stuttered, "I ... I can pick another horse if there's going to be a problem."

He said, "You'll be okay."

The hostler was correct. After giving a quick tutorial on how to control the horse's movement and speed, we started our journey. The hostler led the way. The experience made me feel like a real cowboy. I don't think I ever connected with an animal as much as I did with the horse.

***

WE RETURNED TO THE YURT AFTER OUR HORSE-BACK RIDE. Then we packed up. Before heading out, we thanked the family for their kindness and hospitality.

Next, we visited the Genghis Khan Statue Complex. There stands a gigantic stainless-steel statue of Genghis Khan[53] atop a horse. Also, the complex has a history museum, art galleries, and gift shops. After getting a glimpse into Mongolia's history, purchasing souvenirs, and taking photos, we were on to our next destination.

We drove for roughly thirty minutes on a dirt road before the driver veered off and started driving on grass. At first, I thought he had fallen asleep behind the wheel. However, when I looked at the rearview mirror, his eyes stared ahead. Soon, we arrived at our destination, two yurts in a more secluded area than the previous location.

This place stretched beyond the boonies. We entered the twilight zone. I've encountered some rural locations, but nothing like

---

53   Founder of the Mongol Empire.

Mongolia. The countryside in Mongolia makes even the smallest town feel like New York City.

Our guide said, "We are going to have lunch with Mongolian nomads. But first, I'll show you around."

Soon, I learned that each yurt had a purpose. One served as a kitchen with a dining area inside. The second served as the area where the family slept. The insides of the yurts were beautifully decorated. Also, the nomads constructed them to be sturdy and well insulated.

I asked the guide, "How long does it take to assemble a yurt?"

He replied, "Thirty to forty-five minutes."

It was crazy to think that a nomad could build their home in the same amount of time it would take me to put together a sofa from IKEA.

I really didn't understand much about the life of the nomads, other than they were people who moved from one place to another. Until that point, I considered myself a nomad. I had lived in four countries in the past ten years. I served on a ship that moved about the oceans. When I vacationed, I always chose new lands to explore. Still, I was not even close to being a nomad after learning what their lives were like.

I asked the guide, "Why do nomads move around so much?"

His answer was obvious, but I had never even considered it.

He said, "Nomads live off the land and their livestock. Their animals provide them with meat, milk, as well as clothing. Also, their animals live off the land and can't endure the temperatures of the winter months. So before colder weather approaches, the nomads move to warmer places or places more sustainable for their animals. Sometimes, this means relocating three to four times a year."

A nomad's survival depends on constantly packing and moving everything they own to the next location.

The *Cinco Amigos* (I was finally one of them), the guide, and the driver had lunch with the family. We had Mongolia's national dish called *tsuivan*, a hearty meal consisting of noodles mixed with mutton and vegetables. We, the guests, sat at the table with the father and son. The mother served us generous portions of her delicious food. She went on to clean and joined us later.

When she returned, she invited us to try horse milk. Maybe it was milk from a horse like cow milk comes from a cow. It was my first time ever hearing of horse milk. Needless to say, nothing appropriate or mature came to mind when I imagined the process of milking a horse; therefore, I passed on the opportunity to drink the white, foamy liquid.

After lunch, we thanked the family and stepped outside. A 360-degree view showed nothing but isolation. Still, the three Argentines and I took photos of the landscape. The Spaniard and the driver conversed about traditional Mongolian wrestling called *Bokh*. The Spaniard practiced MMA, and the driver had wrestled in the past. That was a recipe for a challenge. It was fun watching the two attempt to take the other down. I would've bet my money on the Spaniard because he was taller and muscular, whereas the driver was short and chunky. In the end, the two were evenly matched.

I wanted to challenge the Spaniard so badly and test my grappling skills against him, but I didn't because I didn't want to sweat. I had not showered or pooped since arriving in Mongolia. There were no restrooms, showers, or Western-style toilets. In reality, it would have been nice to have a tree. We were pissing on grass and cleaning our bodies with sanitary wipes. I didn't even know where the Mongolian family members were going. I wasn't sure when my next shower would be, so I held off on the wrestling.

After that, it was time to go our separate ways. The *Cuatro Amigos* got into the van that we all arrived in and left with the driver. The guide and I took a smaller car. The driver of our smaller vehicle drove us far away. In the twilight zone, neither time nor distance existed.

***

THE DRIVER DROPPED US OFF AT THE DESTINATION AND SPED OFF. I asked the guide, "Where are we?"

He said, "I don't know."

I tried again, "What's the name of the city or state?" He shrugged his shoulders again, suggesting that he had no clue about our location in the world.

The guide's name was Jochi. Although Jochi didn't know where we were, he did understand why we were there.

He said, "Earlier, we had lunch with Mongolian nomads. We're going to spend the rest of the day with Kazakh nomads."

The Kazakh nomads, who migrated from Mongolia's western neighboring country Kazakhstan, are different from Mongolian nomads in many ways. The most distinguishable cultural differences are obviously language and then religion. The Mongolians practice Buddhism, whereas the Kazakhs nomads practice Islam.

Like earlier, we were in the middle of nowhere. Jochi introduced me to the family. There was an elderly woman and a child, who may have been her grandson. Although the family was kind, it was more of a "hi and bye" introduction. They greeted me in a language unlike anything that I'd ever heard and then went about their daily lives. Even the guide disappeared like a pen when you need one. I really don't understand where he went because there was nowhere to go.

I was there to spend the rest of the day with the family and experience the nomadic life; however, it was like I wasn't even there. I was a glitch in a world far from my own.

This family had three yurts. The first served as the kitchen and dining area. The second yurt was the family's room. The third was for guests. The family's yurt had a large satellite dish right outside the door. It was good to know that even nomads had access to cable television and could watch *Keeping Up With The Kardashians*. Generators supplied electricity to their homes. I felt terrible for the donkeys that had to carry the generator and satellite dish.

The yurts are spacious for what they are, but they aren't rooms at the Hilton. I spent most of the day outside, taking photos of the pastures. There was nothing in the area except for vast landscapes and hills. At first, I thought the hill closest to me was unique. However, once I reached the top, I saw even more hills. The nearest and only other yurt was approximately four hundred yards away. Maybe there were more beyond the hills, but I couldn't see.

From the top of the hill, I saw cows and sheep owned by the Kazakh family. I went down the hill to get photos and videos of the animals. Each time I attempted to get close to the sheep, they just ran away. Later, a young herder came along and led the sheep somewhere else.

Around sunset, I headed back toward the yurt to capture the way the sun's stunning rays pressed on the tents. While taking photos, I saw the older woman again. The fifty-something-year-old woman stood around four feet and eleven inches. She lifted an ax over her head and swung with enough force to break the firewood.

She repeatedly smashed the wood until there was enough to burn and warm everyone throughout the frigid night.

I thought about how this elderly woman has probably never had to worry about paying an energy bill or having the heat cut off. In contrast, I wondered what worries were associated with being her age and having to gather and laboriously chop firewood to stay warm throughout the winter months.

After dark, the woman and her grandson came into my yurt. She wanted to make sure that the inside was warm enough to protect me from the cold and brawling winds. The nomads accompanied me as they sat on a pull-out bed next to me. The high-spirited boy spoke to the woman as she just watched and smiled at the stranger who showed up at her home. Also, I watched her. She was incredibly mesmerizing, like a character out of a magical realism novel. She had a round and reddish sun-kissed face. Looking into the iris of her eyes was like seeing two galaxies of green-grayish sunflowers. The woman's most powerful features were the wrinkles on her face. They told a story and tracing the lines would recall a nomad's journey of thousands of miles.

Unable to communicate with the woman and young boy, I pulled out my camera and showed them pictures that I'd taken. The boy attempted to aggressively grab my camera, but I pulled back quickly before he could take it. He used his hands as if he was taking a photo and made a shutter noise, "Chicka chicka!" He wanted to take pictures with my camera. I gave him the camera and let him "*chicka chicka.*" Then we went outside, and once again, I took photos of the stars.

Morning arrived, and my stomach was fighting me. I hadn't pooped in almost three days. Finally, it was time to go. Unlike the previous homes that I visited, this family had a recognizable place to do business. Two hundred meters from the yurts, there was a hole in the ground. There were no walls to protect from the elements or provide privacy—just a three-foot hole that would be covered with dirt once it was filled by human feces. I won't describe what I saw when I looked down.

In Japan, I used sophisticated noise-canceling toilets that hid embarrassing fart noises. Some sprayed pretty scents that covered ferocious smells. These electric toilets had heated seats and built-in bidets that sprayed warm water to clean the bum. I'm absolutely serious. Most homes in Japan have these toilets.

Not in Mongolia.

I lowered my pants and squatted above the hole. As I looked around, I could see everything that could see me.

It was a mind-altering experience, pooping in the open, that is. It was the norm to everyone except for me, and I had to adjust my reality to realize that. No one even cared, nor did it mean anything to anyone that I was relieving myself in a vastly open field. As odd as it may sound, it was an emancipating experience.

I was just an unadorned piece of flesh with blood flowing through me, living on a remote planet shared by eight billion others like me.

Just like that ... I had felt human in the most primal way. There was nothing wrong or embarrassing about it. In fact, it felt reassuring to execute one of the most natural bodily functions out in the open and not be understood as anything other than a person.

The trip to Mongolia allowed me to reflect on what it's like to be human. It was an eye-opening experience seeing first-hand how humans can adapt, survive, and make an adequate living almost anywhere on this God-given planet.

In my world of unlimited distractions, Mongolia reminded me to appreciate the simpler and more valuable aspects of life. In addition, it was a reminder of how life could be without the conveniences that I'd been accustomed to. I didn't have the resources to browse the World Wide Web; however, I could go outside and see the Milky Way thousands of lightyears away.

***

IN THE MORNING, THE DRIVER ARRIVED. Jochi and I left with him.

I remained with Jochi, and he showed me around different cities throughout the tour. It's hard to know all the places we visited. We'd drive for hours on paved roads and then dirt roads. Suddenly, we'd arrive at a destination.

We visited the ruins of Buddhist monasteries destroyed by the Soviet Union[54] during an intervention to fight against anti-communist factions in the early twentieth century.

We drove through towns built based on Soviet urban planning. In these cities, we visited more families. For all I knew, Jochi was visiting aunts and uncles. As I sat on their couches, they offered me drinks and food. Popular activities among tourists who visit Mongolia include visiting national parks, exploring the Gobi Desert, seeing the monasteries, and passing the time with the nomads. I was really enjoying the role of an observer peeking into the lives of not only the nomads but also the people in the cities.

As anti-climactic as this sounds, I've come to the realization that all people are the same across the world. We're flesh, bones, and spirit. We may belong to different cultures, appear physically different, have different beliefs and perspectives, speak different languages, eat different foods, and live in different geographical regions. Yet, even with those differences, we all eat, sleep, fuck, poop, work, feel, live, and eventually die. Even if it's oversimplified,

---

54   The Soviet Intervention of Mongolia from 1921 to 1924 resulted in the establishment of a pro-Soviet communist state.

the real thing that makes us different is how we spend our time accomplishing those things.

Like my girlfriend could take me to her friend's home, Jochi could take me to a complete stranger's house, and both hosts would think nothing of it. Both parties would be warm and hospitable. Similarly, a Black guy like me could walk down the streets of Ulaanbaatar and get as many stares as a Mongolian nomad walking the boardwalks of Miami. Both situations are not common, and people would be curious.

Indeed, people were curious as I spent my last days in the coldest city capital in the world without a jacket.

CHAPTER 17
WAIT, PAY, LOATHE

~~~~~~

*It's your own expectations that hurt you. Not the world you
live in. Whatever happens in the world is real. What you
think should happen is unreal. So people are hurt by their
expectations. You know, you're not disappointed by the world,
you are disappointed by your own projections.*

—Jacque Fresco

Travelers always get asked the question, "What's the best places you've been to?"

The more a person travels, the more difficult it becomes to answer the question because every place resonates with the traveler. Each destination offers something different that makes it unique. While it's difficult to answer the question about my favorite country, India is nowhere near the top. In fact, it's at the very bottom. Initially, I looked forward to visiting India more than any other country in my itinerary. However, it was the biggest disappointment of my entire traveling experience, and no one could pay me to return there.

Before I continue, I must share that my girlfriend Kaori accompanied me on the trip to India. She couldn't take off as many vacation days as me. Therefore, she chose to spend a week in India with me. Kaori was there every step of the way. Although we did the same trip, she enjoyed it, and I did not. So, while I expect to entertain and leave readers somewhat more informed, don't let my experiences, good or bad, determine whether you visit a country.

For me, it was a letdown from the very beginning, which is sad because I was in high spirits after Mongolia.

Kaori arrived in New Delhi one day before me. She spent the night at a guesthouse hotel. My flight would touchdown in India around 10 PM the next day; therefore, Kaori scheduled a taxi affiliated with the hotel to pick me up from the airport. After going through customs, I waited outside Indira Gandhi International Airport for the hotel's taxi. After thirty minutes, I grew tired of waiting. Eventually, I used the airport's taxi service. I arrived at the hotel at midnight.

Upon arrival, I was ecstatic to see Kaori there. She introduced me to the staff. The owner asked why I didn't take the hotel's taxi. I explained that I had waited, but no taxi came for me. She insisted that I pay for the cab that I didn't even take. It was after midnight, and I didn't want to make a big deal over a few bucks. I handed the cash to the manager. Then she said I had to pay double because the taxi driver had left and then returned to look for me. That pissed me off. Since an angry me was not a good thing, I handed over more money and took the loss. In hindsight, getting cheated would, unfortunately, become the theme of the trip.

The primary purpose of our trip was to do a tour of the Golden Triangle. This popular tourist route allows travelers to explore the cities of New Delhi, Agra, and Jaipur. Additionally, Kaori and I wanted to visit Rajasthan. Due to time constraints, I purchased a local tour package through TripAdvisor to make the experience go smoother.

Surprisingly, we had a personal driver who escorted us around and a guide. The following day, they picked us up early from the hotel in New Delhi. The driver introduced himself as Rishi, and the guide was Jai.

Our first stop was India Gate, a large arch-like memorial monument that honors the Indian soldiers that died in World War I. We walked around and took photos of the monument and surrounding area. Whereas Mongolia didn't have much exciting architecture, India was full of ancient sites. This presented an excellent opportunity to take photos and record 4K videos.

Next, we headed to the Red Fort[55], and this is where things started to become somewhat suspect. Jai (the guide) told me that we had to pay to enter the Red Fort. Initially, I thought it was an all-inclusive package; nonetheless, the tickets only cost $5 per person. *Maybe Kaori and I will be driven to the attractions, but we still have to pay to go inside,* I figured. I didn't think of it as a big deal. I was in India standing in front of a resilient fort made of red sandstones built strong enough to withstand the test of time. For it has existed for nearly four centuries.

We passed by vendors and walked through large crowds, making our way into the fortress. When we were inside, I witnessed a variety of cultures as I saw Hindu women wearing saris, Muslim women in Hijabs, and Western women in pants.

Jai's tour included an eye-opening history lesson. First, I learned that ancient India's territory once included the countries known today as Afghanistan, Pakistan, Nepal, Bhutan, and Bangladesh. Also, Jai talked a great deal about the Mughal Empire and its influence on India. In fact, it was a Mughal emperor named Shah

---

55   Built in the 1640s, Red Fort served as the main residence for Mughal emperors. The empire declined steadily until it was dissolved in 1857.

Jahan who commissioned the Red Fort. Jai was a well-versed historian who spoke of Mughal emperors as if they were his cousins.

In Mongolia, I learned about Genghis Khan and how he built the Mongol Empire, one of the largest empires to ever exist[56]. It stretched across an extensive portion of Asia as well as Europe. Later, descendants of Genghis Khan traveled to Afghanistan, where they adopted Islamic beliefs. These descendants built the Mughal Empire. Surprisingly, Shah Jahan was a descendant of the great Genghis Khan. It seemed like the more I traveled, the more the world was coming together.

***

LATER, WE MADE A THREE-HOUR TRIP FROM NEW DELHI TO AGRA. First, Kaori and I checked into our hotel room. Although the surrounding area appeared shabby, the hotel was nice. After dropping our belongings in the room, we headed to a restaurant. Lunch ended up being a letdown, not because the meal was terrible; on the contrary, the restaurant was quite fancy. That's what Kaori or I didn't like. We wanted authentic Indian food and not overpriced, westernized meals.

We told Jai (the guide) and Rishi (the driver) that the food was okay; we also made it clear that we wanted a more local experience. They were understanding and made some adjustments to meet our needs.

Later in the afternoon, Rishi and Jai took Kaori and me to stores to potentially do some shopping. It took a while to figure out, but eventually, I realized that Jai seemed to be good friends with the owners of the shops that we went to. We visited jewelry, clothing, and spice shops. I could understand sending customers' business to friends, but the shops had costly products. Most of

---

56   After Genghis Khan's death, the Mongol Empire became the largest contiguous empire in history.

the owners had this phony-friendly approach. They made poor attempts at persuading Kaori and me to buy their products.

"Welcome to my shop, brother."

"What do you want to drink. I have soda and masala tea. I make the best masala tea."

I swear that every shop owner used the "masala tea" line. All of them claimed to make the best masala tea. When they served it to us, all of it tasted similar. Nonetheless, the tea was damn good! I give them much credit for that.

What annoyed me the most was that all (I'm not exaggerating by saying "all") of the shops' owners said something along the lines of, "I'm going to leave you and let you shop around. Don't feel pressured to buy anything." Then, like hawks, they watched as we walked around. As soon as we touched anything, they'd come over and try to sell us their products.

Again, I understood that Jai was just looking out for his homies. The homies were just trying to make money. If I were them, I would have done the same thing. This is why, in one instance, I paid $70 for a shot glass made from the same marble and precious stones as the Taj Mahal. It was a gift for my mom, so I didn't mind paying the price and helping out the homies in the same instance.

In the evening, we visited Agra Fort[57], another magnificent fortress made of red sandstone. We spent several hours touring the inside and getting history lessons from Jai. There were people everywhere. As we walked around, I saw other tourists with guides. Some people meditated. Also, teenagers relaxed in the shade to escape the burning sun. I was able to take some astonishing photos of the fortress. After witnessing the sunset from Agra Fort, we returned to the hotel.

---

[57] The main residence of Mughal emperors prior to building Red Fort and moving the capital to Delhi.

The next day, we woke up early and left the hotel before breakfast could start. It was still dark outside. We were on our way to see India's most famous attraction as well as one of the Seven Wonders of the World—the Taj Mahal. When I had previously seen the Taj Mahal in books or pictures online, I thought the design was beautiful, but I didn't see it as anything special. When we got there, I sat on the bench that all tourists sit on to get their photo in front of the Taj Mahal. Still, I didn't understand people's fascination with the mausoleum. It wasn't until I was close enough to touch it that I understood why it's one of the Seven Wonders of the World.

At close range, I saw that the mausoleum was more than a beautiful structure made of ivory-white marble stones. Many moons ago, highly skilled carvers meticulously chiseled intricate designs into the white marble stones that make the Taj Mahal. Additionally, with great precision, they cut shapes out of precious stones to fill the spots carved into the marble stones. Due to the Taj Mahal's white color and untold amounts of precious stones, the structure changes colors depending on how the sun or moonlight touches it. Additionally, the Taj Mahal is perfectly symmetrical on the outside and the inside. It's mind-blowing.

Jai told us the history of the Taj Mahal. Shah Jahan, the same Mughal Emperor that I mentioned earlier, commissioned the mausoleum.

Shah Jahan had built the Taj Mahal to house the tomb of his favorite wife after she died. It took seventeen years to complete.

Kaori was in awe, "He built this for his wife. How romantic!" I could tell by her derisive facial expression that it was a direct attack on my lack of romantic capabilities.

I was quick to engage. "You know he had multiple wives, right? Maybe if I had more girlfriends, I'd be more romantic."

Kaori and I spent several hours marveling at the extraordinary structure and preserved the moments through hundreds of photos. I don't think she wanted to leave. Could I blame her?

***

AFTER RECOVERING OUR BELONGINGS FROM THE HOTEL, WE HIT THE ROAD FOR JAIPUR. Along the way, we stopped for snacks at a gas station. The drive took over four hours. I knew that we had arrived in a major city upon encountering noisy and chaotic traffic. That city was Jaipur.

Once we made it through the traffic jam, Rishi drove down lively streets with a wide variety of shops and street vendors. Finally, Kaori and I exited the vehicle with Jai. Our first stop was the Hawa Mahal. It is a famous palace known for its reddish-pink color and hundreds of small windows that form a unique pyramid-like architectural structure. The palace was originally built so that royal women, who had to adhere to strict social policies, could observe everyday life by looking through the windows.

Next, we drove to Amber, a city in the state of Rajasthan. There, we visited the Amber Fort. Although the fort has an amber tint, it's actually named after the city. The fort palace sits above the town, on one of the many hills throughout the city. Kaori and I had the option of walking up the path to enter the palace or riding an elephant. Who could resist the opportunity to ride a beautifully decorated elephant? As we rode the large animal, we were able to look past the fort's walls and oversee the city. The experience felt magical. Almost everything went perfectly.

When we arrived inside the palace, the mahout (elephant rider) guided the elephant to a high platform where Kaori and I stepped down from the animal. As I thanked the mahout, he rubbed his fingers together and quietly whispered, "Hey, tip." The back of his shirt read, "Do not tip." There were signs on the platform that read the same thing. I thought, *Ah, he's trying to be inconspicuous. The elephant ride was cool. Let me give him something as a token of appreciation.* I reached into my pocket, pulled out $3 (American), and handed it to the mahout. Expecting more, he looked at the bills in dissatisfaction and rudely waved me away. I was so upset with myself for being nice by tipping that ungrateful idiot.

Eventually, the resentment subsided, and I focused on the beautiful palace around me. Yet, deep down, I felt these incidences beginning to taint my perception of the country and weigh heavily on my temperament.

After an hour or so of learning about the palace, we walked down a path to leave. We crossed the street and walked along a park area and boardwalk of Man Sagar Lake, an artificial lake. We saw the amber Jal Mahal Palace, which rested above the lake. While looking at the palace, I noticed a beggarly middle-aged woman holding a baby who came over to ask for money. Jai asked if I wanted to help her. I couldn't find it in my heart to give anything. Next, a man missing an arm approached us. Realizing that I wasn't in a charitable mood, Jai waved his hand in a manner, telling the guy to go away. I understood that Jai may have felt some pity for his unfortunate compatriots; however, it all seemed like a hustle to me.

The following situation didn't do anything to change my mind.

Kaori and I wanted to experience camelback riding in the Rajasthan desert; therefore, we decided to book the tour through Jai's company. Jai and I went to a private area where I could pay for the addition. The payment process went smoothly, and everything seemed good. Then, unexpectedly, Jai said he made a mistake when listing the Golden Triangle tour on TripAdvisor. He said that the tour was supposed to be double the price I paid. He made it clear that it was his mistake, and he wouldn't charge me extra. In my head, I was sighing while thinking about how he was trying to guilt-trip me into paying more money. I listened to him, but there was no way I was getting ready to pay double for the trip. Nonetheless, he was a great tour guide. For that, I ended up giving him a hefty tip. Even so, I was tired of people trying to take advantage of me.

Jai informed us that he had to return to New Delhi to meet a new group of travelers, and Rishi would continue to drive us around. Before returning to New Delhi, Jai accompanied us on several more stops. First, we visited Panna Meena Ka Kund, an extraordinary step well[58] that looks like something out of a fantasy movie. The architecture of the staircases gives the illusion that a person could walk upside down on them, like in the film *Labyrinth* with David Bowie.

Next, we headed to the Jantar Mantar, an observatory made of ancient technology consisting of several large instruments. Jai led Kaori and me to Samrat Yantra, one of the world's largest sundial clocks. He looked at the sky to locate the sun. Then he observed the shadows on the sundial. He said a time and told me to look at the time on my phone. They were identical. Our final trip with Jai was to Pushkar.

Previously, I believed India to be a place of spiritual enlightenment and imagined that it would be a soul-enriching experience. How could it not be? It's the birthplace of Hinduism, the world's oldest religion, as well as the birthplace of Buddhism. I remembered watching the movie *Eat Pray Love* and seeing Julia Robert's adorable self. She wore a sari as she sat in a yoga pose, practicing the art of meditation. Now, I was in India, ready to find myself and experience the sacredness that enriches the soul.

---

58   As the name suggests, a step well is a well in which the water is reached by descending stairs.

After arriving in Pushkar, Rajasthan, Jai handed us over to another guide. The small, dark-skinned man with silky, black hair wore a blue polo shirt tucked into his jeans. He wore the famous red dot known as *ajna* (the third eye chakra) between his eyes. Kaori and I went with our spiritual guide. We meandered through small, crowded streets, home to dozens of local shops.

Along the way, Kaori stepped in cow dung. Since she was wearing flip-flops, the poop smeared all over her foot and between her toes. That gave me a nice laugh. The guide led us to where water was leaking from the roof of some random building. Kaori washed her foot as much as she could using the small drips of water. Once her foot was somewhat cleaner, we continued our journey until we arrived at Brahma Temple.

The guide explained that the Brahma Temple is dedicated to Brahma, the creator-God in Hinduism. Each year, thousands of people across India make pilgrimages to visit the holy site and pay tribute to the creator.

Before entering the temple, Kaori and I removed our shoes since the site is sacred ground. We left our shoes near the entrance. Then we walked up the steps leading into the temple. The guide gave Kaori and me a tour, and we saw small rooms with statues of Hindu gods inside of them. Later, the guide led us behind the temple. There was an outdoor area with wide steps leading down to the divine Pushkar Lake.

All around, devotees prayed and meditated. Topless women bathed in the holy waters of the lake. The guide invited me to pray, and I accepted. Kaori went with a different guide to receive prayer.

My guide found a quiet area and then we sat. He tied a cloth bracelet around my wrist. He told me to close my eyes and repeat after him. The prayer was in Hindi, and I tried as best I could to speak the language.

Then the guide prayed in English. First, he prayed for my health. Then he prayed for prosperity in my life and work. Next, he prayed for my family. Finally, he told me to pray for my family. Similarly, I prayed for their well-being and success.

After some time, the guide told me to open my eyes. Like earlier, he explained that the Brahma Temple was a sacred site. He said that not only Indians visited, but also people from all over the world made the pilgrimage to the holy place. The guide noted that the temple received donations from people all over the world. He politely asked if I could donate to the temple. Of course, I didn't mind contributing to one of the most renowned Brahma temples in the world. I reached in my pocket and pulled out 1,000 Japanese yen, approximately $10 (American). It was the largest bill I had in my pocket, and I gave it to the guide. Then he repeated himself, "This temple receives large donations from people all around the world." I told him that was all I had to donate. Then he caught me off guard by asking me, "How many siblings do you have?"

Distracted by such a random question, I answered, "Three."

Then he said, "You have three siblings and two parents. You can donate 5,000 yen, 1,000 for each family member." That's when I became enraged because I felt that the guide was swindling me during the most spiritual moment of the trip. There was nowhere in the country where I was safe from scammers. My heart hardened. I snatched the donation from his hand and donated it back to myself. I took off the bracelet that he put around my wrist, handed it to him, and walked off to find Kaori. When I saw her, she was still praying with her guide. I interrupted the prayer, "Hey, it's time to go."

She responded, "Huh? Why?"

I said, "Let's go. I don't want to be here anymore."

The guide attempted to speak to me, but I just ignored him. Kaori asked, "What happened?"

I said, "I'll tell you later."

I held her hand as we made our way out of the temple. Our shoes were right where we left them. The guide finally caught up to us. I mean-mugged him so that he understood that I was not in the mood to be bothered. Unfortunately, I had no idea where we were, so I had to speak to him. "This tour is over. Take us back to Jai." After the Brahma Temple, Jai separated from us, and Rishi drove Kaori and me to a desert town in Rajasthan.

Throughout my travels, I've been to many places that I believed were overrated. Fortunately, this was not the case with India. The subcontinent had so much to offer in terms of history, culture, culinary arts, and the like. Unfortunately, my high hopes had quickly come crashing down. It was almost impossible to appreciate the experience because I felt like I had to constantly be on guard for scammers. This didn't make me happy. In fact, it brought out the worst in me.

I came to this realization on the final day of our tour. After checking out of the hotel near the desert where we rode camels, Kaori and I headed to Rishi's vehicle. He would escort us to Jaipur, where we'd visit Birla Mandir Temple before taking a train back to New Delhi.

There was a little girl wearing old, raggedy clothes sitting on the curb close to where Rishi parked his vehicle. She was no older than six years old. As I prepared to enter the van, the downhearted girl looked over at me. She extended her small, fragile arm as if she wanted money. I felt conflicted as I didn't want anything to do with her. I was tired of giving to what seemed like an endless amount of helpless and unappreciative people.

This poor little girl was too young for any of life's hardships to be any fault of her own. How could people decide to create a life and leave it to fend for itself in such dreadful conditions? I could not help but conclude that at the moment, her parents, community, and representatives had failed her.

I was unbiased enough to realize that the issue wasn't exclusive to India. This was a global problem, and a reminder of how indiscriminately merciless life could be. Unfortunately, children don't realize that adults are just as lost and vulnerable as they are.

By traveling around developing nations, I understood the rules of giving and operated by them. 1. Don't give money to beggars. It only encourages poverty by creating a source of dependence. 2. Instead, support locals by purchasing their products or services. 3. Never give out of guilt. Instead, give out of righteous desire. 4. If choosing to give, give the less fortunate what they need, such as food. Eventually, I handed the little girl a pack of salted crackers from my backpack. There was nothing righteous about it. I just wanted the problem to disappear from in front of me. Perhaps, I had failed her too.

There was a time when I'd see impoverished children in countries like the Dominican Republic and feel like it was my responsibility to change the entire world. Still challenging, I realized it was much less complicated to change my own beliefs, behaviors, and how I respond to situations. Somewhere along the way, I accepted that changing the world was beyond my control. Worrying about every single problem would destroy me. Everyone had to be accountable for their own decisions.

I pondered, *Protagonists may not save everyone. Even so, was I slowly transforming into the villain of my own story?*

Later in the evening, Kaori and I took a train from Jaipur back to Delhi. The train was old and suffered a mechanical issue before taking off. We waited on the train for two and a half hours for the mechanics to fix the problem. Once the train ran, it took us four hours to return to Delhi.

***

THE LAST FEW DAYS KAORI AND I SPENT GETTING TO KNOW DELHI WITHOUT A GUIDE OR DRIVER. Honestly, I enjoyed this experience better. Although I learned so much about India's compelling history and rich culture with a guide, it was exhausting having to adhere to such a strict schedule. It was kind of boring as well. Nonetheless, it was nice being able to choose our restaurants and shopping outlets. Overall, we had more flexibility to see India for ourselves.

We stayed at a guesthouse near the Khan Market. The area was spirited and beautiful Indian people, dressed in colorful garments, filled the streets. There was no shortage of restaurants or shopping. Artificial lights and glowing balloons brightened the night and decorated the streets. Each night, some bands blessed the ambiance with pleasant music.

With only a few days left, we spent time sightseeing. My favorite place was the Lotus Temple, a Bahá'í[59] House of Worship whose architecture resembles a white lotus flower. Although there were dozens of visitors, the temple was peaceful and quiet.

Also, we did some last-minute shopping for souvenirs. We visited a few shopping malls and local markets, including Dilli Haat Market. The outdoor vendors sold traditional bags, clothes, blankets, and so much more.

In one shopping district, we passed a shoe store with a sign, "50% Off Everything!" Kaori went to the women's section, and I

---

59   Originating in 1844 in Iran, the Baha'i Faith believes many founders of world religions to be Manifestations of God. These include Jesus, Buddha, Muhammad, and others.

looked at the men's shoes. I came across a pair of nice boots, similar to the ones Jochi had in Mongolia. I asked the manager if he had the boots in my size. After I tried them on, the manager noticed my interest. Then he said all the shoes were fifty percent off except those on the shelf where I pulled the boots from. Those were full price. I would've believed him, except there was an Indian woman who was also shopping in the store. She called the manager's bluff.

"The sign outside says everything in this store is fifty percent off!"

"The shoes on the top shelf are excluded," the manager said nervously.

"That's not what the sign in front of your store says." Then the woman spoke angrily in Hindi to the manager. He just stood there looking pitiful. I didn't feel one ounce of sympathy for the bastard.

After my surrogate Indian mom cursed out the manager, he had the nerve to tell me that he'd take forty percent off. At that point, I didn't want to give one cent to his business. Kaori and I left without purchasing anything. I felt good knowing that at least one person stepped up and protected me from a con artist. She couldn't change the world just by helping one person either, but she could add a little decency.

***

KAORI LEFT INDIA ONE DAY BEFORE ME. A few hours after she departed the guesthouse, I decided to check out and find a hotel closer to the airport. For $2, the staff worker let me borrow his phone to call a taxi. Upon arrival, I realized that I'd be staying in a gated community of hotels, malls, and restaurants. I felt pretty safe in the area, not that I felt unsafe in the other locations where I'd been. Each time I left and returned to the hotel, the security guards made me take everything out of my bag, including my camera. They ran the belongings through a scanner. I don't know what kind of electronic scanner they used, but it somehow ruined my camera. The camera showed a permanent pink screen with black vertical lines across it. I could no longer use the $1,000 camera that I bought specifically for the trip to take high-quality photos. Of course, it had to happen in India.

***

I DIDN'T HOLD ONLY INDIA ACCOUNTABLE FOR THE CAMERA. I emailed Panasonic's customer support team. I explained that my three-month-old GH4 camera had failed during my trip across Asia. My email basically said, "Your product failed. I want my money back and a free GH5 (their newest camera model at the time). Meet these demands, and I'll continue to buy your products." Their response was something like, "Sorry about the camera, but you ain't getting nothin' from us."

Panasonic really messed up. They didn't realize that I had purchased the camera and lenses via Amazon; therefore, I had Amazon reimburse me for all my Panasonic products. Later, I would buy a Sony camera and never look back.

Unfortunately, I wouldn't be able to take quality photos for the remainder of my trip through Asia. Still, I had the camera on my iPhone 6.

CHAPTER 18

THE TOP OF THE WORLD

The moment you doubt whether you can fly, you cease
forever to be able to do it. —*J.M. Barrie*

After India, the next destination was Kathmandu, Nepal. An
unusual story led me to visit Nepal.

Months earlier, I was having a conversation with my friend
Dustin. He was also my coworker on the USS *Shiloh*. Something
in our conversation triggered a random thought in my mind.
However, I couldn't think of the word or idea in my head. So, I
waited for the conversation to pause.

Then I said, "Hey Dustin, I'm trying to think of a specific type
of plane, but it's not coming to mind."

Right away, he said, "A jet."

"No," I replied.

"A drone," he tried again.

"No, it's an actual plane," I said. "But what the hell is it called?"

"Ultra-light!" he responded with confidence.

"What's that?" I asked.

He explained that it was a tiny and light aircraft.

"Maybe," I said, but I was tired of thinking about it.

There was no Wi-Fi on the ship; therefore, I removed my cell phone from my pants pocket, opened the Notes app, and started typing the letters "U-l-t-r-a L-i-g-h-t." By the way, the word that I was trying to think of was "seaplane."

Days passed, and I almost forgot about the word I typed into the Notes app. But then, something led me to open the app. That's when I came across "Ultra-Light." Before I deleted it, I thought, *Wait! There's a reason why this is here. My past self left this here to remind the future me of something.*

I went to Google and searched "ultra-light." I saw mixed results from jackets and bikes to suitcases and lawn chairs. Then I clicked "Images" and saw a small aircraft that looked like a combination of a three-wheeled motorbike and a hang-glider flying through the sky. I'd never been a fan of heights or flying. Turbulence has always made me feel uneasy. This is why I took twenty-four-hour bus rides to cities including Buenos Aires and Rio de Janeiro versus four-hour flights when I lived in Paraguay. However, the discomfort had rarely been enough to dissuade me from doing what I wanted.

Still on Google, I searched where I could experience the fear and thrill of flying in an ultra-light plane. Pokhara, Nepal, appeared first in the results. The flight was within budget, and that's how Nepal became a part of my trip.

Although I didn't know much about Nepal, I knew someone who did. His name was Jaysha, the manager of my favorite Indian–Nepalese restaurant in Zushi, Japan. A few months before the trip, I visited the restaurant. I ordered my favorite curry set, including chicken saag curry and mutter paneer, tandoori chicken, and cheese naan. Of course, an Indian meal wouldn't be complete without mango lassi. Jaysha, born in Nepal, came over to chat with me as always since I had been a loyal customer for several years.

I told him about my trip to Nepal. "The plan is to spend a few days in the capital Kathmandu and then head to Pokhara for a couple more days."

"You're going to Nepal!" he exclaimed.

"Yeah, I plan on sightseeing, but I really don't know much about Nepal," I said.

"Pokhara is beautiful. Do you enjoy hiking?" he asked.

I nodded my head.

He continued, "Then, you'll have to do one of the trails in Pokhara. Here's what I propose. From Kathmandu, travel to Chitwan National Park. Then, go to Pokhara and make sure you go for a hike while you're there. The views that you'll see are unreal!"

Jaysha gave me his friend's contact information, who was a tour guide. I contacted Jaysha's friend, but the tour prices were steep for my budget. In all my years of traveling, I learned that local hostels offer some of the best and most cost-efficient tour packages. Many of them offer single rooms with amenities just like hotels. While searching for a hostel in Kathmandu, I asked each property about tour packages in Chitwan and Pokhara. Finally, I came across one that could arrange everything I wanted to do.

***

MONTHS LATER, I HAD FINALLY ARRIVED IN NEPAL—THE BIRTHPLACE OF BUDDHA[60]. Although I would only be there for a week, I had an ambitious itinerary. There was no time to waste.

After a two-hour flight from New Delhi to Kathmandu, I stood outside the small international airport, waiting in muggy weather.

---

60   Historians disagree on the exact date of Siddhartha Gautama's birth. Some place it between 563 and 483 CE. Others believe he was born circa 400 CE. Most agree he was likely born in Lumbini, a city in modern-day Nepal.

Finally, I saw a young fellow wearing blue jeans, a white polo shirt, and tennis shoes—holding a sign with my name.

I walked toward him. He asked, "Are you Mike Nixon?"

"Yes," I said

"Hey, my name is Sushil, and I'll be your tour guide today. First, I'll take you on a city tour where you'll get to see some world heritage sites. Next, we will go to lunch. Then we'll return to the hostel where you'll be staying. Okay?"

"Sounds like a good plan," I replied.

The driver chauffeured me around the city in an illustrious 1992 Toyota Corolla with no AC for much of the day. Toyota should go to countries like Nepal and make commercials of their older vehicles to demonstrate the reliability of their cars. If I saw a commercial that guaranteed a car would last almost thirty years, I'd be the first person in line to buy it.

The first stop was Boudhanath, a stupa[61]—a large white mound-shaped infrastructure with a golden pyramid at the top. The base of the pyramid has eyes painted on it. Today, it is located along the ancient trade route that extended from Tibet to the Kathmandu Valley. For centuries, merchants visited the site to relax and pray.

Next, we visited Kathmandu Durbar Square, part of the Royal Palace from the ancient Kathmandu Kingdom. On April 25, 2015, Nepal experienced a devastating earthquake that caused nearly ten thousand deaths and left Kathmandu in ruins. The quake spared nothing—not even the country's ancient sites. While walking around the Square, I realized much of it was still being rebuilt.

The driver escorted me around the city from one site to the next. I felt more like a loaf of bread than a passenger as I sat baking in a car whose cooling system depended on how fast the

---

61   Typically, stupas hold holy relics, such as the remains of Buddhist nuns and monks.

vehicle was moving[62]. I could feel the sweat escaping from my pores and seeping through my shirt into the seat. The two-way roads we took were narrow. I don't understand how cars weren't sideswiping one another. Like so many other developing nations and Washington, D.C., the traffic was chaotic and jam-packed with vehicles. Drivers were honking their horns as if the noise was going to miraculously get traffic moving again. I watched a guy in a military uniform exit his truck to yell at another driver who was honking at him.

Suddenly, my chauffeur removed the keys from the ignition and exited the vehicle. He poked his head through the window and said, "I'll be back. Just wait here." Then he ran off into the traffic jam. I had been in the country for less than three hours. He told me to wait as if I had a better option.

Ten minutes later, he returned, and traffic was moving. He explained that one of the company's drivers had been drinking and passed out behind the wheel. He recognized him in the traffic ahead and went to wake him. Then he drove the car to a nearby lot before returning to where he left me. *Thank God that you're my driver and not the other guy*, I thought.

Next, the driver dropped me off at a site known as the Shri Pashupatinath Temple. My chauffeur pointed to the ticket booth, said he'd be back in an hour, and drove off. It took me ten minutes to walk the smoke-filled area. I would have had to pay more to enter additional parts of the temple. But still, I would have been prohibited from fully exploring since I was not Hindu.

Suddenly a friendly-looking gentleman approached and introduced himself. His name was Hari, and he was a tour guide. Hari offered to give a one-hour tour for $5. His English skills were

62   In the Southern United States, this is often called "4-60 air conditioning", meaning four windows down as you drive 60 mph.

sufficiently decipherable, and he was a very polite young man. Frankly, I just wanted companionship. At times, traveling alone felt like a lonely experience.

Hari explained how the Shri Pashupatinath Temple hosted outdoor cremations and the significance to Hinduism. He told me that I was lucky to come on a day when bodies were being cremated. I didn't think of that as lucky; however, things were starting to make sense. The smoke came from the incinerated bodies. As promised, Hari showed me around the area. In the end, I was satisfied with Hari's tour and companionship.

Two hours later ...

I returned to the location where the chauffeur said he would meet me. He wasn't there. I waited a bit longer. Next, I went to a nearby convenience store, where I grabbed a bottle of water. The owner was an older man, and he seemed happy to keep me company. The entire time, he spoke about Ronald Reagan's visit to Nepal in the early '80s and Clint Eastwood movies.

Eventually, the chauffeur returned. He explained that he had to take the drunk driver home. That's why he was late to pick me up.

***

THE NEXT DAY, THE BUS RIDE FROM KATHMANDU TO CHITWAN WAS SPECTACULAR. There was what seemed like an infinite road that curled around the mountains. Traveling along the narrow curves of the mountains felt like a scary roller coaster. I noticed several passengers holding plastic bags. Later, one of the local passengers confirmed that riding through the mountains caused nausea for many Nepalese passengers; therefore, people brought vomit bags. Although sickening, passing through the valleys provided rewarding views of the country's landscape.

Across from me, sat a foreign lady who looked noticeably different than the Nepalese women. After traveling so much, I gained a superpower to identify other tourists.

Being in the military is like being a superhero or villain, depending on whom you ask. There's a strong dichotomy between being a world traveler and a sailor in the military. On the one hand, I was a free-spirited adventurer connected to the world. On the other hand, I was a small mechanism associated with the military-industrial complex. I was a part of a polarizing organization that people either admired or despised. I had an identity that I couldn't openly share with everyone.

Before continuing, I'll tell an old story.

In 2014, the day I graduated from boot camp, my parents came to the ceremony. They drove from Virginia to Illinois to see me. After graduating, new sailors were required to wear uniforms everywhere. In boot camp, everyone was issued the underwear known as tighty-whities, or skivvies, in the Navy. Those were the only underwear that everyone wore for two months. Post-boot camp, the first thing I wanted to do was go to Walmart to buy a five-pack of Hanes boxer briefs for $16.99. I told my family to wait in the car while I went inside to buy some boxers. Two unfriendly-looking guys stopped me in the parking lot. After two months, this was my first encounter with anyone outside of the military. They warned me to be careful wearing my Navy uniform in their neighborhood.

Although I did get my boxer briefs, the experience taught me an important lesson. If fellow Americans in a Walmart parking lot had a problem with me being in the military, I would definitely need to be careful in other countries. That's why I traveled like a spy with a secret identity.

Again, I looked over at the lady sitting in the seat across from me. It's not so hard to start a conversation.

"Are you going to Chitwan as well?" I asked.

There were only two things she could say. She said, "Yes."

The hard part is continuing the conversation. "How long have you been in Nepal?"

Time is experience and knowledge. I wanted to see what helpful information she could provide me about the country.

She said, "Only a few days."

Keep her talking, I thought to myself. "What do you plan to do in Chitwan?" I asked.

We got ourselves a conversation now.

Her name was Mari. Her parents were from China and immigrated to Canada. Mari was a Chinese Canadian in her late forties, maybe early fifties. Although she did not tell me her age, she had a daughter in college. She appeared healthy and exceptionally good-looking for her age, especially after discussing her profession. Mari was a doctor who worked in developing countries.

This interested me. "Wow! Which countries have you worked in?"

First, she explained how she did relief work in Haiti after the 2010 earthquake. Later, her organization sent her to Iraq, Libya, Afghanistan, and Tunisia. She recently worked in Syria, where she provided medical assistance to primarily children and women who suffered war injuries. The nations that Mari named were no ordinary developing countries. Mari worked in war zones and not just any kind of war zones. Each one had U.S. military involvement. She was a woman who had seen war by placing herself in the most dangerous situations to be able to heal others.

I knew what it was like to be on the cusp of war as my ship's commanders awaited orders on whether to respond to a hostile

North Korea conducting nuclear tests and firing missiles over Japanese territories. I wondered what Mari would've thought to know that I was in the military.

Instead of revealing the warfighter in me, I went another route. Being a former Peace Corps Volunteer, I could relate to her humanitarian work by sharing my experience as a volunteer in Paraguay. She listened to my stories and inquired about my projects as a Community Economic Development Volunteer.

For a while, I had been in control of the conversation. When I worked in the hotel industry, my manager used to tell me that the person asking the questions controlled the conversation. It was the strategy I used to keep the conversation on Mari. Suddenly, her barrage of questions came. My only objective was to not reveal that I was in the military. The less said, the better.

"What made you travel all the way from the United States to Nepal?" she asked.

"I just love to travel. I started in Mongolia. I just came from India, and now I'm here in Nepal. After this, I'll go to Myanmar and finish up in Laos," I responded.

Mari was interested in my trip to India because she thought about visiting there. I didn't hesitate to tell her why it was my least favorite country. Nonetheless, I showed her photos of the trip to India. When Mari saw a picture of me standing next to an Asian female in front of the Taj Mahal, she inquired about my companion. I explained that she was my girlfriend, Kaori. I told her that Kaori didn't have as many vacation days, so she could only travel to India with me.

Then the conversation got more interesting.

Mari replied, "Well, your trip sounds amazing! And then you head back to the United States? What's it like to live there right now?"

I would have loved to have answered, "The United States is the best it's ever been! Everybody loves President Trump and what he's doing for the country and world." Sadly, that was hardly the case. Instead, I asked, "What do you mean?"

Mari said, "You don't seem like you're from the United States. You've traveled around the world and have a lot of experience with different cultures. You're well-spoken and polite." She explained that the United States seemed like a difficult place to live. She discussed faults that she saw in President Trump's policies on immigration, trade, and isolating the United States from the rest of the world. She talked about the lax gun laws, mass shootings, violence, and racism. Things got heavy real fast.

Then she asked me, "Being African American and having an Asian girlfriend, what is that like? Do people look at you or treat you differently?"

At the time, I hadn't lived in the United States for nearly three years. I had only resided in the States for two of the past eight years. Everything I knew about my home was from reading online articles, international news, or friends' posts on social media. Considering the information that I came across, it seemed like a depressing place, and I really did not miss home.

I understood Mari's stance on many issues, especially the violence. In the military, the U.S. flag is placed at half-mast or lowered for several reasons, including remembrance, respect, and mourning. Many times, the flag rested at half-mast, and someone would ask why. Someone else would sarcastically respond, "There probably was a mass shooting," for it only to be true.

Regarding immigration, I told Mari that I supported anyone's pursuit to improve their lives through any means necessary as long as their actions are morally just. I also let her know that countries have laws. People who break them must be prepared to face the consequences. I gave her examples. In almost every country I visited, I looked noticeably different from the rest of the population. In Paraguay, law enforcement would sometimes stop the buses and conduct identification checks. After showing some identification, I was good. U.S. Immigration and Customs agents have interrogated me like a drug lord when both leaving and returning to the country. Furthermore, I explained how I had successfully written several letters inviting foreigners to visit the United States and helping them to obtain visas. The process can be bureaucratic and time-consuming, but it works. Unfortunately, it doesn't benefit everyone.

After rambling about my experiences and opinions on various topics, I answered Mari's question about having an Asian girlfriend in America.

"Actually, I don't live in America. Currently, I live in Japan."

"Wow! What kind of work do you do in Japan?" she asked.

"I work with computers?"

I was prepared to answer any question without compromising my identity.

Mari was a professional questioner and threw a curveball. She asked, "What is the process like to get a work visa in Japan?"

The question caught me by surprise. Hesitantly, I replied, "I applied to the company ... and—"

Mari cut me off, "Oh, the company assisted you with the visa process?"

Relieved, I replied, "Yes, I applied, completed the necessary paperwork, and the company took care of the rest."

It was nice conversing with Mari during the bus ride. Once we ran out of juicy stuff to talk about, she took a nap, and I enjoyed the scenery from the window.

***

HOURS LATER, WE ARRIVED AT CHITWAN'S BUS TERMINAL. A driver from the hotel met me at the station. He escorted me to a pickup truck. There was a young Chinese native named Zhang. He wore colorful, loose clothing like a hippie but without the bandana. He spoke English very well. We introduced ourselves and chatted during the fifteen-minute ride to the hotel. After checking into the cool jungle hotel, the staff informed us that lunch would be in an hour. Before going to our separate rooms, Zhang invited me to his room. I told him that I'd drop off my belongings, and then return.

Minutes later, I was knocking on Zhang's door. He invited me in, and I sat on the sofa next to his bed. He was friendly and easygoing.

The first thing I learned about him was that he was an ardent listener of music. His favorite genres were blues, jazz, and reggae. We talked as he played an incredible playlist of artists including John Coltrane, Muddy Waters, Miles Davis, and Jimi Hendrix. Zhang's musical preference blew me away. This twenty-something-year-old Chinese fellow had the musical taste of a sixty-year-old Black man born in Mississippi. He knew more about African American blues legends than I did. Also, he introduced me to Chinese music influenced by American jazz. Then he played Bob Marley, an artist that I was more familiar with.

Whenever you want to play music, but you're not sure how others will react, you can never go wrong with Bob Marley. I did the same thing when I met Sonia at Chicago's airport. Now, a Chinese person had reversed the role.

He asked, "You like Bob Marley?"

I replied, "Of course! Bob Marley's the man."

Then he asked, "Do you smoke marijuana?"

Before I could say "No," he pulled out the sticky icky. That Mary Jane. The skunk. Ganja. Yep, I used to listen to a lot of rap music. Honestly, I have never smoked marijuana in my life. Being in the military with a zero-drug tolerance policy, I damn sure wasn't getting ready to start. There were random drug tests every week. By the way, guess who the most suspicious person on the ship was. Me ... the guy who was always traveling to strange places and doing God knows what. Those random drug tests never seemed random to me.

As Zhang was lighting the joint, I didn't even have time to process whether marijuana was legal in Nepal. So, I assumed it was legal. I pondered what would happen if the housekeeper came in or someone smelled the pungent odor of Asian chronic. Before I could decide to leave, I was already smelling like a hippie in the sixties. The point of no return had already passed.

Some minutes later, he asked if I minded his smoking. "Buzz Kill" Mike told him that I'd feel more comfortable he if wasn't do-ing it. He took one last puff and place the joint on the nightstand.

"You want to know what I like most about music, especially jazz?" Zhang asked.

"What's that?" I inquired.

He said, "It's free. The freedom of expression when the artists are singing, dancing, or performing. In jazz, if you really listen to it, you'll notice that the musicians improvise playing their instruments. It's one song with many sounds, but the sounds are unique to each musician."

I had no idea where he was going with it, but I continued to listen.

"In China, whether it's an actor or musician, you only watch or listen to what the government wants you to see and hear," he said.

I interrupted, "When I visited Beijing, I'd spend the nights in my hotel room browsing through the television channels. I thought the programs depicted a positive image and representation of China and its culture. I turned through news programs and movies. I settled on the programs that showed traditional Chinese dance performances."

"Most of the programs are sponsored by the state-run media," he said.

I replied, "Well, I prefer those programs to some of the trash I used to see on American television. I can't even listen to the music that people make nowadays. Two of my favorite singers are Lauryn Hill and Laura Izibor. Both walked away from the music industry because they didn't want to conform to the standards set by record companies. Now that I think about it, American media is run more so by big business than the government."

Zhang broke eye contact with me as he looked over at his joint by the nightstand. The blues played in the background. He reached toward the spliff and grabbed his phone that was next to it. After a couple interactions with his phone, I felt his eyes return to me.

Then he asked, "Do you know the Dalai Lama?"

I replied, "I've heard of him."

"I have a friend in India who knows the Dalai Lama. When I was in India a few months ago, my friend introduced me to him," he said.

Then Zhang unlocked his phone and showed me a photo of himself standing next to the most prominent Buddhist leader in the world. Impressed, I stared at the image of the small and happy elder wearing a red robe. Zhang began to speak.

"If the Chinese Government knew I had this photo, I'd probably be in prison."

I quickly looked up at Zhang and thought, *Who the hell is this guy?* The only word that came out of my mouth was, "Why?"

Zhang explained that, in the 1950s, the Dalai Lama[63] was the spiritual and political leader of Tibet. The Chinese Government didn't agree with his teachings and leadership, so they sent soldiers to invade Tibet. Eventually, the Dalai Lama fled Tibet to escape imprisonment and potentially death. India provided him political asylum. The disdain from the Chinese remains to this day. That was the reason Zhang could've been arrested for taking a photo with the Dalai Lama.

Afterward, there was a moment of silence. At the same time, I reflected on my own life, not to compare, but realize that it now was somehow a part of Zhang's life and story—just as his own life was intertwined with and affected by the life of the Dalai Lama. Interestingly, I was now connected to the Dalai Lama through Zhang. It would become a part of my story.

Suddenly, there was on knock on the door!

Fuck, I thought.

Zhang grabbed his cannabis cigarette, placed it in a bag, and hid it under the pillow. There was not much we could do in a short time to hide the smell. Zhang was getting ready to go to jail not for knowing the Dalai Lama, but for possessing illegal drugs[64] in Nepal. And I was his accomplice by default.

I went to the door. Without opening it, I asked, "How may I help you?"

There was a reply, "I'm part of the hotel staff. I would like to inform you that your lunch is ready."

---

63 Believed to be a reincarnation of the Bodhisattva of Compassion, the Dalai Lama leads the most dominant denomination of Tibetan Buddhism. The Chinese Government rejects Tibet's claims of independence.

64 Marijuana has been used in Nepal for religious, therapeutic, and recreation reasons for hundreds of years. It has been illegal since 1960.

"Okay, we'll be there soon," I said.

The next couple of days, I passed touring Chitwan's National Park. I kayaked through crocodile-infested waters, rode an elephant through the jungle, and saw rhinoceroses for the first time in my life. I did cross paths with Mari and Zhang throughout my excursions. Nearly a week earlier, I had ridden a camel in India's Rajasthan desert. A week before that, I was with a nomadic family in the middle of Mongolia. Only traveling could provide such unique experiences and adventure.

***

AFTER CHITWAN, I TOOK A BREATHTAKING TWO-HOUR BUS RIDE THROUGH THE MOUNTAINS AND VALLEYS OF NEPAL TO POKHARA. When I arrived in Pokhara, it was so beautiful that I fell in love with it instantly. There was a city somewhere between the lakes, mountains, and heaven. That city was Pokhara. The local hotels, shops, and eateries catered to tourists and mountaineers. I loved how Pokhara maintained its true nature and did not feel touristic.

A day after arriving in Pokhara, a guide picked me up from the hotel. He was a short, older gentleman. He introduced himself as a Sherpa. I thought that was his name, so I referred to him as Mr. Sherpa for the entirety of my trip. Actually, Sherpa is an ethnic group of people who live in the mountains in Nepal. I didn't realize this until after my trip. My guide, Mr. Sherpa, explained that we would leave town and spend the day hiking. The hike would lead to a peak that would reveal an incredible view of Annapurna, the deadliest mountain in the world.

We arrived at the start of the trail, and there was only one problem. The gloomy clouds had selfishly taken over the skies, and nothing was visible beyond those sad-looking bastards. Mr.

Sherpa said that we would continue, hoping the weather would clear. However, it had only grown worse as a light rain began to fall.

While we hiked, Mr. Sherpa explained that he used to be a mountaineer. After spending his youth hiking Mt. Everest, he gave it up. He now only accepted less strenuous treks like the one we were doing. I thought, *Funny, this is pretty damn strenuous to me.* After a while, we were above some clouds. Still, there were layers of clouds above us. Also, no matter how much we ascended, I saw small homes that belonged to the isolated communities of people who lived there.

Mr. Sherpa was a quiet guide. He wasn't a small talker, which I didn't mind. I'm not much of a talker myself, which is why I encourage others to do the talking. However, when Mr. Sherpa did speak, his stories were fascinating and had profound meaning. Listening to Mr. Sherpa was like listening to a Vietnam veteran tell war stories.

"I've been doing this a long time. I can't even tell you how many times I've guided mountaineers to the top of Mt. Everest. Although Mt. Everest is the highest mountain in the world, it's not the most dangerous. There are far more challenging mountains, and I've climbed several of them. Sadly, I've also lost some coworkers and good friends along the way."

I could see Mr. Sherpa's eyes water as if he was going to cry. He continued.

"Climbing mountains is not the most dangerous thing that I've done.

When I was a lot younger, a small group of Russians visited my company's office, searching for a guide to assist them in climbing through nine glaciers. This was unheard of. Glaciers refer to the ice that forms over and runs down the sides of mountains. The ice is slippery and can collapse at any moment. If a person falls into a crevasse, there's no rescuing them. No one in my company wanted to do it.

The Russians made a lucrative proposal to my company—the kind of money that's life-changing. To accept the offer would be like accepting death. On the other hand, successfully making it through the glaciers would be financially rewarding and bring notoriety to my company. My boss tried his best to recruit someone for the assignment, but no one wanted it. He begged me to do it; however, I didn't want it either. I was young with a wife, and we had just had a baby. That was a reason to both do it and not do it. In the end, I decided to do it.

Those Russians were crazy. It seemed like they carried more vodka than climbing gear. They drank vodka as if it was water. They'd go '*Gulp, gulp, gulp*' and pass the bottle. They'd drink and try to hand me the bottle, 'Sherpa, have some vodka.' We were on the cusp of death in those glaciers, and they were drinking. I couldn't do it. We had our meals in the glaciers and slept in the glaciers. It took about a week to climb through each glacier, and we did nine. There were moments when I thought I was going to die. But, when we made it out of the last glacier, it was one of the most rewarding experiences.

I didn't find out until later that they were filming a documentary. After they completed the film, the Russians sent me a copy. I was in it. I couldn't believe it. As I watched it, I just cried."

I could see Mr. Sherpa's eyes tearing up again. The sky must have felt Mr. Sherpa's emotions. Like tears, the rain began to come down.

"There's a Sherpa hotel nearby where we can take shelter," Mr. Sherpa said.

Again, not knowing that Sherpa referred to an ethnic group, I thought he implied that his relatives owned a hotel. Nonetheless, it was a family-owned hotel with four or five rooms. The family occupied several of the rooms. Mr. Sherpa led me to a decently sized dining area. It resembled a conference room more than a place for eating. There were long tables but also a lot of unoccupied space. There were large glass windows that covered most of the wall and provided a nice view of the outside. Mr. Sherpa presented me with a lunch menu with only four options. I chose Nepalese curry chicken served with white rice. Once the meal arrived, he left the room, giving me privacy.

I didn't anticipate I'd be staying in a hotel in the mountains; therefore, I didn't pack any clothes. I didn't bring a phone charger. *Why would I need a phone charger on a hike*, I thought before leaving the city. Once I realized that I probably would be spending the night at the hotel, I limited my cell phone usage to only taking photos. Little did I know that there would be a small family-owned hotel with Wi-Fi in the mountains of Nepal. Unfortunately, I couldn't benefit from it because I had to preserve the battery.

Thankfully, there was a bar in the dining room. Instead of drinks, dust-covered books disorderly occupied the shelves. Talk about a thirst for knowledge. After lunch, I grabbed a novel and began reading. It must have felt like an hour had gone by. When I checked the time, only fifteen minutes had passed. What was this place? Time had slowed down[65].

Later in the evening, Mr. Sherpa took me to a luxury hotel that was still in its construction phase. However, receptionists were working at the front desk. Mr. Sherpa talked them into giving us a tour of the property. It was a magnificent property funded by a Japanese investment firm. The rooms were large and, even with

---

65   Gravity affects time; therefore, time moves imperceptibly slower at the top of a mountain. Time had actually sped up.

the clouds, the views were amazing. We spent a short amount of the evening at the property.

The weather never cleared up. So, I didn't get to see the sun kiss Annapurna's majestic peak.

By the time we returned to the small Sherpa hotel, it was almost dark. Mr. Sherpa led me to a room to get clean before dinner. Since I didn't pack any clothes, I showered and put on the same clothes that I had taken off before showering. Afterward, I returned to the dining area. The windows that provided lovely views of the outside in the day were now black walls reflecting the night.

After dinner, I went to the roof. The weather was chilly but tolerable. The darkness and the absence of sound bothered me the most. I stood outside for a few minutes and couldn't tolerate being out there any longer. The darkness frightened me. I felt that if I had stayed there any longer, I would begin to see things that I didn't want to see. I once read about the anechoic chamber[66] in Minnesota and how it cancels out all sound. If a person stays in the chamber long enough, their senses can become distorted, causing them to hallucinate.

This is what I thought as I stood outside. It was terrifying to be in the abyss of darkness and silence. I felt so lonely and vulnerable. A melancholic wave brushed me, and I lost control of my emotions and my eyes began to tear up. There was only darkness, emptiness, and quietness. My mind could not interpret it. Finally, I couldn't take it any longer, so I returned inside.

Once inside, I realized how shaken up I had been from the events leading up to the experience. I could feel my hands trembling. I recalled climbing the mountain and seeing the clouds below me and above me. I remembered how the day slowed down

66   Test subjects have reported hallucinating within fifteen minutes in a sensory deprivation chamber. Interestingly, schizophrenic subjects experienced fewer hallucinations than neurotypical subjects.

as if I was stuck in time. There was no communication with the outside world. A family was living in the hotel, and I was just a brief disruption in their everyday life. On the other hand, this wasn't my usual way of life.

Life interrupted my plans. I was supposed to hike the mountain and return to my hotel in the town. I wasn't supposed to be here. I regained control of my senses. I closed my eyes and said my famous prayer, "God, give me strength." I opened my eyes, rose, and went back outside into the darkness. I stayed there until I didn't feel afraid.

***

THE FOLLOWING DAY, MR. SHERPA AND I LEFT THE HOTEL EARLY TO CATCH THE SUNRISE OVER ANNAPURNA'S PEAK. It was still too cloudy to see anything. We descended the mountain and headed back into town. Mr. Sherpa drove me to the aerial sports center, nothing more than a small-scale airport for small aircraft, including ultra-lights. The opportunity to fly in an ultra-light led me to Nepal.

After going through security, a receptionist escorted me to the back of the airport. There was an aluminum structure that housed different types of crafts. There, I witnessed how small the ultra-light crafts were and how vulnerable I'd be to the elements. I was frightened and no longer wanted to fly.

The staff asked, "What ultra-light do you want to fly in?"

I noticed that some were bigger than others. Several kinds had doors and windows that would provide protection from the elements. Those looked like mini jets. Although I almost selected the less terrifying ultra-light, I stuck with the original plan, which was to fly thirty minutes in a craft resembling a motorcycle's sidecar.

I would not have been able to live with myself for traveling so far, only to become a coward.

Next, the staff brought me protective gear, including a thick jacket, gloves, and a helmet. After suiting up, I headed outside to the runway.

The pilot allowed me to enter and sit in the back seat of the craft. Next, he helped strap me in.

Then he said, "If at any point you get nervous and need me to lower altitude, just tap me." I nodded my head in acceptance of his offer.

He sat in the seat in front of me and buckled up. There was as much space between us as there would be between two people riding together on a motorcycle. He started the ultra-light craft. The blade was on the back of the vessel and began to spin. It was so close that all I had to do was reach back if my goal was to lose a hand.

It took seconds for the craft to ascend to altitudes that were far beyond my comfort zone. I probably would have been more comfortable if E.T. was the third passenger. About a minute into it, I tapped the pilot on the shoulder. I didn't even care about not getting my money's worth. I just wanted down. Fortunately, there was some redemption. Maybe the pilot didn't think I was serious or he didn't feel my taps because he kept going higher. I had the chance to rethink my decision. Rethinking it did not make things better.

In only a few minutes, I learned three things. Turbulence is wind, and the wind blows very hard at high altitudes. Two, the wind can become so loud that it's deafening. Three, the sky is frigid. Well, I guess I already knew those things. Nonetheless, it was more obvious as the pilot expertly guided the craft through the raging air currents. I'm sure skydivers, hang-gliders, and those alike know the feeling. As someone who becomes nervous during turbulence when flying in a commercial airplane, being in a tiny plane with no doors or windows was petrifying.

Apart from the terror, the plane ride was an unbelievably adrenaline-filled adventure. The stunning landscapes helped to distract me from the fear. The ultra-light craft flew like an eagle as we got a bird's-eye view of the city as well as sites such as the Peace Pagoda and Phewa Lake. Although the skies were cloudy, I could still catch glimpses of the majestic Himalayan Mountain ranges. Below, I saw valleys populated with homes and tributaries that flowed into lakes.

After we landed, my legs and hands shook uncontrollably. At that point, fear no longer mattered. I had conquered it and felt accomplished.

CHAPTER 19

IF I WAS FREE

I just go with the flow, so any style can be in my music—
that makes it exciting. —*Yoko Ono*

Originally, I booked the flight to Myanmar with the intention of flying in a hot air balloon over the iconic red-brick and honey-colored pagodas and temples located in Bagan. After contacting agencies to inquire about prices, I quickly learned the hot air balloon flights were not being offered during the days I'd be in Myanmar. I had missed the season by only a few weeks. Since I had already purchased the flight to the country formerly known as Burma, I would have to wing the trip.

I've enjoyed previous trips where I didn't plan as much. Personally, the planning phase is one of the most exciting parts of the trip; however, the planner sees everything beforehand and has a general idea about what will happen. Although the trip ends up being enjoyable, it can feel like you're just going through the motions. Things tend to be more interesting when the traveler shows up at a place and doesn't know what to expect. That's what I loved; however, I'll admit that it can be more time-consuming and costly to travel without much preparation. That's where experience and a little luck come into play.

The lodging where I stayed was right across from Mandalay Palace[67], located in the city of the same name. From the rooftop, I had an incredible view of the royal palace and fortress. A water-filled moat surrounded the palace. Outside of the moat were parks and a trail, where the locals walked and exercised. I observed the beautiful sunset as it set above the palace and lovely people.

The rooftop contained a bar area with an assortment of tables with chairs where guests could sit. There, I relaxed as I watched guests come and go. Most guests came in pairs, so I assumed they were friends or couples traveling together. Starting a conversation with a small group presented a more significant challenge because I didn't want to interrupt the intimate moments between others.

Finally, a presence filled the chair at the table next to mine. The small woman wore her golden-brown hair in a bun. She sipped her drink with authority as she concentrated on her smartphone. I pretended not to look at her as the screen's light reflected on her face. *Did she feel me watching her?* If so, she didn't show the slightest care in the world. Once she appeared somewhat distracted from the phone, I asked, "How many days have you been here?" She turned her attention to me and answered. For a while, she divided her attention between me and her phone as we conversed across tables. Minutes later, she invited me to her table.

"Excuse me, but I'm working on my plans for tomorrow. I'll be a few more minutes. Do you have a phone?" she asked.

"Yes," I replied. Then the lady offered me the name of her personal pocket Wi-Fi network and gave me her password. I thanked her before mentioning that I was already connected to a network. My first impression of her was how kind and trusting

---

67   The palace, built in the 1850s, was the residence of the final two kings of Burma. Great Britain colonized the country in 1885 and ended the monarchy.

she was. Before that moment, we didn't even know one another's names. Soon I'd learn that her name was Kim.

Kim was a Korean American. Born to South Korean parents, a White American family adopted her when she was a child. Although from different backgrounds, Kim grew to love her parents and siblings very much. As she got older, Kim yearned to know her Korean heritage. Eventually, this led her to travel to South Korea, where she made a living as an English teacher for seven years. When I met her, Kim only had a few years left on her teacher's contract; therefore, she wanted to maximize her time in Asia. That desire led her to vacation in Myanmar.

Around 7 PM, Kim mentioned that she was hungry. We walked a few blocks from the hotel, searching for restaurants until we found one called Mary-Min that catered to her dietary needs. Kim was a diehard vegetarian. Our table was on the balcony of the second floor, allowing us a view of the narrow street decorated with tangled power lines. She ordered a vegetable soup, salad, and strawberry lassi. Earlier, I'd eaten an overly portioned lunch that still occupied my stomach, so I settled for papaya lassi.

Kim and I had a few things in common. For one, we were both '80's babies. We both grew up on the east coast, Virginia for me and New Jersey for her. Like me, she was an ardent R&B music listener and acknowledged the '90s as the golden age of R&B. Everyone knew of TLC, Mariah Carey, and Montell Jordan. It took a particular fan to appreciate the likes of Tamia, 112, and Jodeci. Kim was no ordinary fan.

"You know a lot of those artists were really young when they began their careers," she said.

"Yeah, I know. Monica was fourteen years old when she recorded "Why I Love You So Much." She's only like six years older than me. It's crazy to think that the song would've been dedicated to me had I been born in her city," I replied.

"You think fourteen-year-old Monica would've dated a third grader?" Kim inquired.

"Probably not, but she had some hits! And Babyface ... Babyface made the '90s! He wrote everybody's favorite '90's song," I said.

Kim laughed.

"It doesn't matter if the song was sung by Toni Braxton, Boyz II Men, Whitney Houston, Tevin Campbell, or Madonna, Babyface wrote it!" I continued. Kim looked at me like she wanted me to shut up, but she knew it was true.

We were so into the conversation that we hardly noticed when our drinks arrived. Kim grabbed the papaya lassi and drank from the straw. "Umm, this is good!"

"I think you grabbed my drink. I'm pretty sure I ordered the papaya lassi." I said.

"Dude, I'm so sorry!" she responded and laughed. Then she gave me my drink. "You can sip some of mine if you want."

I loved her sense of humor. She could joke around with a straight face. I do the same thing, and sometimes it confuses people because they can't tell if I'm joking or being serious. So, I easily connected with Kim's comedic genius and laughed as we conversed.

At that moment in my life, Kim was just the person I needed. She was down-to-earth. Her personality was cooler than a twelve-pack of Modelo on Super Bowl Sunday. Most importantly, she was a planner. She shared her plans for the next day and invited me to come along if I was free. I could not help but smirk at the thought of *If I was free*. As I mentioned in the very beginning, I was improvising the entire trip, and this was still my first day in Myanmar.

After a healthy dinner filled with fun conversation, Kim and I walked back to the hostel. When we returned, we said our goodnights. While she went off to shower before bed, I went up to the rooftop. I needed a moment to reflect and thank the travel gods for introducing me to someone as pleasant as Kim. The gods weren't done with me yet.

On the roof, I met a young guy from the Philippines named Orly. Orly was also on vacation with a flexible schedule. We spoke briefly. I told him about Kim and invited him to join us on the following day. Orly accepted the invitation.

***

THE NEXT MORNING, EVERYONE ASSEMBLED EARLY IN THE LOBBY—DRESSED TO IMPRESS. Kim wore a comfortable gray shirt and burgundy harem pants. It looked like she had taken her clothes straight from Aladdin's wardrobe. Also, Kim sported these aviator sunglasses that made her look like a total badass. Anytime I think of her, I picture her wearing those iconic shades. Orly was like the Filipino Fonzworth Bentley. The guy dressed in a way that I could only dream of. Impressively, he wore cargo shorts, a stylish buttoned shirt, and sandals. I've always sucked at fashion. A long time ago, I adopted the "Steve Jobs" swag. After all my years of traveling the world, you'd think I was in the same location from the photos because I wore the same clothes all the time.

Kim's plan involved traveling to Mingun to visit some popular tourist attractions. We took a taxi to Mingun Jetty, an archaic boat harbor in Mandalay. The harbor made me feel more like Jack Sparrow from *Pirates of the Caribbean* than a tourist. After purchasing round-trip tickets, we walked across a thin, unstable wooden brow to board a vessel that resembled a pirate ship. Then we sailed for forty-five minutes along the Irrawaddy River until we arrived in Mingun.

It was common for tourists to hire guides to show them around Mingun; however, we had Kim. She seemed to have done her research and had a clear idea of what was there. First, we visited Mingun Pahtodgawgy, a large, incomplete stupa. Although unfinished, it's quite impressive because it looks like a red-brownish temple carved out of a gigantic stone. We climbed the steps to the top, where we had a spectacular view of the ancient city. Next, we stopped by Sat Taw Yar Pagoda, a white Buddhist temple with a golden top. Mythological dragons sit at the bank of the Irrawaddy River, protecting the temples. Lastly, we visited Hsinbyume Pagoda, a large white pagoda with an unrivaled architectural style. The primary reason Kim chose to visit Myanmar was to see this great pagoda first-hand. The awe-inspiring design filled her with deep contentment as she gazed in wonderment at the pagoda's wave-like structure.

After all the temples and pagodas, we shopped at the local markets for souvenirs. Dozens of stalls sold traditional garments, including conical hats and colorful bags. Some vendors sold fruits and food products. Others sold decorative products and embellishments for the home.

Most travelers have a special collection of souvenirs that they acquire when abroad. For me, it's bills of the local currency. It's easy to carry and doesn't take up a lot of space. Also, I purchase shot glasses for family members. For Kim, it's elephant-related gifts such as small statues or paintings of the large animal that's admired throughout Asian culture. That's what she searched for at the markets.

Around noon, Orly, Kim, and I left Mingun for Mandalay. After the boat ride, we took a taxi to the Kuthodaw Pagoda, a golden Buddhist stupa known as the site of the world's largest book. When told that Kuthodaw was home to the world's largest book, I imagined an enormous book sitting on top of a sturdy table; however, hundreds of five-foot marble tablets surrounded the outside of the golden stupa. Each stone tablet served as a page in the book[68]. Afterward, we walked to the Sanda Muni Pagoda, another white and golden stupa. We continued to travel by foot as we spent the afternoon visiting pagoda after pagoda. We passed by dozens of monks who smiled politely as we walked through quiet streets that led to sacred sites.

Finally, the time arrived when Kim had to separate from Orly and me. It saddened us to see our guide and friend leave. She planned to leave Mandalay for Bagan that night. Hence, she needed to get back to the guesthouse and pack. In our final moment together, I gave Kim a warm hug of appreciation and wished her luck. Orly did the same. Now, it was just the two of us. We continued visiting the temples recommended by our beloved Kim. Our final stop for the day was a Burmese restaurant called Mingalabar. Even though the restaurant was pricey, the portions were generous, and the restaurant offered a relaxing atmosphere. Orly and I ordered more than we could eat. We indulged in a variety of curries, salads, and vegetables.

By the time Orly and I returned to the hostel, Kim was gone. Before the night ended, the two of us agreed to continue sightseeing the following day.

Although Orly was only a few years younger than me, he looked like he could have been born a decade before me. Orly was from Cebu, where he still lived and worked as a nurse. When he was younger, his dream was to travel and know the world outside

---

68   There are 730 tablets for 1,460 pages. Each tablet is roughly 3.5' × 5', about the size of a standard American flag.

of his archipelagic nation. Orly knew that travel required money; therefore, he studied nursing and achieved his professional goal. He worked fruitfully and saved until he could finally afford to travel. When he and I met, he was treating himself to a birthday gift—a trip to Myanmar. After a few weeks in Myanmar, he'd make his way to Australia.

First, we owed each other another day of sightseeing. Since Mandalay's Royal Palace stood across the street from the hostel, we started there. Then we visited more Buddhist sites, including the Mahamuni Buddha Temple and Eindawya Pagoda. Our last stop was Mandalay Hill, an attractive destination for international travelers and Buddhist pilgrims who visit the temples and monasteries. Since Mandalay Hill is a sacred site, visitors must remove their shoes before doing the forty-five-minute climb. After taking off my sandals, the ground felt like a hot skillet, warmed by the sun. The stunning golden Sutaungpyei Pagoda sits at the top of Mandalay Hill. It's only rivaled by the breathtaking sunset over the city.

Orly's scheduled had him leaving the next day. Like Kim, he would make his journey to Bagan. I couldn't help but wonder, *If the season had been open for hot air balloon rides, would I have been able to meet Kim or Orly in Bagan? Maybe, I'd be traveling to Bagan with them.*

With Orly gone, I was alone and had to come up with a plan for my last few days in Mandalay.

***

MY HOSTEL WAS NOT TOO FAR FROM THE TAXI STAND. The first time I walked by it, I met a driver. He told me that he offered reasonable prices if I ever needed a taxi. Each time I passed by the stand, the taxi driver greeted me. Unlike annoying cabmen or aggressive businessmen in other countries, he never tried to sell me a ride other than our first encounter. For this reason, I felt comfortable going to him after Orly left.

I had passed by him so often that he didn't realize I was seeking his services. Really, I think he just wanted to practice speaking English with me. He asked what I thought of Myanmar. I shared that I was enjoying his wonderful country. I asked him, "How's business going?" He told me business was slow. The European and Chinese travelers, whose business he had always enjoyed, were not there this year. He was surprised to see an American.

"Today, I need transportation," I said.

"Where do you want to go?" he responded.

"I was hoping you could tell me," I said.

He reached into his vehicle, grabbed a stack of laminated papers, and handed them to me. "These are the tours that I offer." As I looked at the tours, I noticed that I had already visited many of the places shown. He made a fair offer (around $20) to allow me to rent his taxi services for the entire day. Again, I looked through the sheets with tour packages. I showed the driver all of the places that I'd been to already. He came up with a plan to drive me from one place to another.

Like the previous days, I visited more Buddhist pagodas and temples. One particular temple was the teak Shwenandaw Monastery, famous for its traditional Burmese architecture and carvings of Buddhist myths. After I explored the inside of the monastery, I walked around the surrounding areas.

There were plenty of vendors. Being a collector of postcards, I came across a table with beautiful pop-up cards. As I looked at the cards, the vendor seemed so happy that she had a customer. She was a young lady with black hair and deep brown eyes. After looking, I decided not to buy anything. That's when the vendor made this playfully sad face and put up her index finger, indicating that I please buy one card. Not only was it the cutest thing I'd ever seen, but it was also a good selling tactic. After purchasing a few postcards, her body language expressed a tremendous amount of joy.

The driver waited precisely where he dropped me off. That's how it was throughout the day. He'd take me to a site and encouraged me to take as long as I wanted. When I finished seeing one place, he'd take me to the next one.

The final stop of the day was the U Bein Bridge. Located in Amarapura, it stretches across Taungthaman Lake. The almost two-hundred-year-old bridge is famous for being the longest teakwood bridge in the world, which makes it a popular tourist site. Due to the influx of visitors, there are all kinds of restaurants along the lake. The restaurants were quite busy as people competed to dine at the ones that provided the best view of the water and U Bein Bridge.

Since it was a challenge finding an uncrowded restaurant, I strolled the surrounding area. I checked out the markets. Then I walked across the narrow bridge, populated with dozens of people. Upon returning, I was lucky enough to find a nice seat at a seafood restaurant. There I enjoyed fried fish, salad, and a Coca-Cola while watching the sunset.

My trip to Myanmar could not have gone any better. For one, I got to meet Kim and Orly. Orly and I kept in contact for as long as we were in Myanmar. After Myanmar, he continued his travels by going to Australia while I headed to Laos. We sent photos of our experiences to one another. Kim and I kept in contact for much longer. Years later, she would leave South Korea and return to the United States, but not before taking off three months and traveling solo around the Middle East, North Africa, and Europe. She was brave, bold and something incredible.

One thing that made Myanmar one of my favorite countries was how friendly the Burmese people were. When I was there, I did not feel like a foreigner. The people were welcoming and genuinely warm. I remember walking around Amarapura and hearing a guy yell, "Hey, my Brother!" as he drove by on his motorcycle. When I noticed him, the Burmese fellow was smiling and waving at me. I remember a group of young female monks smiling at me, Kim, and Orly as we walked the streets leading to the temples. I recalled a group of high school students politely asking to take photos with Orly and me when we visited the Royal Palace. They appeared star-struck when we agreed to the pictures. I remember eating at restaurants by myself and the staff coming over to talk with me. I left with a beautiful impression of the country. This is why it saddened me to learn about the deadly coup that occurred at the beginning of 2021[69].

---

69   On February 1, 2021, Myanmar's military overthrew the democratically elected majority and installed a government run by military officers.

CHAPTER 20
LAST STOP

~~~~~~

Be easy. Take your time. You are coming home. To yourself.
—*Nayyirah Waheed*

When I take time off work to travel internationally, I leave the day my vacation begins, and I'm at work the day after I return. This hardly allows any recuperation time, which can be helpful, especially when jumping across different time zones. Therefore, Laos provided the perfect opportunity to rest and reflect on my previous travels and what lay ahead. I didn't necessarily expect it to be this way. Like Myanmar, I didn't plan anything past the flight and hotel. Unlike Myanmar, I didn't meet any phenomenal travelers to explore with.

My five-country trip across Asia ended in Luang Prabang. Before arriving, I didn't know much about the city. By *tuk-tuk*[70], it took approximately ten minutes to travel from Luang Prabang International Airport to my hotel, which was in the heart of the old town. The hotel was in a convenient location, parallel to the main road.

Being in Luang Prabang gave the impression of being on a tropical island. Palm trees covered an extensive portion of the

---

70   Also known as an "auto rickshaw," this is a three-wheeled motorized taxi.

hot and humid city. Across the street from my hotel flowed the transboundary Mekong River. The river's muddy brown waters brilliantly complemented its naturally green surroundings as it flowed through a jungle town with a hint of French Colonial influence. It's beautiful, and there's no wonder why practically the entire city is a World Heritage Site.

A vast portion of the city can be explored by foot. The road behind my hotel was the welcoming Sisavangvong Road, the main street of Luang Prabang. It's home to a wide range of restaurants, cafes, shops, museums, and Buddhist temples. I made it a priority to not only enjoy the infamous cappuccinos but also visit sites, including the Royal Palace, Wat Xiengthong, Haw Pha Bang, Wat May Souvannapoumaram, and so many other places that I have no idea how to pronounce.

Also, there's beauty in peace. This was evident on the days I woke up early enough to observe the monks performing their morning rituals. They wore saffron robes and carried baskets. Each morning, the monks walked barefoot on the serene streets and collected alms from Buddhist followers. Several times, I saw them while I performed my own morning ritual.

In the morning, I'd visit a deli cafe close to my hotel. Obviously, I'd start with an iced coffee with milk. Additionally, they had the best damn croissants in the world. My favorite was their croissant sandwich which had a plain omelet, a thick slice of mozzarella cheese, and tomato slices; however, the game-changer was a generous layer of pesto spread. This revolutionized my idea of breakfast sandwiches. Luang Prabang introduced a brother to pesto and had me eating it on a breakfast croissant sandwich of all things. I absolutely loved it.

Luang Prabang offered a range of outdoor activities for nature lovers.

The most famous climb in the city's center is Phousi Hill. Although it wasn't a strenuous hike, the heat made it seem like a challenging workout. By the time I made it to the top, sweat leaked from my pores like water through a broken faucet. The view of the city from the hilltop was unreal. There existed a city somewhere buried underneath the omnipresent palm trees. The peanut butter-colored Mekong and Nam Khan Rivers brought life to Luang Prabang. Beyond the city were massive rolling hills that made it difficult for the city's beauty to escape.

Twenty miles south of Luang Prabang, there's a spectacular area home to the Kuang Si Falls. There, I went on what began as a splendid adventure, climbing steps and crossing wooden footbridges as I ascended past countless shallow pools of turquoise waters fed by glorious waterfalls. If I remember correctly, it was the *tuk-tuk* driver who told me about a secret cave somewhere near the falls. "Secret cave" sounds cool, *right*? However, it was nowhere near the falls because I walked an additional forty minutes through a deserted forest to get there.

When I arrived at the end of the creepy forest, an old Laotian woman was sitting at a table. There was nothing or no one else around. Before I could analyze the situation, the *sorceress* had already read my mind and knew what I wanted. She pointed in the direction of a flight of steps. Then, she pointed to the box on the table. It had flashlights inside it. The dollar sign written on the box insinuated that the flashlights weren't complimentary, so I rented one for a dollar.

After climbing the steps, I saw the cave's entrance. The five-foot black hole in a rock captured the quintessence of horror. The black scorpion on the ground didn't help the case. If I was Dr. Doolittle and could understand animal talk, the scorpion was probably saying, "Bruh, I wouldn't go in there if I were you."

Even after shining the flashlight toward the darkness, I couldn't see anything except three feet of the muddy floor. I had never seen a comedy movie or family drama that took place in a cave. I had seen some horror movies, though, and I didn't want to be the main character in that true story.

I wasn't upset at myself for paying a dollar to rent the cheap flashlight. I wasn't even upset with myself for chickening out. However, I had walked so far to get to the cave, and now I had to go back under the broiling sun.

Luang Prabang seemed to attract a more mature and sophisticated travel crowd. *Was I a part of that crowd?* Probably not, as I secretly sniffed my sweaty armpits when no one was looking. I hid from the sun in coffee shops, on shade-protected benches along the Mekong River, and surprisingly in my hotel room. Apart from cooling off, I frequented my hotel room to change clothes. Since I only packed half a small carry-on suitcase for a month-long trip, I often hand-washed clothes in the shower. Instead of Tide or Gain detergents, I used the small bottles of hotel shampoo if I was lucky. If I wasn't so fortunate, I used the bar soap. Clothes like jeans and cotton shirts would have been a laundry nightmare; therefore, I ensured that I packed quick-dry items.

Perhaps, my favorite part of the trip was the visits to the night market. It could have absolutely been because the sun was busy shining in some other part of the world, making the night a good time to go out. Over one hundred tents sprung up on the narrow Sisavangvong Road. Vendors placed blankets on the ground and their products on top. They sold everything imaginable: clothes, shoes, jewelry, art, decorations, and souvenirs. The vendors didn't hassle customers, so it felt enjoyable to walk around.

In Luang Prabang's center, restaurants were pricey; therefore, the market provided the opportunity to buy inexpensive street food. There were all kinds of food carts on the main road and narrow side streets. It's appalling how, before traveling, I associated cheap food with lower quality or not tasty. Abroad, the cheap street food has been some of the best, and Laos was no different. The atmosphere was pleasant as tourists and locals bargained with vendors for deals on products.

Of all the countries and cities, I visited on my trip, Luang Prabang would have been the best place to bring Kaori. I'll admit that not many things compare to the timeless Indo-Islamic architecture that India acquired over centuries. However, Luang Prabang had a romantic vibe that made me want to play some Marvin Gaye and take my lady on a cruise on the Mekong River before sunset. It was a fantastic way to end an enthralling journey.

CHAPTER 21

FROM PARAGUAY TO JAPAN

A person is a person through other persons; you can't be
human in isolation; you are human only in relationships.
—*Desmond Tutu*

***

It was the spring of 2019. I was going on five years in the Navy, three of which I passed in Yokosuka, Japan. In the fall of 2018, I went on my trip across Asia. In the first few months of 2019, I went to San Diego to train and that's when I ran into Andrei. Now, I was back in Japan, where I would be stationed for two more years. Between transferring ships, I was eligible for a few weeks of vacation. During this leave period, I would have special guests coming to visit: my Paraguayan sisters Lilian and Adriana.

***

SOMETIME IN LATE 2018, KAORI AND I WERE AT HOME WATCHING TELEVISION. We watched a program about a Japanese family who migrated to Paraguay to escape the harsh conditions brought by World War II. The immigrant family planted seeds for posterity in the landlocked South American country. The show followed the life of their modern-day Japanese

Paraguayan family that lived in a district called Yguazú, known for its Japanese population. I knew Yguazú very well.

In late August 2010, I had arrived in Juan E. O'Leary, where I served for two years. A day after arriving, my host family had invited me to an annual Japanese festival in Yguazú. That had been nine years ago. As I watched, I took photos of the television screen and sent the images to my friends back in Paraguay. The nostalgia overwhelmed me. I had a strong urge to relive those memories or at least feel their comfort. So, I contacted the only person whose desire to travel was as strong as mine and someone I loved dearly—my Paraguayan sister Lili.

I sent her an email, "Would you and Adri travel to Japan if you had the opportunity?" She replied, "Of course." I responded, "If you're serious, consider the tickets purchased."

Lili was sixteen years old when her parents rented me a room and accepted me into their home. By the time I left Paraguay in 2012, Lili was preparing for her freshman year of college. Her plans were to study tourism and hospitality and travel the world.

Despite both of us beginning in different places in the world, we both developed a love for travel. Since elementary school, Lili enjoyed the art of folklore dancing. By the time she reached high school, she was a prominent member of O'Leary Jeroky, the most well-known dance group in her city. What began as a community dance group recognized by the local municipality became an international group and a member of the International Council of Organization of Folklore Festival and Folk Arts (CIOFF).

Dance not only allowed O'Leary Jeroky's members to perform at events in neighboring communities but also paved the way for international opportunities. The group traveled abroad and danced in various cities in Argentina, Brazil, Mexico, Venezuela, and countries across Europe. Moreover, they invited dance groups from Brazil, Colombia, Togo, and Hungary to dance in their town. Of course, they started doing all the cool stuff after I was long gone.

After graduating college, Lili's passion for travel led her to a job with a tourism agency. Her job entailed selling tour packages to travel lovers who enjoyed seeing the world as much as she did. Additionally, she traveled and served as a tour guide on numerous international trips. Lili went on to eventually start her own travel business, *Embarque Seguro Turismo & Negocios.*

***

YOKOSUKA NAVAL BASE IS A DECENTLY SIZED BASE WITH THOUSANDS OF SAILORS. Being assigned orders to a foreign country may seem like a dream come true. Just because a sailor ended up stationed in Japan didn't necessarily mean they wanted to be there. A surprising number of sailors didn't even go to Tokyo, although it was easily accessible. If you were my friend, you had to put down the Nintendo Switch and go somewhere with me. My first experience as a guide in Japan was escorting my shipmates around the local areas.

Then, my family visited me for a week. There was no sitting around the house. I made sure that they got a taste of Japan. In fact, taste was the first sense that I focused on when playing the guide role. Everybody had to eat.

For travelers (particularly Paraguayans) without a lot of experience with Asian cuisine, Japanese food can be quite the experience and take time to appreciate. When I was in Paraguay, there were two ways that Paraguayans served a steak: well-done and overcooked. With that said, I couldn't really expect Lili and Adri to eat raw fish after taking them to a sushi restaurant. Even the first time I ate sushi, I didn't like it and was convinced that I'd get a tapeworm.

On their first night in Japan, Lili took a tiny nibble of the raw salmon before deciding it wasn't for her; however, looking at it was enough for Adri.

Nonetheless, they loved ramen. If you grew up like me, there was no such thing as ramen; it was either "Raymond noodles" or "oodles and noodles." Similarly, Lili and Adri didn't realize ramen was a Japanese soup with noodles. Back home, it came in a plastic wrapper or Styrofoam cup. In Japan, chefs simmered seasoned meat and pork bone in a larger pot overnight to generate the perfect soup broth. When we went into my favorite ramen shop in Zushi, the chef mixed the hot broth with soy sauce, added thick, freshly cooked noodles, and topped it with spinach, pork slices, chives, and a boiled egg. For the less experienced, using chopsticks was often a problem; however, most restaurants had forks. For $7 (American), ramen was the king of Japanese cuisine.

Still, sushi reigned as god.

***

KAMAKURA WAS ONE OF MY FAVORITE PLACES IN JAPAN. The city includes a little of everything that Japan has to offer: great restaurants, shopping, ancient shrines and temples, beaches, and scenic hiking trails. Kamakura was only two short train stops from my residence, so I frequented the historic city[71]. Also, it was a spectacular place to take visitors to introduce them to Japanese culture. Lili, Adri, and I first visited a shop that allowed people to rent kimonos. The girls dressed in alluring kimonos, and the staff gave them makeovers that complemented the traditional attire. After that, they would spend the day walking around like this.

---

71 Sugimoto-dera is an ancient Buddhist temple in Kamakura built circa 700 CE.

Next, we headed to Komachi Dori Street, a famous street at the heart of Kamakura. The pedestrian street is approximately three hundred-fifty meters and home to a myriad of restaurants, street vendors, boutique shops, and cafes. Every day, around fifty thousand people (local and international) visit the narrow street. It ends a block away from Tsurugaoka Hachimangu Shrine, a red Shinto[72] shrine. Many people go there to pray, sightsee, or both. Beautiful gardens, that change with the seasons, surround the area. While enjoying the sights of Japanese architecture and culture, the Paraguayans didn't miss the opportunity to take countless photos.

Later, we took the Enoshima Train Line to Hase. Hase is a city in Kamakura. It's known for its many shrines and temples. Its most famous attraction is the Great Buddha statue at Kōtoku-in Temple. The Great Buddha is one of the largest bronze statues in Japan.

✹✹✹

LIKE PLUNGING INTO ARCTIC FREEZING WATER, TOKYO COULD BE A SHOCK FOR COUNTRY GIRLS FROM LANDLOCKED PARAGUAY. The entire country of Paraguay has a population of around seven million people. As the largest city in the world, Tokyo is double that.

Therefore, we started small. Yokohama was the closest big city to where I lived. Being larger than Paraguay's capital, Asunción, Lili and Adri would get their first experience of a Japanese city encompassed by unique buildings, including the Yokohama Landmark Tower, InterContinental Grand Hotel, and Marine Tower.

First, we walked around Yokohama Chinatown, the largest Chinatown in Asia. From there, we made our way to the Red Brick Warehouse. Once a vital warehouse along Tokyo Bay, it's now filled

---

72   Japan's indigenous religion which centers around veneration of kami, spirits that live in all things. The religion emerged between 300 BCE and 300 CE, predating Buddhism in Japan.

with fancy restaurants and shops that were beyond my budget. Then we visited the Cup Noodles Museum, which tells the history of cup noodles. Also, it includes a display with hundreds of cup noodles and types of ramen from all over the world. We created our own variety of cup noodles and took them as souvenirs. Next, we went to Cosmo Clock 21, a famous amusement park home to a giant Ferris wheel with a clock that lights up at night. Finally, since it's impossible to take out young ladies and not shop, we visited Queen's Square Mall and World Porters.

***

THE PARAGUAYAN SISTERS VISITED JAPAN DURING THE KANAMARA MATSURI FESTIVAL, ALSO KNOWN AS THE PENIS FESTIVAL. It's an annual fertility festival. Previously I avoided it because, *Why would I go to a Penis Festival?* Nonetheless, I thought it would be a fun experience for the conservative Paraguayan girls.

Thousands of local tourists and foreigners had already filled the streets by the time we arrived. They lined up and formed an almost impenetrable crowd outside of the Kanayama Shrine in Kawasaki. Once the shrine's gate would open, participants in the parade would come out carrying giant penis statues. Those closest to the entrance would be the first to see the start of the parade and be the first ones to enter the gates. This meant that they'd have the best chances at buying penis memorabilia, such as penis-shaped lollipops, penis-shaped hats, glasses with penis-shaped noses attached, and chocolate-covered banana snacks shaped like penises. This was a fertility festival, so there would be pink vagina-shaped lollipops. That's what I wanted.

Again, we were at the very back. Thousands of people stood in front of us.

On that day, Lili and Adri wore traditional Paraguayan dresses laced with colorful spiderweb-liked designs called ñandutí. Likewise, they wore make-up and jewelry and decorated their hair with flowers. They may as well have been naked because they attracted a lot of attention. People in the crowd wanted to take photos with the girls, including this creepy-looking old Japanese man.

After taking a photo with the man, he grabbed Lili's hand and tried to pull her away. I said, "No, no, no!" Then he looked at me, pointed to the entrance, and made the hand gesture for, "Let's go!" Finally, I understood. He led us through an ocean of people until we were some of the first ones at the gate. Once the gate opened, most people focused on the gigantic penis statues that Japanese performers carried out. The old man took us to the stalls where Lili and Adri purchased penis-shaped lollipops. Unfortunately, the sweet vagina candies were already gone.

Afterward, the ladies and I walked a couple of blocks to the Kawasaki Daishi, a famous Buddhist temple built in the twelfth century. Since it was the day of the Kanamara Matsuri, dozens of food vendors were catering to the tourists. Adri ordered a fried cheese stick, and Lili ordered a hotdog that unintentionally resembled a penis. My taste being a little more experienced, I selected *takoyaki* which is octopus pieces fried inside a ball of batter. We relaxed there for several hours and then took a train to Kawasaki's shopping district.

***

THE HONCH IS A POPULAR AREA RIGHT ACROSS FROM YOKOSUKA NAVAL BASE. It's known for its shops, restaurants, and notorious bars. When sailors get in trouble in the Navy, they go to Captain's mast. Captain's mast is like court on a ship, but probably more severe and less entertaining than *Judge Judy*.

The captain gets the facts and decides whether the sailor's offense is punishable under the military justice code. Definitely less fun than *Judge Judy*. Almost ninety-five percent of the Yokosuka sailors who went to captain's mast, their stories began in the Honch. The number one culprit was the mischievous *chūhai*, made by mixing the Japanese liquor *shōchū* with juice or carbonated beverages. It was a dangerous drink because of the high alcohol content, and it went down as smooth as juice.

Lili and Adri couldn't leave Japan without visiting a *chūhai* stand in the Honch. My coworkers called me "One Cup" because one cup was all I could drink and still feel confident I'd make it to my house (and not captain's mast). Eventually, I worked my way to one and a half cups. Unfortunately, one and a half was a little too much for *las Paraguayas*. I carried them both home, one on each of my shoulders.

That night, while relaxing with Kaori, I heard shouts coming from the downstairs bathroom. When I arrived, the bathroom door was open. The two sisters were wrestling on the floor. Lili was trying to stick an unopened tampon into Adri's mouth. I had to break them up and take them to their room. The following day, Kaori saw that a few tampons were outside the box. She asked me if the girls were okay. I said they were okay and then asked, "Why?" She thought that one of them was experiencing their "time of the month." In reality, they had experienced the *chūhai*.

***

LILI AND ADRI SAW A MAJOR JAPANESE CITY IN YOKOHAMA, RODE CROWDED TRAINS, SAW ENORMOUS PENIS STATUES, AND SURVIVED THE *CHŪHAI*. I thought the girls were ready to visit Tokyo. Tokyo is a massive city, and it's impossible to see even the main attractions in one day; therefore, we visited popular sites over the course of several days. Tokyo was an hour-long train ride from where I resided; therefore, it wasn't much to get up and go.

The first stop was Meiji Jingu Shrine. At the entrance of Meiji Jingu stands a tall wooden *torii* gate. *Torii* gates are at the entrance of shrines and remind visitors that they're entering a sacred site. After passing underneath the *torii* gate, we walked along a wide gravel road passing astonishing gardens. It's quite the trek to the Meiji Jingu Shrine. Wealthy people usually have their weddings at the holy location. If lucky, visitors can capture the noteworthy events.

After Meiji Jingu, we crossed the street and headed to Harajuku. Harajuku is home to the famous Takeshita Street. It's one of the most popular areas in Tokyo for fashionable youth fascinated with pop culture. Also, it's on this street that you're guaranteed to see someone dressed up as an anime character or rocking some flamboyant hair color like megaphone-green. As a tourist, that's exactly the person you want to take a photo with. However, the narrow pedestrian street is so packed that you can't even make it through the crowd to take a picture with Super Saiyan 5 Goku. Therefore, I escorted Lili and Adri inside the clothing stores and souvenir shops to get a break from the crowds.

Next, we walked to Omotesandō Boulevard, one of Tokyo's most prominent luxury shopping districts. It's the perfect place to go if you want to feel broke. This is where they have Gucci, Louis Vuitton, Prada, and all the other brands that Kanye West raps about. As we passed by the stores, I observed the workers in their tuxedos. I wore a $30 pair of Old Navy jeans and a $40 off-brand North Face jacket. The real reason I took Lili and Adri on the boulevard was for them to experience the suffocating crowd. This was Tokyo to me.

The sun was setting.

No visit to Tokyo would be complete without visiting the Shibuya Crossing. It's the NYC Times Square of Japan, but probably cleaner ... and a lot safer. Lili and Adri crossed the road several times as I took photos from the Starbucks on the second floor of a building in front of the crosswalk. Now, it was dark. The buildings were outlined with colorful and glowing neon lights. The Paraguayans were finally in Japan.

***

LILI AND ADRI HAD A FRIEND NAMED ALEM, WHO WAS A JAPANESE PARAGUAYAN BORN IN YGUAZÚ. They went to school with him in Paraguay. Alem had arrived in Japan a few weeks earlier than they did. He moved to Japan to live with his father in Hakone and search for better job opportunities. The second or maybe third time we visited Tokyo, Alem took a three-hour train to meet us in Asakusa. The Kaminarimon Gate is a large lantern that hangs over the entrance. After passing through, Lili, Adri, and I entered Nakamise Street. The narrow street is popular because it has dozens of old-fashioned shops; additionally, it leads to Sensō-ji Temple, the oldest Buddhist temple in Tokyo. Likewise, Asakusa Shrine is nearby and one of the oldest in the city.

Once Alem arrived, the girls' interest shifted from sightseeing to catching up with an old friend. I thought Alem was a cool and smart guy; I'd let my daughter date him if I had one. He spoke Spanish, Guaraní, Portuguese, English, and Japanese. He was exactly what we needed, someone who could read and speak Japanese. With Alem, I could sit back and let him lead the way. After sightseeing in Asakusa, we grabbed lunch at a hole-in-the-wall restaurant on some random side street. We were the only foreigners, and the menu was in Japanese. Luckily, we had Alem to translate.

After eating rice and seafood, we continued walking until we reached Tokyo Skytree[73], the second tallest structure in the world. Although we didn't purchase the $20-tickets to go to the top, we walked around the mall below the tower.

Later in the evening, I invited Alem to spend the night at my place. That way, he could maximize time with his friends.

***

TRAVELING DOESN'T COME WITHOUT DISAP-POINTMENT, AND PERHAPS THE BIGGEST DISAP-POINTMENT CAME FROM VISITING A PARAGUAYAN RESTAURANT. The restaurant was located in Tokyo. I knew of it because after telling Kaori about my Peace Corps Paraguay experience, she wanted to try their food. Lili and Adri were ecstatic about visiting a restaurant owned by a former compatriot. They wanted to eat some familiar food, hear about the owner's experience, and know what led her to Japan.

One day while in Tokyo, we decided to take a train to the part of the city where the restaurant was located. When we arrived, the restaurant had just stopped serving lunch. So I knocked on the door, and the Paraguayan owner answered. Lili and Adri expressed tremendous happiness upon seeing this old woman. I told the owner that they were Paraguayan. Her stoic facial expression read, "Ok, and ..." Then, in Spanish, she asked Lili and Adri what part of Paraguay they were from. They spoke briefly in their indigenous language *Guaraní*. Then the owner gave this unbelievably fake laugh as if she was happy to see fellow Paraguayans and said, "We're closed now. We open again at 5 PM." We didn't go back.

---

73   A broadcast tower reaching 634 meters (2,080 feet).

Luckily, the restaurant was located in Akasaka, an upscale district in Tokyo with many attractions that made the trip worth it. Likewise, it wasn't so far from the famous party district Roppongi. Although we visited the shopping areas in Roppongi, I doubted that I could've gotten into any club dressed like Kanye West on a 2004 *The College Dropout* tour. I had on my favorite Old Navy jeans, a collared shirt, and a backpack.

I carried a backpack everywhere because there aren't any public trash bins on the streets in Japan. Therefore, I never wanted to get stuck carrying a plastic bottle or candy wrappers. In case you're curious, most public trash cans were removed from the streets in the mid-90s after a doomsday cult carried out deadly sarin gas attacks[74] in Tokyo. What's more surprising than Japan not having public trash cans is that the streets are very clean.

***

ENOSHIMA WAS ANOTHER FAVORITE SITE I EN-JOYED TAKING VISITORS. Enoshima is a small island located in Sagami Bay. From the mainland, we reached Enoshima by crossing a short bridge about twenty minutes by foot.

After crossing the bridge, there's a bronze verdigris-covered *torii* gate. Looking beyond the gate truly feels like another world. Past the *torii* gates, there's the famous Benten Nakamise Dori Street. Like most pedestrian streets in Japan, there are shops, restaurants, and street vendors. Additionally, there's a place called Dr. Fish where tourists can pay to have small red garra fish nibble on and exfoliate their feet. Then the fish are cooked and served in a soup. Of course, I'm only kidding about the fish being cooked

---

74   The attacks were perpetrated by Aum Shinrikyo, a syncretic cult based on the idea of a coming Third World War. Twelve people died in the attack, and over five thousand were injured.

and served in soup; that part was a fib. Lili and Adri went there to let the small fishes suck on their toes.

Benten Nakamise Dori Street is inclined and requires some effort to climb. At the end of the climb, there's the power-projecting Enoshima Shrine.

From this point, there are several ways to go, and all of them involve more climbing. Visitors can pay to use the escalators. I took Lili and Adri on the scenic route, which involved walking upstairs, past temples, and through thoroughly kempt gardens. Next, there were more stairs leading past more shops and restaurants. At the very top of the hill, which takes at least thirty minutes to climb, is the most famous garden known as Samuel Cocking Garden. Each season, professional gardeners remodel the area by creating a variety of pleasing flower exhibitions. Additionally, the gardens are decorated with lights and displays that look spectacular at night.

The most popular attraction can be seen from the garden. In fact, it can be viewed from miles off the island. That is the Enoshima Sea Candle lighthouse and observatory. After taking an elevator to the top, we had a breathtaking panoramic view of the bay and dozens of cities. Next, we made our way to the back of the island, which consisted of large sea rocks. Also, there are caves in the area. We relaxed on the rocks, marinated in the sea breeze and listened to the sounds of the crashing waves.

We made our way back to Enoshima's entrance just in time to observe the stunning sunset. The sky was pink and blue, and the bay reflected the colors magnificently. In the background stood a purple silhouette of the god-like Mount Fuji.

***

AFTER A WEEK OF SERVING AS THEIR GUIDE, I GAVE THE GIRLS THE LAST FEW DAYS TO EXPLORE

WITHOUT ME. Lili just wanted to go back to the *chūhai* stand; however, that was the only thing I prohibited. I couldn't risk her killing her younger sister by sticking a tampon down her throat. I really didn't want to have to explain that to their parents. If they returned to the *chūhai* stand, I never found out. They were shopping or hanging out with their friend Alem for all I knew.

The Paraguayans' time in Japan was coming to end. Before they headed back to their country, I couldn't let them leave without introducing them to my friend Bara-san and his crew.

CHAPTER 22

FAIR WINDS AND FOLLOWING SEAS

~~~~~~

A bad day sailing is 100 times better than a good day at work.

—Anonymous

O n December 3, 2015, I arrived at Yokosuka Base in Japan to begin my career as a Sailor in the United States Navy. However,
I could not leave the base and explore my sixth country until I
completed a week-long orientation. December and early January
were holiday periods, which meant no orientation courses were
held; therefore, I was stuck on the base. In mid-January, I finally
attended the orientation class. A well-aged Japanese *obasan* (older
woman), with a great sense of humor, hosted the class. The only
thing I remember from the orientation is her telling the audience,
"Look to your right. Now look to your left. One of the people next
to you is going to marry a Japanese national."

A month later, I was dating Kaori, a Japanese national.

❋❋❋

THREE YEARS BEFORE KAORI AND I STARTED
DATING, SHE PERFORMED ADMINISTRATIVE
WORK AT A HOSPICE. Despite her duties, Kaori developed

positive relationships with the patients living at the hospice and with the patients' families.

Every weekend, Hirono-san (in Japanese *san* is added at the end of a person's name and means Mr. or Mrs.) visited the hospice to spend time with her mother, who lived there. Each visit, Kaori checked Hirono-san into the hospice and escorted her to her mother's location. Over time, Kaori and Hirono-san became friends. They remained so even after Hirono-san's mother passed away. It was Hirono-san who introduced Kaori to Bara-san (Hirono-san's husband). Likewise, Kaori introduced me to Bara-san.

***

"HEY HONEY, DO YOU WANNA GO SAILING?" Kaori asked.

"I make a living working on a ship and being out to sea for months at a time. No, thank you," I responded.

She didn't stop. "I have a friend who owns a sailboat, and he wants to meet you."

The U.S. Navy has boats too, and it met me first, I thought.

Eventually, I decided to go and meet Bara-san, and it was one of the best decisions I'd ever made. Bara-san was in his early-60s and on the heavier side for a Japanese fellow, but still smaller than the average U.S. citizen. He had retired as a news director from Japan's international broadcaster NHK World Television[75]. Bara-san owned a fifteen-passenger sailboat; every weather-permitting Sunday, the socialite gathered a crew and headed out into Sagami Bay.

The usual crew was made up of anything but usual people. For one, most were old enough to be my grandparent. They had graduated from prestigious Japanese universities such as Waseda

---

[75]   NHK is a public broadcaster in Japan. Since 1995, NHK World has produced content for North America and Europe.

University[76] and Keio University. Lastly, they were either retired or worked part-time. Essentially, these were some pretty wealthy individuals. Every Sunday, the regulars included Captain Bara-san, Ikeda-san, Kenchan, Kudo-san, and me, if my Navy ship wasn't underway.

Perhaps, the most interesting of all was Ikeda-san. Ikeda-san met Bara-san while working as an international news reporter at NHK World Television. Ikeda-san traveled all over the world to cover stories affecting Japan. He spoke several languages, including English. He had the opportunity to meet Jimmy Carter, Ronald Reagan, and other world leaders. When Ikeda-san was not working on new stories, many of his travels involved strange, intimate quests that would result in either hilarious or ridiculous stories decades later. Bara-san's number one goal seemed to get Ikeda-san drunk enough to share those stories.

Ikeda-san once told a story: "In the late seventies, my work had taken me to Rio de Janeiro, Brazil. When I was there, I met a lovely young Brazilian lady at a bar. She was very beautiful. And she seemed interested in me as well. We conversed for quite a while. After a few drinks, I invited her to my hotel room, where we made love. Later, I woke up to her attempting to steal money from my pants pockets. That's when I learned that she was a prostitute. She wanted money from me, but I told her, 'No.'"

"Did you pay her?" I interrupted while laughing.

"No," Ikeda-san said and continued the story, "Listen … a day later, I began to burn down there. You know, the private parts. I could not stop rubbing it. After a couple of days, I went to the hospital. The doctor gave me medicine and said I would be ok. At the time, I was married. My wife was in Japan. When I returned, I

---

76   Notable graduates include nine Japanese Prime Ministers, Haruki Murakami, and two presidents of Nintendo.

ended up passing the burn to my wife. That's how she found out that I had cheated, and she divorced me. I'm a bad man."

Sometimes I didn't know whether to feel bad for Ikeda-san, or humored by his stories.

Bara-san referred to the seventy-something-year-old Ikeda-san as "Super Playboy." In Ikeda-san's youth, he was quite an attractive and charming young man with lovers worldwide. Even in his seventies, Ikeda-san dated girls half his age. The youngest I had known him to date was in her twenties. I had never seen him sadder than the day he told me that the girl's parents didn't want her dating an old man.

Ikeda-san was the only one who spoke English; he served as the verbal bridge between me and everyone else, as our translator.

Another faithful crew member was Kenchan, who was in his sixties and retired. Kenchan was the CEO type who had headed a marketing firm; in addition, he had amassed a fortune in real estate. He was undoubtedly the wealthiest of the group; however, he was also the alcoholic of the group—the kind of alcoholic who gets the shakes. The liquor made him stop shaking. Sometimes, my girlfriend would see Kenchan passed out on benches around town. Just to give you an idea of how safe Japan is: Kenchan wore a $20,000 Rolex, and each time he woke up, it was still on his wrist. A couple of times, the police found Kenchan passed out and took him to the station until he sobered up. Despite his alcohol addiction, Kenchan managed to date a kind actress who starred in Japanese dramas. She came along on numerous occasions.

Once Kenchan invited Kaori and me to dinner. Before we guzzled three 750 ml bottles of wine, he ordered olives as an appetizer. I thought, *Who in the hell orders olives as an appetizer?* I was used to the fried macaroni balls and southwestern spring rolls. But Kenchan changed my world with those olives. I didn't even know olives were fruits. Those rich and savory little balls of goodness were quite different than the ones I used to eat from the can.

Then there was Kudo-san. He was the quiet one of the bunch. Kudo-san never said much, but he sailed the boat most of the time; he taught me how to sail. Also, he'd laugh at Ikeda-san's silly stories.

Then there was me. I'm sure you know this guy by now.

Additionally, I had the pleasure of meeting so many interesting people. One of Bara-san's good friends, Chef (as I called him), owned a restaurant in Tokyo. When Chef came along, he prepared delicious Japanese food and delicacies like *fugu* (blowfish). Blowfish is deadly if prepared incorrectly[77]. Also, there were guests from countries including Spain, Brazil, the United Kingdom, and now Paraguay. It was a mystery to me how or why they had come to Japan and ended up on Bara-san's sailboat. Then again, I was there too.

As a random side note, one of my travel regrets was not traveling to Bhutan, and it wasn't for lack of effort. It took way more coordination and money than I could justify getting there. Later, Bara-san told me that if I ever wanted to go, he'd talk to his friend in Bhutan, a member of the royal family. Whomever this prince or princess was had previously sailed on Bara-san's boat.

***

EACH MONDAY, I'D TELL MY NAVY FRIENDS ABOUT "SAILING SUNDAYS" AND MY LATEST ADVENTURES. I could've just said I knew someone with a sailboat. However, it

---

77   The Japanese Government tightly regulates fugu. Chefs must train for at least three years before they are licensed to prepare the dish. The lethality comes from tetrodotoxin, a lethal neurotoxin contained in the organs and skin of the fish.

sounded cooler (and somewhat boastful) telling my shipmates, "I have a friend who owns a yacht."

Bara-san allowed me to bring guests anytime I wanted. On many occasions, I invited friends and coworkers. At first, they were like me: "I'm in the Navy, live on a ship, blah, blah, blah." It took two-and-a-half years of me inviting others before the first person accepted the invite. There's just something enchanting and addicting about sailing toward a beautiful snowcapped Mt. Fuji.

After the first person went, everybody in my division wanted to go. Soon they realized the huge differences between being on a sailboat and a warship: relaxation, booze, and paddle boarding.

It was a fantastic cross-cultural experience. These older, affluent Japanese gentlemen served us delicacies like oyster, caviar, and *shikasashi* (raw venison). Ikeda-san even gifted me a bottle of homemade, aged *umeshu* (Japanese plum wine made with Brandy)[78]. It took more than a year to make it. Whenever I'd bring a twelve-pack of Bud Light Platinum or a bottle of Crown Royal Apple, from the Commissary grocery store on the Navy base, they'd get so excited. Japanese stores didn't sell those types of liquor, and they were "exclusive." Most Sundays consisted of sailing, booze, lunch, and these old men's stories.

Again, Ikeda-san was the most interesting out of all of us. He was a world traveler and, in his younger days, spoke fluent English, Spanish, and Portuguese. By the time I met him, he had struggled to speak English; however, I could understand him, and his stories were always engaging, humorous, and outrageous.

"One time, I went to Texas to cover a story on the beef exports from the United States to Japan. I met with some farmers to interview them. They took me into the barn to show me the

78   Unripe, green plums are steeped in shōchū (or other white liquor) with sugar. Umeshu can be consumed after three months, but it's better to wait. Six to nine months is considered preferable.

animals. After the interview, they told me to climb on a stool behind one of the cows. When I did it, one of the farmers told me to pull my pants down."

"What!" I said as I laughed uncontrollably. "Are you serious?" "What did you do?"

Ikeda-san continued, "I pulled down my pants. Then the farmers told me to make love with the cow. So I made love with the cow."

"What did the farmers do?" I asked.

"They made love to the cow, too," Ikeda-san responded. "I'm a bad man."

Poor cow, I thought.

Each Sunday, we would take off into Sagami Bay around 10 AM and spend two to three hours at sea. After sailing, there was always lunch. Sometimes, Chef cooked. Then there were the times we dined without the flow of the ocean beneath us.

Right across from the marina where Bara-san docked his boat, we would dine at the place that became my favorite restaurant. It was a small, local fisherman restaurant. Every Sunday, I saw the same loyal customers and afterwhile, I became one of them. My Navy buddies and I were the only foreigners who were ever there. Each dish they served was the best: *sashimi*, Japanese pork cutlet with curry, fried chicken, noodles. I constantly challenged those I invited, a sort of initiation. It made me nervous every time I made the offer. I told my friends, "I'll give you $50 if this isn't the best Japanese food you've ever had." Even if they lied, I would have paid them. Then the slurping, the "mmm mmm," and the "oh my God" let me know that the food was the best. After lunch, I'd pull out $50 in Japanese currency and ask, "Do I owe anyone?" No one ever accepted the money.

Several times, I invited Ikeda-san, Bara-san, and his wife Hirono-san to Yokosuka Naval Base. Each year, the base celebrates

251

Friendship Day[79] by allowing Japanese nationals to walk around the base, tour the ships, interact with military personnel, and purchase food and souvenirs. Once again, I was a tour guide as I escorted my friends around the base.

Bara-san's hospitality extended beyond his sailboat. Bara-san's wife, Hirono-san, and my lady, Kaori, were friends. They invited us to their home for lunch and dinner numerous times throughout the years: New Year's, Christmas, as well as Japanese holidays.

Each summer, the local city hosted a big fireworks' show on Sagami Bay. It was an extraordinary event. The fireworks were launched from a barge floating off the coast of Zushi Beach. Streams of light ascended toward the sky and then exploded into colorful and bright illuminations taking off in all directions. Even more impressive, some of the fireworks burst into famous Japanese characters from cartoons, including Pokémon and Doraemon.

These thirty-minute shows of nonstop fireworks attracted thousands of local residents. Most of them relaxed on the beach as they enjoyed the flashy lights and thunderous explosions. However, Bara-san invited guests to his boat. Everyone watched the show pier-side at the marina where his sailboat was docked. In previous years, I had attended Bara-san's boat parties, and we drank and enjoyed popular Japanese foods such as *yakitori*[80].

One particular summer, Bara-san invited Kaori and me to watch the show; however, I could not join. The fireworks show occurred the same evening that my naval ship was going out to sea. Although I could not join the party, I could see the same fireworks as I stood on the forecastle. As my ship headed underway, I watched the bright, colorful star-like explosions. I knew that I

---

79   Friendship Day was proposed in 1930 by the founder of Hallmark as a day to celebrate friendships and, of course, sell greeting cards.
80   Skewers of meat typically grilled over a charcoal fire. Beef, chicken, pork, and liver are all common.

was sharing the experience with thousands of others, including Bara-san and his guests. If not for my ship's schedule, I would have celebrated with them.

It's interesting how sharing special occasions with other humans make life all the more worthwhile. There were thousands of people watching the fireworks, and I felt connected to all of them. There were possibly people I had sat next to on the trains. Maybe some of the people worked at restaurants or stores I visited. Some of those people were U.S. Sailors who worked on the same base as me. Some of those people I would probably see in the future and could've befriended if I'd only said, "Hi" or "Kon'nichiwa." While we all witnessed the fireworks show together, I stood on the weather deck with one of my mentors, Petty Officer Rivers. As we watched the fireworks, I listened to Rivers as he shared his experiences in the Navy and spoke about his family. He wouldn't see them for months.

The most fascinating thing about it all, and what I've been able to personally learn and experience, is that it's not culture, religion, race, or even language that brings us together. All of those things play minor roles. It's not listening to Whitney Houston while cooking pizza with a group of newfound coworkers. It's not MMA, sailboats, traveling, or even serving in the military that draws us together.

The one thing that absolutely brings all of us together is as simple as it is misunderstood, and that is life. We can be from countries on opposite sides of the world, be from different socio-economic statuses, and be decades apart in age. Somehow, we were all miraculously born and brought together by this thing called life. Everything else is a matter of timing, decision-making, and indeed a little luck. Each time we move beyond our own mental and physical boundaries, we live a little bit more by pursuing experiences that can potentially make our lives more fulfilling.

After half a decade of friendship, Bara-san and I barely understood one another. Bara-san spoke limited English and, even after five years of living in Japan, I spoke embarrassingly little Japanese.

"*Kon'nichiwa*," I'd say to Bara-san.

"Hi, Mike," he'd respond with a warm smile.

To say anything else presented a struggle for either of us. Most of our conversations were translated by others, particularly Kaori, Ikeda-san, and sometimes Google-san. Nonetheless, we developed a close-knit bond just as meaningful as life itself.

Kaori once told me that Bara-san and his wife Hirono-san didn't have any children.

She said, "I think they like spending time with us because it reminds them of what it would be like to have kids."

We were in our early thirties. Kaori, our invitees, and I were among the younger guests; sometimes, Bara-san's married friends brought their younger children.

I remember traveling abroad for the first time to study in the Dominican Republic. One of the first things I did was go online and search, "What is it like for Black travelers in the Dominican Republic?" This wasn't the first or last time I had asked Google the question. The real question was, "What was it like to be 'me' in a world outside of my home country? How would I be treated, and would I be accepted?" These were questions that only I could answer. If my experiences had been as unfavorable or negative as many of the responses that came up in the searches, I would have stopped traveling a long time ago. In Japan, like so many other places I've lived, I found much comfort in strangers who became friends and the families that treated me as their own.

*****

IN JULY 2021, I FINISHED MY TIME ON THE USS *CURTIS WILBUR*. The time had come for me to return to the motherland after five and a half years—the longest I'd ever spent outside of the United States. By this time, Kaori was now my wife and would be returning with me as the *obasan* from the orientation predicted almost six years earlier.

A few nights before leaving Japan, Bara-san and his wife Hirono-san invited us to dinner. It was special because it was our going-away dinner. Hirono-san made homemade sweet and sour pork, my favorite Chinese dish. Bara-san prepared *okonomiyaki*, a savory Japanese pancake with vegetables; it was the dish that Kaori and I had on our first date. Bara-san and Hirono-san went all out for us. The food tasted delicious, and everything was going well until it wasn't.

Earlier that day, Kaori and I went to Coco's Curry, a famous Japanese curry restaurant that all the drunk sailors thought was the best restaurant ever. To its credit, it was a damn good restaurant as far as fast food was concerned. Coco's had a wide variety of meats and veggies that customers could order with their curry. The most important thing was the spice level which ranged from one to ten. Anything higher than a five burned the tongue enough to make the meal intolerable to anyone who wasn't crazy. In Japan, I developed quite a tolerance for spicy food. So before leaving, it was only fitting to test my tolerance by ordering a meal with a spice level of ten. Surprisingly, I got through it. Sadly, it just happened to fall on the day of Bara-san's dinner.

It occurred after dinner, right before the meaningful conversations, sharing of memories, and laughter takes place. Out of nowhere, the spicy curry kicked in, and my stomach said, "Bruh, we gotta find a bathroom."

Bara-san's bathroom was not too far from the kitchen; however, the walls weren't as soundproof as I needed them to be, and I couldn't risk the smell making its way to the dining area. I tried to hold it, but my gut was experiencing a nuclear meltdown. I whispered to Kaori, "Baby, can we go?" From my serious facial expression, she could tell something was bothering me. In Japanese, she informed Bara-san and Hirono-san that we had to go.

She wanted to say bye to her friends who she would be leaving as she was getting ready to begin a new life in the United States. Understandably, they continued to talk and hug it out while my (and my stomach's) patience vanished. Kaori and Hirono-san went into a room where there was a photo of Hirono-san's late mother. They went to pay homage to the mother because they met through her when Kaori worked at the hospice. Kaori met Bara-san through Hirono-san, and I met everyone through Kaori. It was an emotional moment. The entire time, my facial expression read, "Please, hurry up! I need to leave." Literally and figuratively, I felt shitty about the whole situation.

Finally, we left and were waved off by Bara-san and Hirono-san. As soon as they were out of sight, I attempted to run, but that was not a good idea. Leaving Kaori behind, I walked as fast as possible, looking for the nearest bathroom before finding a 7/11 convenience store.

After Kaori found out what my problem was, she thought it was the funniest thing in the world. She purposely made me feel bad by saying that we didn't even get to take one last photo together. That was our final moment with Bara-san and his wife.

In this life of travel and the people in between, sometimes shit just happens—no pun intended.

CHAPTER 23

THE ROLLER COASTER

~~~~~~

You must meet with triumph and disaster and treat those
two impostors just the same. —*Les Brown*

C herry blossom season was coming to an end in the land of the
rising sun. A few weeks after my Paraguayan sisters departed
Japan, I checked in aboard the USS *Curtis D. Wilbur*. A month
into my new command, we headed out to sea—near Guam to
participate in the 2019 Pacific Vanguard Exercise.

Life at sea is routine. There's daily maintenance, training,
drills, meetings, and watches. A watch refers to one of the many
workstations always manned by sailors since the ship operates
twenty-four hours a day. The watches continually rotate between
three to four people throughout each day. All things considered,
a sailor could easily work between twelve to fourteen (or more)
hours a day. If there isn't much maintenance or the day's schedule
is light, that could decrease the number of hours worked. Sailors
find moments for meals, showers, sleep, and personal time somewhere between work. Ultimately, sleep trumps everything. After
long workdays, I would choose rest over a meal. While a civilian
with a more traditional job has the opportunity to partake in an

extracurricular activity, there's not much to do as a sailor living inside a floating chunk of metal on the salty ocean.

When I did get a moment to myself, I took advantage of the ship's internet service, considering it was available. Sometimes, the mission dictated whether it was accessible. When it was, I read news articles to find out what was happening in the world. Additionally, I checked my favorite MMA site to find out the results of fights that I missed or upcoming events. More importantly, I'd log in to Facebook because that's how I maintained contact with family and friends.

Checking social media was a double-edged sword. Although it was nice receiving messages from family or seeing photos of friends, it often felt like the world was moving on without me. Also, if people didn't hear from me, they began to worry and had reason to. There was always something happening between the United States and nations like Russia, China, and North Korea that always made it to the news. We were in those nations' backyards. Furthermore, I wanted to know how my family was doing. Even with the best intentions, I had to be careful because everyone had their problems, and there was only so much I could do from the other side of the world.

On May 29, 2019, I logged into my Facebook account from a computer in my workspace. Immediately, I saw photos of my uncle Edward. As I scrolled down, it seemed that everyone had posted pictures of him. The Messenger icon showed that I had several messages waiting. My heart broke as I read and learned that my Uncle Ed had recently died. "Edward is dead," read the message sent by my grandmother. It was a direct and sharp blow right through my heart. This old woman, who was suffering, was in too much pain to use decorated words to inform me of her son's death. Her second youngest son was dead at the age of fifty-one.

I thought back to my childhood and what it was like growing up in Saint Louis, a city plagued by poverty and violence. Of all the places I've been to, it's a wonder that my family and I escaped that city. But, growing up, I did have an angel to protect me. When my nineteen-year-old mom was at work, Uncle Ed babysat three-year-old me. When I was an unfocused, undisciplined kid, flunking the fifth grade, Ed signed me up to play football and took me to all my games. When I was hungry, he'd give me a couple of dollars, so I could go to the corner store and buy a bag of Doritos and a soda. When a gang of neighborhood bullies attacked me, he wanted to take a concussed me to fight them one on one. Thankfully, my mom talked him out of that one. Getting beat up again didn't sound fun.

That's who Uncle Ed was. He took care of everybody, and everyone loved him. I could only dream of being the person he was. While I was traveling the world and being an "inspiration" to everyone, Ed was at the graduations, birthday parties, and cookouts. I wish I could have been as strong, supportive, funny, and loved as my uncle. Instead, I was at sea while everyone else was mourning the loss of our family's heart.

As I stared at the computer screen, overwhelmed by the news, one of my coworkers entered the space. I shouted, "Get out!" I didn't mean to say it so rudely. He forgave any offense or confusion that he may have felt as he witnessed me burst into tears. I let out a painful sob and put my hands over my face. My coworker came over, gave me two pats on the back, and walked out. After responding to my family's messages, I logged out of my account before anyone could have the chance to respond. I needed the moment to myself.

Later that night, I went to my rack (bed) in the berthing. I put my headphones and listened to Sam Cooke. "Ease my Troublin'

Mind" and "Nobody Knows the Trouble I've Seen" played on repeat that night.

Uncle Ed passed away due to complications during a weight loss surgery; he had always been on the heavy side. When I played pee-wee football, Ed challenged me to a race. Kid me laughed and thought, "There's no way this fat dude can win," but he embarrassed me. "Let's do it again! Let's do it again!" I pleaded. He never allowed me to redeem the loss.

Historically, many of my family members have struggled with weight problems. In the light of Ed's passing, it seemed like everyone made resolutions to lose weight. However, the sadness followed them like a shadow, and they were so broken that they lacked the willpower to follow through. For me, it was heartbreaking to witness from afar the living lose track of life.

I would like to believe that everyone is the protagonist of their own story. It's strange how life continues whether or not the protagonist survives. Uncle Ed left this world a hero.

The weight of Ed's death crushed the family. I had my own ways of grieving and dealing with death. For one, I kept my body and mind focused on the immediate tasks. At sea, those fourteen-hour workdays didn't feel so tedious compared to the loss of a relative. Also, I spent time reflecting on what Ed's death meant to me and how I would carry it forward.

I reflected,

If dying is inevitable and everyone dies, then why do people fear anything about living when eventually it'll all go away? Why not take chances? Is it fear alone that prevents us from living a more fulfilling life? Or is it the pain caused when we act on our fears by taking risks, but we still fall short? What if we don't fall short? Doesn't success come from pain and adversity as well? What difference does it make? Fulfillment and dissatisfaction are one and the same, just like living and dying.

In the end, I concluded that nothing really mattered to the wider world. However, much mattered to me, like my health, relationships, time, experiences, and how I could make the best of it all.

I contemplated, *Life is one big contradiction. Take the sea, for example; it's neither alive nor dead. The same typhoon that causes death and destruction also brings forth life and replenishment.*

***

EVENTUALLY, MY SHIP RETURNED TO JAPAN DURING THE SUMMER OF 2019. I made my best efforts to maintain healthy communication with all of my family. Around New Year, my Uncle Jeffery reached out to me. We shared some new year's resolutions. My goals were as unconvincing as anyone else's: stop drinking, get in shape, read more and save more money. In one of the emails, he wrote, "Are you close to reaching the million-dollar mark?" In my family, being financially independent meant you weren't buried in a monstrous amount of debt and had a few dollars to your name.

I responded, "Not yet."

I thought, *Why not?*

I reread his message; it was no longer an inquiry. It was a challenge to me and my new belief. I wanted to see what could happen if I began living my life as if things didn't really matter, not even failure or death.

***

WHILE I MAY HAVE NOT BEEN A MILLIONAIRE, I WASN'T FINANCIALLY STUPID EITHER. Although, I had made a lot of stupid financial decisions. Before I continue, this is a disclaimer that I'm not a financial advisor. This is not financial advice.

In 2017, I had a fair amount of money saved in my bank account. It wasn't "Elon Musk" money or anything, but I was comfortable. I thought, *Maybe, I should invest some of my money.* Then another thought came to mind, *Maybe, I should invest someone else's money*! That sounded like the better idea.

Next, I went to the bank and took out a $30,000 personal loan. I invested the entire loan in the stock market. I'll make this story quick. After about three years later (2020), I finally paid off the loan. At the end of three years, instead of $30,000, I now had $19,000 times inflation; in addition, I had to pay interest on the loan. I took a risk and lost. Instead of transferring the money to my savings account, I just left it invested in whatever lousy stocks I purchased. For a moment, I almost believed that I'd never do it again.

Some months later, I looked at my investment portfolio, and it was worth about $23,000 and rising. Eventually, it climbed past $30,000. At the time, I didn't understand what was going on.

In March 2020, the stock market had bottomed as a result of the COVID-19 pandemic. Once the market began rising, it did so at a historical rate. I saw the value of my portfolio increase significantly. Then, I invested some of my savings. Then I started borrowing money from my brokerage company. By borrowing money, I increased my buying power. This is known as marginal investing. Basically, it allowed me to increase the value of my investments from money that I didn't own. It was paying dividends, literally.

Sometimes, I'd see daily losses over $10,000, while other times, I'd see weekly gains greater than $50,000. It was insane. The thing about stocks is you really don't have the money until you sell them. *Why would I sell the stocks if the dollar amounts were doubling and tripling?* So instead, I just kept borrowing money and investing in companies that showed promising returns.

Even before my investments exploded, traveling taught me to be a minimalist, and I already felt comfortable with everything I had. Now I was at a point in my life where I could quit my job, travel the entire world, and afterward spend a decade living in a bungalow in the Philippines. Of course, there were a few small issues. 1. Nobody really quits the Navy (there are contractual obligations). 2. It was the height of the COVID-19 pandemic. Many countries closed their borders. 3. Then, there was the IRS.

The most frightening realization of it all was knowing that I could've done anything that I wanted. Besides traveling, there was no greater experience that money could buy me. *Then, what was next? What would I do after visiting every country on my bucket list?* And my bucket list was a world map. Again, there was a global pandemic, and I was still in the navy.

As a sailor in Japan, I spent most of 2020 quarantining on a ship, at home, or at sea. When fall hit, we went out to sea for a strenuous period. There's nothing like being on a boat for months and not knowing when you'll see land again. We couldn't return to Japan or visit any ports because of the threat that the COVID-19 pandemic posed to our mission-ready capabilities. With this, I couldn't spend any real money even if I wanted to.

Instead, I'd shop online and send care packages to family and friends. My favorite gift to send was handmade Japanese knives that were beautifully hammered and inscribed with *kanji*. Also, I ordered snacks from websites and had them delivered to friends and family.

I recalled my Uncle Jeffery's email, "Are you close to reaching the million-dollar mark?" I could finally tell my uncle that I was closer. On the same note, I had a mortgage's worth of borrowed money that I was paying interest on. Risk and reward were the same, like life and death. That's the state I was in after Uncle Ed passed.

Intelligence and idiocy, all the same. Okay, maybe that's a stretch, but that's the direction I was heading. In an attempt to become the family's first millionaire, I was also on track to become the first member with a million dollars in debt—all for the subtle art of not giving a f*ck.

With money comes an increased level of responsibility. If you want to keep or increase it, then you need the education to make the best decisions. It's strange the way things happen. Soon after I read how terribly risky marginal investing could be, it became a practical lesson. The same way that margin multiplies gains, it multiplies losses. It didn't happen immediately, but it happened fast. I was following Warren Buffet's "buy and hold for life" strategy. While that may work for a multi-billionaire, it didn't go so well for me and my borrowed money. Like magic, my "travel the world and bungalow" money evaporated into the thin air of the stock market.

Nonetheless, I wasn't completely financially reckless. Before I could lose everything, I took heed to what I was learning from the financial books. Instead of staying heavily invested on the roller coaster of individual stocks, I went the more boring route via an S&P 500 Index Fund. Instead of beating the market, the fund just mimics the S&P 500 index.

If you're considering investing, below are some books that I enjoyed.

The Millionaire Next Door—Thomas J. Stanley
The Simple Path to Wealth—J. L. Collins
The Automatic Millionaire—David Bach
Rich Dad Poor Dad—Robert Kiyosaki

***

THE YEAR 2020 WAS A ROLLER COASTER RIDE FOR SO MANY REASONS. The financial roller coaster was definitely the wildest one. The catalyst for boarding that roller coaster was the New Year's email from my Uncle Jeffery. The fire inside me came from seeing how paralyzed my family was by the loss of our dear Edward. They were dedicating their goals (e.g., losing weight) to Ed; however, he was gone, and they were still alive. They had to desperately want it for themselves and act in accordance with their desires.

My own state of despair led me to make some aggressive and risky decisions. A decision is just a choice, a combination of thought and action that leads to a consequence. But desperation … desperation breaks down a person's choices until only the most extreme options remain to choose from. Benjamin Disraeli once wrote, "Desperation is sometimes as powerful an inspirer as genius." At times, it was the reason I grabbed ahold of the most immediate opportunity available to me, especially in regard to travel.

I must mention that my own travel experience has been a roller coaster ride in itself. I would have loved to have begun with a $500,000 annual salary and the ability to quit my job and travel the world. Likewise, it would've been nice to get out of college, sell everything, and take my chances around the globe—even with five digits of student loans trailing behind. Ultimately, we all have to do what we can until we reach the point where we can do what we want. The decisions I made led me down other paths. I can't exactly say I don't regret any of it; however, I wouldn't have had it any other way.

Still, there were things I desperately wanted far more than riding a reckless financial roller coaster of uncertainty. I wanted my family to be happy. And I wanted them to know that even though they were down, it wasn't too late to get back up. I wished for COVID-19 to go away, so I could travel again. Furthermore, I desired to stop wanting in excess. I longed for the return of a grateful spirit.

CHAPTER 24

TAKE ME HOME

Home is neither here nor there. Home is within you, or

home is nowhere at all.

—*Hermann Hesse*

The first time I heard the song "Take Me Home, Country Roads" by John Denver, I was in a hotel lobby in Beijing, China. It played as background music, but I really loved the tune. As I listened, I recognized the places in Mr. Denver's lyrics. The Blue Ridge Mountains and West Virginia.

During my early years in the Navy, I met a sailor from West Virginia. He was the first person I'd ever met from the state. There's a stereotype associated with people from there. After learning that he was from there, I asked him, "Is it true what they say about people from West Virginia?"

Without hesitation, he said, "Yep, we all sleep with our cousins." We both shared a laugh.

How does the song "Take Me Home, Country Roads" and stereotypes of West Virginians marrying cousins fit into my story? I haven't quite figured that out yet. But sorry to anyone I offended.

Although I'd never been to West Virginia[81], my home was its eastern neighbor, Virginia. There, I'd been to Shenandoah National Park in the Blue Ridge Mountains with my friend Dan. Shenandoah is one of the most beautiful places I've ever been to. Likewise, it was one of the most profound trips I've ever experienced. My adventure spirit had been shaped by the rugged trails and baptized in the expansive river of trees. I left there, reborn and set to explore the world.

As much time as I lived abroad, I've rarely encountered homesickness; however, if there was anything that made me nostalgic, it was listening to Mr. Denver's song.

Now, the moment had arrived. Life was getting ready to take me home.

***

I HAD SPENT OVER FIVE YEARS IN JAPAN. One of my biggest travel regrets is not exploring the country as much as I should have. Missed opportunities that I let slip away included visiting Kyoto, Okinawa, Osaka, Hiroshima, and every other place that pops up when you Google, "places to visit in Japan." Similarly, I regret not purchasing the $200 ticket and taking the three-hour flight to South Korea. I thought, *There was no way I could be stationed on a ship in Japan for so many years and not make a port visit to Seoul or Busan.* Well, I miscalculated terribly.

The Navy provided an excellent opportunity to travel primarily because I somehow successfully managed to get stationed in Japan for two tours. Although my ships didn't visit many foreign ports, I was still able to vacation to nearby countries during the holidays. This allowed me to explore most of Southeast Asia. Nonetheless,

---

81   In 1863, pro-Union counties of western Virginia seceded from confederate Virginia and formed their own state.

I figured that I'd wait my final year before traveling around Japan or taking the flight to South Korea.

During the second week of January 2020, Kaori and I had just returned from a trip to Brunei, the country known as the Abode of Peace. We walked around the quiet capital Bandar Seri Begawan and took boat rides through the tranquil rainforest which makes up Ulu Temburong National Park.

On the day Kaori and I left for Brunei, President Donald Trump ordered a drone strike that killed Iranian General Qasem Soleimani in Iraq. Then, a few days before Kaori and I returned to Japan, Iran retaliated by bombing an Iraqi base hosting U.S. Forces. After the trip, I quickly transitioned from the "that was a nice vacation" mindset to the "we're probably going to war" mindset. For a while, it seemed that way.

A few weeks later, something else happened. There was a horrendous helicopter crash that took the life of basketball legend Kobe Bryant. The news shocked the world. We were no longer going to war; we were now mourning the death of the basketball phenom and those who passed with him. It was almost as if things couldn't get worse. I remember walking through the passageways of my ship and occasionally hearing, "The coronavirus is nothing; the flu kills more people. It'll pass." However, everybody was talking about the death of Kobe Bryant.

Eventually, tension with Iran seemed to dissipate from the media, along with the stories of Kobe Bryant.

COVID-19 emerged, spread, and caused a global pandemic. There went my opportunities to explore Japan and visit South Korea.

***

"IT'LL PASS," THEY SAID.

The only thing that would pass was a period where I had to pause my dream of traveling the world. Traveling was not only one of my life's greatest passions but also something that I was good at doing. One aspect I always enjoyed about traveling was the planning aspect—the booking of flights, accommodations, and searching for activities to do. Constantly having an adventure to look forward to felt like a pleasure in itself. Unfortunately, that was no longer the case.

I believed that the COVID-19 pandemic would pass quickly. It would go away, and I would be free to travel. Instead, it took millions of lives, brought the world to a halt, and tanked worldwide financial markets. Eventually, my investment portfolio would hit astronomical heights and then come crashing down.

Even before the pandemic, I planned to save a decent amount of money and travel the rest of the world. In fact, in the fall of 2019, I created a blog Bro, Go Travel! (www.brogotravel.com) to offer value in the form of free travel advice, helpful resources, and motivation. I had never been a writer. *How could I be motivated to travel country to country if I couldn't even write a travel article? Why would I travel the world and not creatively document the experiences?*

That's when I purchased the Sony camera. Like before, I would take the train to nearby cities like Kamakura, Yokohama, and Tokyo. I made videos and asked random strangers to take photos of them. Then, I'd practice editing the material. Three months before the Brunei trip, Kaori and I took a multi-destination round trip from Japan to Singapore, the Maldives, and Malaysia for under $700. Living abroad made travel incredibly affordable. Anyhow, I had thousands of photos and videos from so many countries to use as content on my website. Additionally, I wrote enough blogs to make three blogs post a month for a year. I was serious about traveling the world.

Everything was going according to plan until the coronavirus. Traveling had become a daunting task. It didn't make any sense to make blog posts encouraging people to travel during a global pandemic when nations closed their borders. Instead, I created an Instagram account called Brogotravel. In quarantine, I edited and posted images from previous trips. As Murphy's Law would have it, my hard drive crashed. It contained thousands of photos across seventeen countries taken over five years.

When the COVID-19 pandemic-related restrictions eased, I could only go to work, the grocery store, and home. The only thing I could do to keep myself sane was to start drafting a book.

I believe that even an introvert would have agreed that it was terrible having to quarantine and not having the option to go out. Even if introverts disagreed, I know they were upset that the pandemic delayed new seasons of their favorite Netflix shows and movies.

As previously stated, the only thing worse than quarantining and not having the option to go anywhere is going out to sea with no plan for returning home. Early October 2020, my ship went out to sea. It remained at sea for Halloween, Thanksgiving, Christmas, New Year's, Valentine's Day, and Easter.

***

EARLIER IN MY LIFE, THE TRAVEL BUG HAD BIT-TEN ME, AND ITS BITE RELEASED AN ANTIDOTE THAT CURED ME OF A LIFE OF DESPONDENCY. Each year, I'd travel to stimulate my soul and boost my spirits. Sometimes, it was a quick trip, and sometimes the stay was more long-term. But it was always enough to keep me going. Travel had given meaning to my life. Up until 2021, almost one-third of my life took place abroad. Nearly two years without traveling due to the COVID-19 pandemic seemed like the perfect amount of time to remove the antidote from my body. Somewhere along the way, I lost the desire to travel.

In the summer of 2021, my time in Japan ended. I would finally be returning to the United States with Kaori. Earlier on, I made requests for assignments in South Korea, Spain, and Italy. I knew I needed to be overseas; even so, I wasn't upset after not receiving the orders. I had seen new sailors arrive in Japan, and not leave the base for a year. I thought about how the restrictions and policies constantly changed. One week, sailors could dine in at restaurants, and the following week we couldn't. Without the freedom to thoroughly enjoy the destination, serving in a foreign country no longer seemed appealing to me.

My next assignment took me to the Eastern Shore of Virginia. After permanently leaving Missouri at the tender age of twelve, Virginia became my home. Even after living there until my mid-20s, I didn't know the Eastern Shore existed.

Like the countryside of Mongolia, the Eastern Shore is the boonies. It's at the border of Virginia, Maryland, and Delaware. Therefore, there's poor radio reception while driving. Whenever I listened to my favorite R&B radio station, it seemed like the songs and white noise competed for listenership. Driving along Route 13, you pass by cotton plantations and endless cornfields. As you navigate through Route 13, there's no shortage of local vendors selling fresh fruits and vegetables from their stands along the road. It's almost like being in a different country. The Eastern Shore doesn't feel like the United States in the twenty-first century.

This is a place rich in history where famous Civil War battles took place. It's a place where my ancestors labored under the hot sun in cotton fields. It's a place where small cities still have colonial-style homes. Kaori and I visited small towns like

Parksley and Berlin. These cities make you feel like you're living in the '60s. As Kaori and I walked through these small towns, we encountered friendly people. We greeted one another as we crossed paths. From vehicles, people waved as they passed by us. This was small-town America.

Every day while driving to work, I had to be careful not to run over chickens that socialized on the roads. At night, I had to watch for deer. In the summer, mosquitoes form gangs that terrorize everyone, including the thousands of tourists that flock to Chincoteague and Assateague to see the wild horses and ponies[82]. With little light pollution, the visible Milky Way displays a bioluminescent river of stars, visible from the beaches of Assateague.

If the name Assateague doesn't make you laugh, there are also small towns with names including Assawoman, Onancock, Middlesex, Little Hell, and Savageville—all located on the Eastern Shore. *And somehow, West Virginia ended up with the stereotypes.*

What's good about living on the Eastern Shore is accessibility. I could drive and touch Virginia, Maryland, and Delaware in an hour. A person could go to cities like Baltimore, Philadelphia, Atlantic City, New York City, and Washington D.C., in a matter of hours. Still, there were things that I found incomprehensible. In 2018, Mongolian nomads had satellite television and Nepalese mountain people had Wi-Fi; however, I had coworkers living only a few hours from the nation's capital who lived in communities without access to Wi-Fi in 2021.

Somewhere out there was a different America; I was aware of it. Perhaps, there were many different Americas. The Eastern Shore of Virginia was my America.

---

82   Chincoteague ponies are feral horses that live on Assateague Island. They are the subject of the children's novel series Misty of Chincoteague and the film adaptation Misty (1961).

Like international travel, going around the United States didn't appeal to me either. I wasn't interested in any road trips or flights to other states. Dining at restaurants that served international cuisines no longer excited me. A quick trip to Arby's to get a roast beef sandwich and curly fries seemed to appease my desire to travel. It seemed wrong. Deep down, I knew that there wasn't anything I could do about it.

Mentally, I was good. I didn't feel depressed about not being able to travel abroad. Nor did I feel like traveling was a thing of the past. At times, I did feel trapped between fond memories of past travel experiences and possibilities expunged by the pandemic. It seems the longest roads are created when we know what's behind us, but we still have to move forward.

Although I didn't feel like traveling, I had to try. I submitted vacation requests to travel to Portugal, Spain, and Morocco. I got pushback from my supervisor for apparent reasons, and I understood why. It would have been easier to go to Puerto Rico since it's a U.S. territory, but I didn't want to go. When my vacation requests to travel within the United States received approval, I just stayed at home. I reserved rental cars to take road trips, only to cancel the reservation a few days later.

The difficult part was being married to a travel lover. While in Japan, Kaori and I traveled a lot. She was there with me on most of my flights across Asia. Like me, she studied abroad when she was younger. She visited African and European countries, both continents with places that had once held top spots on my bucket list. Now she was living in the United States, a place full of new wonders to explore. Not being in the military, she was free to travel as she pleased; however, she just wanted to take a trip to Baltimore or New York City with me.

***

I'M NOT WHO I WAS YESTERDAY. Tomorrow, I'll be a different person as well. Besides my infant years, everything I was and everything I'll ever be revolve around a decision-making process that transforms me over and over again. Like that, I was not the same person who had worked behind the desk at the Comfort Inn.

Thankfully, I can say that I've never traveled to run away from any external problems. For me, it was more about placing myself in new environments. I would travel to new countries to constantly challenge and reinvent myself.

I was no longer the insecure kid who didn't have many friends. I was no longer afraid to open up and share myself with others. I went from thinking the Banana Republic was a country to being able to name almost every nation in the world. The thought of getting on a plane and going to a place I couldn't even pronounce no longer intimidated me. It took traveling way beyond my comfort zone to experience the changes I needed to happen. Along the journey, I fell in love with the process and every beautiful place and wonderful person that was a part of that process.

Traveling has played a significant role in shaping me into the person I've become. That's why it was difficult to accept that it was no longer the primary diversion in my life. It was a constant battle to retain what had given me the most fulfillment. I didn't want to fight anymore. The thing about always fighting is that when you stop, you start to wonder what else is there to do. There was dead silence in my life. Is this what it means when they say, "Some people are living as if they're already dead." *Did my life lose its purpose?* In the years I could not travel, I had to adjust and keep living.

When I reflect, I achieved what I set out to accomplish. Of course, there's always more. Like the guests coming through the

275

hotel, I lived the life of the exchange student who studied abroad, and the volunteer who served in a foreign country. The Navy Sailor ... that was me too. Just as I was the guy making crucial financial decisions. All these things and more defined my identity. I finally transformed into who I wanted to be, a person making the best of their life in their own way. It took tremendous faith. When I stepped back to look at my work, I could see that I created a life that felt meaningful. The life I wanted belonged to me. I now possessed stories to share. I could finally tell them.

CHAPTER 25

DISLOCATED STORIES

~~~~~~

Traveling—it leaves you speechless, then turns you into a
storyteller.
—Ibn Battuta

B efore I leave you [the reader] to go out and continue your own
journeys in this life, I'll share a few more random stories from
my trips.

TRAVEL AND FOOD

If I told you that I went to Hard Rock Cafe in Tokyo and had a
pulled pork sandwich with fries, that wouldn't really be interesting.

In Japan, cowherds massage and feed their cows frat-boy
amounts of beer. These cows eventually become a mouthwatering,
melt-in-your-mouth delicacy known as Kobe beef. For more than
$200, you get a steak portion that teases your hunger and leaves
you craving more. Since you don't want to pay another $200 for
another steak, you consider a McDonald's cheeseburger. The
only thing stopping you from buying a Big Mac is the belief that
a $200 steak and $2 processed piece of meat shouldn't coexist in
your digestive system. That's a little more interesting, *right*?

As I've mentioned previously, traveling is all about experiencing new things. Each country is unique, and the culinary scene is one of the many things that stand out at each destination. Therefore, I made it my duty to try everything, even the stuff that terrifies people.

In this case, I had to contact Kristin (one of my best friends) before committing the ultimate sin by eating man's best friend. Yes, I'm talking about consuming Lassie, Marley, and Balto.

Kristin and I met during our Peace Corps service and have been friends ever since. Also, during the periods that I struggled to find work, she let me stay at her place in Maryland when I had interviews in the area. Sometimes, I'd visit her just to hang out. We'd go for hikes in the mountains, picnic at vineyards, or go to the movies. Kristin was my homegirl.

There were two things about Kristin that made her exceptionally different from me. One, she followed a strict vegetarian diet. Two, she loved dogs. While in Paraguay, she found an abandoned and dying puppy that someone left on the road. It was the size of a hamster. She took that puppy home and cared for it until it was healthy. After the Peace Corps, she brought her best friend, Marta, to the United States.

In another life, Kristin and I were sworn enemies. She was the PETA dictator of a vegan nation surviving from gluten-free trail mix, granola, and Beyond Meat baby back ribs. It was the *literal* Hunger Games. I led the underground carnivorous resistance movement to overthrow her government. We burned propaganda posters that read, "Zombies Live Amongst Us!"

In this life, my bizarre cravings needed Kristin's authorization to go rogue. So, I sent her a message.

"Hey buddy, I'm in Vietnam. You know I eat crazy stuff. Well, here, people eat dogs. Would I lose you as a friend?"

Kristin responded, "Are you freaking kidding me?"

"No. You're the only person I respect enough that if you say 'No,' I won't do it." I wrote.

She messaged, "I can't believe you. I won't hold it against you if you try it. If you do, I don't want to know. Those poor dogs!"

Yes! I had Kristin's blessings. However, when I saw the cooked dog's head and meat in the glass enclosure, I had a change of heart and didn't go through with it. I won't act all high and mighty. It was more of a sanitation concern after seeing insects flying around the meat.

After thirty-plus countries, I built a resume that would rival that of any *Fear Factor* contestant. I've eaten every organ of an animal plus a couple of bones. I've consumed a snake's heart and drunk its blood. Alligator. Capybara (the largest rodent in the world). Kangaroo. Fish eyeballs. Jellyfish. Shark. Squid. Octopus. Sea urchin. Cow tongue. Cow intestines. Pig brain. Bull testicles. Alpaca. Guinea pig. Pigeon. Parrots. Armadillo. Chicken feet. Goat. Frog. Horse. Deer. Rabbit. Navy ship food.

It didn't stop at animals either. I'd eaten insects as well: water bugs, beetles, silkworms, ants, and spiders. Surprisingly, tarantula has little white meat and tastes like shrimp.

Out of all my food conquests, the only thing I could not force myself to eat was durian fruit. I'm the kind of person that'll try something multiple times before deciding whether or not I like it. With durian fruit, it's been all-out war, and I've lost every battle. I've nibbled at the fruit on many occasions. Also, I've tried durian crackers, cookies; and I damned near vomited trying to eat durian ice cream.

Durian fruit has the texture of papaya. It tastes like melon fruit blended with onions, mixed with sour cream potato chips, and marinated in swamp water. In many countries, it's illegal to consume the fruit in places like public buses and hotel rooms because of its pungent smell. Once I bought a pack of durian wafers. I lied and told my shipmates that the wafers tasted delicious. Once I opened the wrapper, the entire office smelled like sweet and musty ass-crack. It was so bad that no one ate the wafers. We triple bagged the wafers before throwing them into the trash bin. The smell lingered for weeks.

There was something far worse than durian fruit. This was Japanese *natto*, fermented beans, and it smelled as such. Japanese people mix it with raw egg and mustard; that's how it's eaten during breakfast, lunch, or dinner. The smell and slimy texture are hideous. I touched *natto* with my tongue, and it went numb. I would have chosen death rather than eat it, and I almost did.

One delicacy made me realize that being the Black Andrew Zimmern would probably kill me. When Kaori and I were still dating, we took a trip to Cambodia. We visited the infamous Pub Street in Siem Reap. At night, things got crazy. Street vendors brought out their food carts serving snakes, insects, and every other weird thing that I had already tried except for one thing: scorpion.

There were backpackers and tourists hesitant to purchase the scorpions. Those who had purchased them were scared to eat. *Rookies*, I thought. I gave the vendor money, and he handed me a black scorpion on a stick. A screaming crowd surrounded me. Some guy was filming. I looked at his camera and said, "The secret is not to think about it and just do it." I put the scorpion in my mouth and pulled it from the stick with my teeth. My eyes began to water as I chewed the crunchy creature as fast as possible and swallowed it. I opened my mouth and stuck out my tongue to show that nothing was there. "Ohhh!" roared the crowd.

Not too long after that, Kaori and I got into an argument about whatever dumb shit couples argue about while on an exotic vacation. I can't remember what it was about. But she left and headed back to the hotel without me. That's the stuff that couples don't post on social media. No one posts angry pictures with the Statue of Liberty in the background. Whatever I did to upset her, I really chose the wrong time to fuck up.

Shortly after she left, I felt this pulsating headache coming on. It felt like the creature from the movie *Alien* was getting ready to explode through my head. While Kaori had a keen sense of direction, I didn't, especially at night. I walked around, and the headache grew worse. The inside of my stomach churned in pain. By the time I made it to the hotel, Kaori had already showered and was asleep. I don't think she heard me puking or doing the diarrhea thing.

The following day, I could hardly move or speak. Rigor mortis was setting in, and Kaori was worried. She said that I had been trembling and sweating all night, even though the room was cool. I couldn't eat or drink without puking. As I lay in bed dying, I was happy for one reason. I thought, *She's worried about my dumb ass and not mad at me anymore*. Although worry didn't prevent her from leaving me alone to go shopping and enjoy her vacation. Shortly after she left, I closed my eyes. I didn't die; it was just a long sleep. I awoke in the evening to Kaori returning. She brought me medicine and Cambodian KFC. The chicken was *finger lickin' good*!

I realized that I didn't get food poisoning from the scorpion; I got poisoned[83]. In another life, that experience may have been enough to convince me to accept a high-ranking leadership position in Kristin's PETA dictatorship.

83　Cooking scorpions should denature the venom, but removing the stinger is advised. Raw scorpion can be eaten but the venom gland must be carefully removed.

SURFER DUDES

This is another story from when Kaori and I were dating. She wanted to go to Bali. Bali is a part of the world's largest archipelago country, Indonesia. Also, Indonesia has the largest Muslim population in the world. However, the Bali population is predominantly Hindu.

Bali had never been a place that appealed to me at all. Stereotypically speaking, Bali was where yoga women on Paleo diets and surfer dudes with eight-pack abs went to Eat Pray and Love it up. People went to Bali for the beaches and to soak in the sun. They went to Bali to take selfies in front of temples. That wasn't my style, but you know how it goes,

"Monkey see, monkey do.

Woman go, and man do too."

We stayed in a fancy (but cheap) bungalow in Canggu, not too far from the beach. The narrow streets were exquisitely decorated with trees. After arriving, we took a stroll until we settled at a nearby cafe. After looking at the menu, it only reinforced my perception of Bali being a place for Paleo women and surfer dudes. I read from the menu. "There's a smoothie made with carrots, banana, kiwi, apple peels, and basil leaf. Who drinks this stuff?"

Kaori said, "Umm! That sounds good." I couldn't believe that I was dating a Low-Carb girl.

For me to enjoy this trip, I needed adventure. Something hardcore. What did I do?

I went online and booked a canyoning excursion for Kaori and me. It would be three hours of meandering through the jungle, jumping from waterfalls, swimming, hiking, and zip-lining from nosebleed heights.

A van picked up Kaori and me from our bungalow the following day. We drove two hours to get to our destination. Bali is a beautiful, mountainous country known for active volcanoes, iconic rice paddy fields, and tropical jungles. After arriving at the company's office, we had breakfast. Then, we dressed in full-body wetsuits, helmets, and boots. Next, we began the course.

Kaori and I were part of a small group, accompanied by two adult sisters from Australia and their fifty-something-year-old mother. Besides the guide, I was the only male on the trip.

Twenty minutes into the excursion, we arrived at the first waterfall. It was also the shortest one. We had to jump from the five-foot cascade into the natural pool below. Being a gentleman, I let the ladies go first. Then I went. I spread out my arms like a flying bird as I fell toward the water. As soon as my right arm hit the water, it dislocated.

I tried my best to pop my arm back into place. I pulled, jerked, stretched, and twisted it. No wonder I didn't have any success in fixing it. The pain made me want to scream like a little bitch, but pride prevented me since I was around women. Therefore, I settled for the more manly sounding groans. This occurred only twenty minutes into the three-hour course. It wasn't like I could just jump back up the waterfall and go home. There were many more jumps, including a thirty-foot one. I got through it, but it came at a cost.

The pain felt like torture. When we returned to our bungalow later in the evening, I asked the hotel rep about their spa services. An hour later, a masseuse arrived at the bungalow. After an hour's massage, unsurprisingly, my dislocated arm was still hurting. I had never dislocated my arm. I didn't even know whether it dislocated. It surely felt like it, so I assumed the worst.

I knew what I couldn't do. I couldn't end the trip and return to Japan. I was going to get my money's worth out of it.

There was only one option. I returned to the front desk rep. "Is there a hospital around here?"

He said, "No, but I know someone who can help you. Come here tomorrow morning at 7 AM. You'll have to get there early. I'll call a taxi for you."

Kaori and I arrived in the lobby at 7 AM. The rep wrote something on a piece of paper. Then he handed it to me. I looked at the name on the paper.

"You'll have to find him."

"What's the address?" I asked.

He replied, "I called a taxi. The driver will drop you off in the area. Once you get there, show someone the name on the paper. They'll point you in the right direction."

The taxi driver dropped us off on some random street. The first person I saw, I showed them the name on the paper, and they pointed me to a Balinese house. I walked through the gate, which led to a large outdoor patio area. There had to have been at least sixty people sitting around.

I didn't know what was happening. I asked people, "Do you speak English?" until I found a Balinese man who did.

I asked, "Is there a doctor here?"

He pointed to a shirtless old man sitting on a marble floor.

"Is that the doctor?" I asked.

"He's a healer," the man informed me.

"I dislocated my arm. Do you think the healer can fix it?"

He said, "If you truly believe that the remedial power of God flows through the healer, you can be cured."

I thought, "This is either witchcraft or a cult. These people are crazy." I wanted assurance. "All of these people sitting around are waiting for the healer?"

"Yes," the man replied.

"How much does it cost to be healed?"

He said, "You give whatever your heart tells you to?"

"How long is the wait? How do you know who's next?"

He replied, "I don't know." Then he pointed to someone. "I came in after him."

Twenty minutes passed, and the healer attended to the same person I saw with him when I walked in.

This is crazy. I'm not waiting for this. I thought. Kaori and I left.

Later, we rented bikes and attempted riding around the city. The bumps on the roads caused my arm to throb in pain. I didn't have a choice.

The next morning, I got there even earlier to meet the healer. Before the gate could open, there was already a long line of people. It was like fanatics waiting at the premiere of a new *Star Wars vs The Avengers* movie; plus, the first ten people get a free Tickle Me Elmo doll.

Again, I thought, *This is crazy. I'm not waiting.* And I left again.

Once the evening hit, I could no longer bear the sharp pains. A day and a half had passed since I had hurt my arm. The pain was becoming more relentless. I could barely move my right arm. I began to move like a zombie from the *Walking Dead*. For a third time, Kaori and I returned to the healer. I think Kaori would've just chopped off my arm with a machete if I had left again.

The healer had only a few people, but he wasn't accepting any more clients. Fortunately, he had a change of heart seeing me in so much pain. After waiting an hour, it was finally my turn.

I pointed to where my arm was hurting. The shirtless old man took a puff of his cigarette. He grabbed my arm and slowly moved it around while studying my face.

"Ouch," I shouted.

He grabbed a thick book, which appeared to be on human anatomy. He continued smoking his cigarette as he flipped through the pages. *What kind of healer smokes Newports*, I pondered.

He pulled out a small metal rod the size of a pen. He put it between each of my toes and started twisting.

"Ouch," I cried as my face expressed the discomfort. "My arm." I pointed to my arm. "Not foot."

He gave me a calm look and smiled. It was a look to reassure me that he knew what he was doing. Then he massaged my shoulders and pressed trigger points along my upper back and neck. Last he started to move my arm around. I was visibly in pain.

Kaori found it entertaining as she laughed and took photos of me.

"Go away," I yelled in anger.

The healer carefully and skillfully moved my arm in specific positions. I could hear pops. Sounded like a good thing to me. After twenty minutes, he finished. He looked at me and smiled. "OK?"

Sure enough, although my arm was sore, it felt much better. I was wrong; it wasn't crazy. This guy was the real deal.

I was the healer's last client of the day. As Kaori and I were leaving, we saw a Balinese man accompanying a Chinese surfer. The tourist had on a wetsuit as if he had come straight from the beach. He was holding his hand and appeared to be in excruciating pain. When I looked at the surfer's hand, his ring finger bent irregularly sideways. But I knew that the healer would fix it. I was finally a believer.

Kaori and I made our way to the beach to catch the sunset.

CHAPTER 26
FINAL PIECE

Life doesn't require that we be the best, only that we try our best. —H. Jackson Brown Jr.

If I could go back in time, I would walk through the doors of the Comfort Inn where I used to work. After all, it was my dream job. I met many interesting people. Many of them helped me understand who I wanted to be. I'd rewind the clock and pass through the front doors of my old employer.

I'd be sure to go there during a less busy time. My past self would probably be checking in a guest or on a reservation call. I'd smile, wave at him, and head to the lobby. Not knowing I'm him in the future, he'd look at me and probably think, "That guy looks like an older, fat version of me."

I've seen the time travel movies: *Looper* with Bruce Willis, *Predestination* with Ethan Hawke, and *Avengers: Endgame*. I learned that you don't interfere with who you were in the past. That's how things turn messy and chaotic.

Anyhow, I'd continue to the lobby. There, I'd fix myself a cup of coffee and add a tiny cup of Coffee-Mate French Vanilla creamer. Finally, I'd grab a pack of Otis Spunkmeyer chocolate chip cookies before taking my seat.

I'd take a quick glimpse of my younger self. Silently, I would thank him for all he had invested in me. As I'd watch him, I'd wonder if he's satisfied with whom we'll become. Am I the person that he wants to be? How would he feel knowing that we were the same person from different times in our life?

I'd take out a pen and pad and begin writing a letter to leave behind. If I remember him correctly, my younger self would probably be too courteous and perhaps embarrassed to read someone else's letter. Nonetheless, I'd take my chances. Even if he doesn't pick up the letter and read it, maybe someone else would. Below is the letter that I would leave:

LIFE
Life is a living word experienced by how each person defines it. Love yourself and your life. In the end, life is nothing more than a culmination of experiences that belong to only you. What's nice is that you play a huge role in determining what a lot of those experiences are and how things turn out. There will be times when you don't have control over a situation, and things turn out differently than you expect them to. However, you can control your attitude and reactions to those situations.

There's no specific moment that's going to come and serve as a catalyst for you to change, for better or worse. You're going to have to go out into the world, interact, and make mistakes. The faster you can make those mistakes, the sooner you'll be able to learn from them. Don't forget that you can learn from the mistakes of others as well. First, you must leave your comfort zone and take chances. Whenever you question, "When is the best time to take action?" The answer is always, "Now."

Speaking of time, it's the most valuable resource you have. Once your clock stops ticking, that's it. A professor once told me,

"Time is the only thing that everyone has the same amount of, at any given moment. What makes each of us different is how we use each second." So, prioritize and use it productively. Your efforts should be greater than your desires. And don't measure time by money but rather the experiences. Although time is worth more than money, make sure your finances are in order. While money can't buy time, it can damn sure free up your time. So, make wise investments.

In order to make the best decisions and best investments, study what interests you and the things you're passionate about. Then, work more on the things that interest you. The greatest investment that you can ever make is in yourself.

If you're willing to work forty hours a week for someone else, you better be willing to give yourself that same amount of time. Don't waste it or sleep it away. Resist complacency and eliminate distractions. Always have goals and make progress in achieving them. The effort that you give makes a difference.

If you fall short, it's okay. It's okay to experience disappointment and have regrets, but don't let them consume you. Just be prepared and have a better idea about what you'd do differently next time. Sometimes there's a next time, and sometimes there isn't. This is why it's essential to take risks.

Do whatever you believe will bring you joy. Don't do things because other people want you to do them. You can do things for others that will make them happy. However, do it only if it's what you want to do. In the end, you're the only one who's responsible for your actions and how your life turns out.

Life is good. No matter how hard life gets, things will always get better. If it seems like the situation isn't getting better, you do have the power to change your perspective and take action.

TRAVEL

I wrote that you have to work on the things that interest you. If you don't know what you're interested in or need more options, traveling is a great way to discover your passion.

First things first: get a passport!

Travel as much as you can. The purpose of travel is to get away from what you're used to. Travel is about exposing yourself to people, environments, and situations you normally wouldn't consider. Doing so will open you up to new ideas, unique ways of seeing the world, and different ways of experiencing life. Likewise, you'll gain skills, knowledge, and values that'll assist you in facing everyday challenges. First, you must get up and go.

There are many ways you can travel. You can travel by simply expanding your horizon of the types of music you listen to and books you read. Read *The Alchemist* by Paulo Coelho or *Siddhartha* by Herman Hesse. I know you'll love those books. Reading and music may not be what you're thinking of when travel comes to mind. So, go downtown and walk around, or go to the countryside and take photos of animals. Maybe that seems boring and not exotic enough for you. You determine what's boring or fun and exotic—not the destination.

Take the initiative to begin the process. Start simple. Find the cheapest and safest country. Learn a little about it before you go, and you'll be all right. Buy the cheap ticket and go. The worst-case scenario is that you have a bad experience. Maybe you'll get lost or you'll come across bad people. Let me tell you a secret: the worst-case scenarios can happen anytime and anywhere.

If, for whatever reason, you have doubt about doing anything, act immediately. Doubt is like mold: the longer you let it sit, the more of it grows. Just do it. Just travel.

To travel internationally for cheap—travel during the off-season, be a CouchSurfer, stay at hostels, work at hostels for room and board, volunteer for room and board. Offer your skills in exchange for room and board. Teach a language, cook, dance, sing, write, take photos, fix computers. If you have friends with family in other countries, ask to stay with their family. There's so much you can do. Think outside of the box.

If you want to live in another country, here are some ways: study abroad, apply for jobs in the hospitality field (hotels, airlines, cruise ships), apply for the Peace Corps, become a WWOOFer (Worldwide Opportunities on Organic Farms), join the military, teach English, start a business, get sponsored by an organization, become a tour guide, play for local international sports teams, etc. The possibilities are endless. There's nothing beyond your reach.

If you ever feel like you don't know how to do something, don't be afraid to ask someone for help. You may have to ask many people before you find someone. Nonetheless, some people are willing to help. With this, never ask someone to do for you what you can do for yourself.

Traveling will bring you experiences, both good and bad.

The best part of travel ... better yet, the best (and worst) parts of life and travel are the same thing. This is the people you interact with.

For example, if you don't like a job, it's most likely because you don't get along with people you work with. If you don't like school, it's most likely because you hold unfavorable views of the teachers or students. If you don't like a country... You see where this is going? Similarly, if you have a great experience, it's because there were great people who were a part of the experience. Don't forget that "you" are a person too. Yes, I'm implying that you can be the reason the experience is good or not.

This leads to the final piece.

PEOPLE

Everyone is unique, and you can learn something from anyone. Even a homeless person can teach you how to live on the streets.

Focus on building relationships with people, and never stop. Don't limit your interactions to people who look like you, speak like you, and think like you. Rarely you will find someone like this. Showing that you appreciate others for who they are is one of the best ways to build relationships.

The easiest way to start a conversation is to ask a person how they're doing and give them an honest compliment. Next, you ask general questions that allow them to talk about themselves and things of their interest. Then, listen. If they meet your standards, keep it going.

Choose kindness as much as you possibly can. Challenges, hardships, and suffering are not unique to only you. One of the worst things you can do is make someone else carry your burden when they're already down and out. Keep this in mind when you feel the need to complain. Actually, learn to not complain. This is not to say don't express your feelings. Everyone is fighting their own battles. They may be able to help you fight yours, and you may be able to assist them with theirs.

People will expect many things from you, just like you'll expect things from them. Unless you borrowed something from someone, you don't owe anyone in this world anything. Likewise, they don't owe you anything. No one owes you friendship, employment, happiness, or anything else. Even so, be kind and generous.

Unfortunately, there are bad people in this world. When the times arrive, be prepared to deal with them. Don't go through life thinking that this entire world is against you and out to cause you harm. You'll be surprised that it's quite the opposite. Really, try to think of all the people who helped you in your life. There were so many people. It may not be the ones who were closest to you as you expected. Therefore, it's easy to think that the world is bad because the people who hurt you the most are those closest to you. Also, think about the people you helped. All of it adds up; all of it matters.

Finally, there's an insatiable hunger in every person, including you. It's not the hunger that nourishes the body. It's the desire that drives the ghost inside of every one of us to pursue what we want in our lives. You must constantly feed it but do so cautiously. What it consumes determines the very essence of who you are and will be. This hunger will always want more: more love, more happiness, more success, more money, more travel, and so on. I once read something that I've found to be accurate, "desire is the root of all pain." This is why you have to be grateful. Be grateful for life, be thankful for the people in your life, and appreciate what you have.

If at any given point you can ask yourself, "Am I at peace with who I am" and the answer is "Yes," then you've figured it all out. If not, keep working on yourself. I'm sure that you'll get to that point.

THE END

THE REQUEST

Dear Reader,

Thank you for taking the time to read the book. If you enjoyed it, it would mean so much to me if you could go on Amazon and submit an honest review ... Recommend it to family and friends ... Share it on social media, and /or tag it #lifetravelpeople. As an independent author, I would appreciate every ounce of support. Your kindness and assistance are the only way others will discover and read the book.

Again, I'm truly grateful for you being a part of this journey. And ... one last time, thank you!

CHAPTER 1:
1. O. Henry (1904). *Cabbages and Kings*. New York City:
Doubleday, Page & Company. pp. 132, 296.

CHAPTER 2:
2. https://www.britannica.com/place/Soweto

CHAPTER 3:
3. "Historia" (in Spanish). Universidad Autónoma de Santo
Domingo.
4. "Origins of Reggaeton Music." Pimsleur.com 6 December
2018. Archived from the original on 3 July 2019. Retrieved 14
June 2019.
5. Lady Brighid ni Chiarain. "An English translation of Ruperto
de Nola's Libre del Coch." Stefan's Florilegium.
6. Columbus, Christopher; Curtis, William Eleroy (1894). The
authentic letters of Columbus. Field Columbia Museum.

CHAPTER 4:
7. "History of Jamestown." Apva.org. Archived from the original
on March 23, 2009
8. https://vfwpost2913.com/2017/12/11/
the-history-of-military-rations/

CHAPTER 5:
10. https://www.peacecorps.gov/about/history/
12. https://www.encyclopedia.com/humanities/en-
cyclopedias-almanacs-transcripts-and-maps/
oleary-juan-emiliano-1880-1968

CHAPTER 6:

13. Central Intelligence Agency (2016). "Paraguay." The World Factbook. Langley, Virginia: Central Intelligence Agency.
14. "Fried Chitterlings (Chitlins) and Hog Maws." The Chitterling Site.

CHAPTER 7:

15. Cervantes, Biblioteca Virtual Miguel de. "En busca del hueso perdido: (tratado de paraguayología) / Helio Vera." Biblioteca Virtual Miguel de Cervantes
17. https://www.britannica.com/plant/common-custard-apple
18. Maxwell, James Clerk (1857). "XVIII. —Experiments on Colour, as perceived by the Eye, with Remarks on Colour-Blindness." Transactions of the Royal Society of Edinburgh. Royal Society of Edinburgh. 21 (2): 275–298.
19. https://www.wondermondo.com/monday-falls-saltos-del-monday/

CHAPTER 8:

20. Musicant, Ivan (1990). The Banana Wars: A History of United States Military Intervention in Latin America from the Spanish American War to the Invasion of Panama. New York: MacMillan Publishing.
21. León, P., 1998, *The Discovery and Conquest of Peru, Chronicles of the New World Encounter*, edited and translated by Cook and Cook, Durham: Duke University Press.
22. León, P., 1998, *The Discovery and Conquest of Peru, Chronicles of the New World Encounter*, edited and translated by Cook and Cook, Durham: Duke University Press.
23. "Nicaragua." Encyclopedia Americana. Grolier Online.

24. https://vianica.com/go/specials/16-augusto-sandino.html
25. "Maná to Receive Icon Award at 2021 Billboard Latin Music Awards." www.billboard.com. 2 September 2021.

CHAPTER 9:
26. https://www.military.com/base-guide/browse-by-service/navy
27. *The Hobbit.*
28. "Lincoln Park Zoo (Zoo, Chicago, Illinois, United States)— *Encyclopædia Britannica.* https://www.britannica.com
29. https://chicago.cbslocal.com/2011/02/10/coldest-days-ever-in-chicago/

CHAPTER 10:
31. https://okinawa.stripes.com/travel/retracing-commodore-perry%E2%80%99s-footprint-japan
32. https://adventurousmiriam.com/10-weird-laws-singapore-get-trouble/
33. https://www.britannica.com/topic/Christ-the-Redeemer

CHAPTER 11:
34. https://www.environment.sa.gov.au/licences-and-permits/wildlife-permits/laws-guidelines/kangaroo-guidelines

CHAPTER 12:
35. https://www.nationsonline.org/oneworld/map/google_map_Shenzhen.htm
36. https://www.nationsonline.org/oneworld/Chinese_Customs/chinese_calendar.htm
37. https://www.britannica.com/place/Ulaanbaatar

CHAPTER 13:

38. https://www.welcomeuruguay.com/puntadeleste/the-hand-monument.html

39. Burger, R. L.; Salazar, L. C.; Nesbitt, J.; Washburn, E.; Fehren-Schmitz, L. (August 2021). "New AMS dates for Machu Picchu: results and implications." Antiquity. 2021: 1–15.

40. Thompson, Robert Farris (2005). *Tango: The Art History of Love*. Pantheon Books.

CHAPTER 14:

42. "Regions of Chinese food-styles/flavors of cooking." University of Kansas, Kansas Asia Scholars.

45. Carroll, John (2007). *A Concise History of Hong Kong*.

CHAPTER 15:

46. https://www.adobe.com/creativecloud/photography/discover/bokeh-effect.html

CHAPTER 16:

47. https://www.worldatlas.com/articles/the-coldest-capital-cities-in-the-world.html

49. Mongolia National Census 2010 Provision Results. National Statistical Office of Mongolia.

50. https://stir-tea-coffee.com/features/frigid-mongolia-warms-to-coffee/

54. https://www.jstor.org/stable/650603

CHAPTER 17:

55. https://whc.unesco.org/en/list/231

56. Morgan, David (June 1989). Arbel, B.; et al. (eds.). "The Mongols and the Eastern Mediterranean: Latins and Greeks

in the Eastern Mediterranean after 1204." Mediterranean Historical Review.

57. https://whc.unesco.org/en/list/231

59. Esslemont, J. E. (1980). Bahá'u'lláh and the New Era (Fifth ed.). US Bahá'í Publishing Trust.

CHAPTER 18:

60. https://www.worldhistory.org/Siddhartha_Gautama/

64. https://www.independent.co.uk/news/world/asia/cannabis-marijuna-nepal-festival-shivaratri-kathmandu-a9349191.html

66. https://www.wired.com/2009/10/hallucinations/

CHAPTER 19:

67. https://www.gomyanmartours.com/mandalay-palace/

68. https://www.hrw.org/world-report/2022/country-chapters/myanmar-burma

CHAPTER 21:

71. https://www.japan-experience.com/all-about-japan/kamakura/temples-shrines/sugimoto-dera-temple

72. https://www.britannica.com/topic/Shinto

74. https://www.history.com/this-day-in-history/tokyo-subways-are-attacked-with-sarin-gas

CHAPTER 22:

77. https://www.bbc.com/news/magazine-18065372

78. https://www.masterclass.com/articles/umeshu-recipe#what-are-umeboshi

79. https://nationaltoday.com/friendship-day-2021/

CHAPTER 25:
83. https://www.vice.com/en/article/kbx5z9/
how-to-cook-bugs-scorpions

www.ingramcontent.com/pod-product-compliance
Lightning Source LLC
Chambersburg PA
CBHW071140130626
46553CB00004B/1455